"I think 24-7 prayer is one of the greatest thin[g]
enced in recent years and we will never be the
—Commissioner Alex Hughes (Territorial Commander, Salvation
Army UK)

"24-7 is brilliant. If you're wanting to combine social involvement
with spiritual intimacy this is an absolutely fantastic tool!"
—Steve Chalke (Director, Faithworks and TV presenter)

"24-7 is making history as an unstoppable global prayer movement,
and has caught the imagination of a rising generation, involving
many tens of thousands in urgent, persistent, continuous, world-
changing intercession, encouraging radical discipleship and effective
mission. This brilliant book will inspire you with practical help on
how to establish 24-7 in your own community."
—Dr. Patrick Dixon (Director, Global Change Ltd and author of
*Futurewise*)

"24-7 is about prayer—a lifeline to our creator God. It helps us to
stand in the gap and intercede for the things we're passionate about,
to see things happen and to witness miracles... lovely!"
—Andy Hunter (DJ/recording artist)

"The 24-7 prayer movement is one of the most out of control God-
things anywhere on the planet at the moment. Whatever you do,
don't just read about it—catch the Fire!"
—Andy Hawthorne (Director, The Message Trust)

"This has to be one of the most exciting movements in the church
today. I'm excited about what 24-7 is teaching."
—Rev. Dr. Rob Frost (Director, Share Jesus International)

"God's mission to save lost humanity is the central theme of
Scripture. Jesus Christ is the key to it all. All of our discipleship, wor-

ship and prayer is part of this great mission. The heart of 24-7 is to bring prayer and mission together and to do this in a way, which flows out of the instincts and culture of the emerging generations. I've been in and around 24-7 since it started. Run by a bunch of nobodies, surfing the 'waves of the Spirit' and making it up as they went along. The rest is history. Check out the story and get involved. Lets see where the waves will take us!"
—Roger Ellis (Director, Fusion, and leader, Revelation Church)

"24-7 was a God idea that has swept around the globe. Prayer has always preceded revivals, the re-evangelisation of people groups and the transformation of society. Throw yourself into this river of prayer, it could be the best thing you have ever done."
—Gerald Coates (Team Leader, Pioneer, Author, Broadcaster)

"It is absolutely thrilling to witness thousands of young people discovering the power of prayer through the 24-7 movement. I believe the key to reaching our world is passion, prayer, practical action and proclamation. 24-7 combines all four! I wholeheartedly commend 24-7 to churches, universities and all those longing for the coming of God's Kingdom."
—Rev. Lyndon Bowring (Executive Chairman, CARE)

# RED MOON RISING

Published by Relevant Books
A division of Relevant Media Group, Inc.

*www.relevantbooks.com*
*www.relevantmediagroup.com*

© 2003 Peter Greig and David Roberts

Published in association with Kingsway Publications, Eastbourne, England

Design by Matthew L. Crowe, Lloyd Kinsley
Relevant Solutions
*www.relevant-solutions.com*

Relevant Books is a registered trademark of Relevant Media Group, Inc.,
and is registered in the U.S. Patent and Trademark Office.

Library of Congress Control Number: 2003096207
International Standard Book Number: 0-9729276-6-2

For information:
RELEVANT MEDIA GROUP, INC.
POST OFFICE BOX 951127
LAKE MARY, FL 32795
407-333-7152

04 05 9 8 7 6 5 4 3

Printed in the United States of America

This is the story of many lives in many cultures over several years.
We dedicate it simply to anyone who's ever done a 3 a.m. slot
in a 24-7 prayer room and found themselves wondering ...

"Why?"

**From Dave:**
For Hugh Bourne, Count Zinzendorf, Lorenzo Dow, Lorenzo Dow
Cunningham, George and Anna Roberts, and all the others
whose past is shaping my future.

**From Pete:**
For Michael Curry who prayed for me faithfully every day of my
weird and wonderful life until he died in the mountains of Skye.
Heaven only knows how much I owe to your example.

And to all those friends not named elsewhere in this book whose
stories are the very heartbeat of 24-7, especially Amy and Casey
Johnson, Andrea Clarke, Andrew Grinnell, Annie Bullen, Ben Hull,
Billy Kennedy, Brian Marriot, Carlotta Verdura, Charlotte New, Chris
Brown, Christian Cheeseman, Dan King, Debra Green, Donny
Tompuno, Farah Stehrenberger, Gill and Peter Greig-Allen, Jesus and
Rachel Repetto, Jonny Smith, Karen Freeman, Linda Warwick, Malc
and Penny Pierce, Mark Markiewicz, Mia Lind, Nathalie Rod-
Coronado, Nathan Staines, Nigel Singleton, Oria Dale, Phil Togwell,
Rachel McKee, Richard McIntyre, Robert and Sue Armstrong,
Rustin Carlson, Simon Mander, Steph Carter, Steve Holloway, Tim
Rose, Tim Sudworth, Tony and Jo Benn, Wogan Heasley.

With thanks to Cara Baker, Richard Herkes, and Sharon Roberts.

*"In the last days," God says, "I will pour out my Spirit on all people. Your sons and daughters will prophesy, your young men will see visions, your old men will dream dreams…The sun will be turned to darkness and the moon to blood before the coming of the great and glorious day of the Lord. And everyone who calls on the name of the Lord will be saved." —Acts 2*

# FOREWORD

In 1722 a rag tag band of several hundred young people gathered on the estate of a wealthy count by the name of Zinzendorf. Five years later, God showed up, and they began to pray. They prayed in strange and creative ways, but they prayed. They prayed 24/7. Their prayer led to compassion for the poor and those who had never heard of Jesus. Their prayer meeting went on for 125 years without ceasing—the longest prayer meeting in history.

God has decided to do again what He did among the Moravians almost 300 years ago. A 24/7 prayer meeting has started again, but now it has circled the globe overnight. We should not be surprised God chose an unlikely candidate to lead the 24-7 prayer movement. Pete Greig struggled to hear God's voice and wasn't very good at praying—but he was determined to chase the Spirit wherever that took him. The chase led to a blue-haired kid in Dresden, who in turn got him to the home of that first 24-7 prayer meeting started those many years ago. God got through to Pete, and the rest is history, as they say.

Pete Greig reminds us that prayer doesn't belong to the stodgy or the religious. Nor can prayer be controlled by religious types who think they have a corner on the right words to use and the correct position to stand. *Red Moon Rising* reminds us that prayer is not something to do, but someone to talk to. It stirs faith in us to believe that when we talk to God, He responds.

In his amazing story, Pete Greig takes us with him as he chases the Spirit, as he dances with God. God initiated the dance; Pete Greig and his wife Samie responded—now God is responding to their response. And what a cool response!

Does this movement have to do with the last days? Is there a red moon rising again? Pete Greig believes so. Guys like Pete have believed Jesus is coming back very soon for years—Jesus has not come back. Does that change anything? Not for me. It just means that the Spirit of God is awakening the hearts of young men and women all over the earth, He is creating expectation. Expectation is necessary for Jesus to return. He is not going to come back for a bride who is not prepared. Expectation is a part of preparation. I see expectation growing in the hearts of people like Pete—and it awakens my heart as well.

*Red Moon Rising* is not just a book; it's an invitation. I have accepted the invitation. I jumped at the offer the first moment I met Pete. I think you will too, once you listen to the Spirit as He speaks through these pages. I invite you to join Pete and myself and many others in giving our hearts to this one thing—to prepare for a great harvest that will usher in the return of Jesus. I would rather throw in my lot with a bunch of crazy lovers of Jesus whose hearts have been awakened and who are building churches that make disciples who love Jesus—than hang back and be safe. As they say, those who hope, lead.

Why all the fuss with prayer and stirring up expectation? So Jesus will be glorified in the earth. It's about Jesus hearing His name in languages He has never heard in heaven. That's the goal. More love for Jesus. More cultures and peoples set free to love him and enjoy Him forever.

When I kneel before the throne of God, I want to look into His eyes and see the joy He receives when I lay crowns at His feet. I found that same desire in Pete and Samie Greig and their friends. They are part of a movement birthed by the Holy Spirit that no one person or organization can claim or control. But anyone can join in. Just listen like Pete did and start chasing the wind of the Spirit.

*Floyd McClung*
*All Nations Family*

# CONTENTS

# INTRODUCTION

Outside the first great prayer room is a fisherman of all people, a guy named Peter who is preaching to the multicultural crowds of Jerusalem. He's explaining with great passion that right here, right now, right before their very eyes, the Spirit of Yahweh is raining down. An era of vision and salvation has begun. Welcome to the last days, he says. Welcome to the end of the movie.

According to the prophet Joel, God's heavenly logo for such an era is the harvest moon, rising blood red and pregnant with possibilities above us. Such a moon rises over every generation awaiting the one that will finally fulfill the Great Commission, taking the good news of Jesus to every culture and ushering in the kingdom of heaven. In our time the Spirit is mobilizing young people with fresh vision, sons and daughters are speaking prophetically to the culture, older generations continue to dream, and many people cry out for salvation in every tribe and tongue.

This is a book about a prayer movement; 24-7 is catalyzing intercession and mission all over the world, and anyone can join in. But the movement has a context, and this book will also introduce you to some of the radical youth churches and amazing people at the heart of this phenomenon. We often laugh; sometimes we're stunned into silence. There are always frustrations. But in the midst of many emotions, a nameless, faceless army meets God on its own in tiny prayer rooms from Alaska to Australia and emerges with a fresh resolve to help people discover Jesus and the timeless message of His life, death, and resurrection.

A red moon rose in the winter sky above the nightclub in which we gathered to launch 24-7 prayer. For us it was a sign, reminding us of Joel's prophecy and Peter's great Pentecostal sermon. We sensed that this movement of prayer, initiated by God, much to everyone's surprise, was somehow something to do with the end times, called to be a portal for fresh vision, a small part of a big picture as the Holy Spirit moves in our time. As we explored the story of what God is doing through people willing to pray 24-7, we continue to see that red moon rising as Joel predicted.

This is not simply Pete's story, although it is told from his perspective of his involvement. This is the story of a group of friends in various countries exploring the power of prayer, mission, and Christian community together. Our prayer is that, as you read this book you will be challenged, encouraged, and changed to become even more like Jesus. This story isn't ultimately about 24-7 or any other movement; it's about what can happen when ordinary people dare to dream extraordinary dreams. Our prayer is that you will be inspired to do the same wherever you live and however inadequate you may sometimes feel.

The prophet Joel tells us that before the "day of the Lord," God will "pour out His Spirit on all people. Your sons and daughters will prophesy, your old men will dream dreams, your young men will see visions. Even on my servants, both men and women, I will pour out my Spirit in those days."

Dare we believe that these are those days? Could a red moon rise once more?

*Pete Greig & Dave Roberts*

*"For each age is a dream that is dying, Or one that is coming to birth."*
*—Arthur O'Shaughnessy (1844–1881)*

# HOW TO USE THIS BOOK

*Red Moon Rising* can be read on three different levels. In each chapter, alongside the main story you will find two types of boxes: Deeper and Journey.

These draw out personal testimonies and deeper teaching from the text without—we hope—interrupting the flow of the main story. It's completely up to you whether you skip these boxes or study them in depth.

## DEEPER

The DEEPER boxes pick up on themes in the narrative and explore them in a bit more depth. You may appreciate these elements of teaching content or choose to ignore them altogether as you sprint through the text.

## JOURNEY

The JOURNEY boxes illustrate the story with personal testimonies and occasional poetry.

# CHAPTER ONE

# ELECTRICAL **STORM**
[PORTUGAL. GERMANY.]

*Let's see colors that have never been seen*
*Let's go places no one else has been ...*
*Well if the sky can crack, there must be someway back*
*To love and only love*
*Electrical storm*
　　　　　　　—U2, "Electrical Storm"

STANDING ON THE SPECTACULAR CLIFFS
of Cape St. Vincent that night, I had no idea that my
life was about to change. We had pitched our little
tent on the most southwesterly point of Europe, far
from the lights of any city and beneath a canopy of
unusually bright stars.

For days Nick and I had been traveling west along
the coast of Portuguese Algarve, camping on cliff
tops looking out to sea and cooking fresh fish on an
open fire. By day we would hit the beaches, often
leaving our backpacks on the sand to plunge into
the sea.

Having recently graduated from university in

London, our futures stretched out before us like those long, straight, empty roads you see in photographs of Montana. We were tanned and dirty, the sea and sun had bleached our tousled hair, and we were having the time of our lives.

After so many days traveling with the ocean on our left, it had been exciting to catch the first glimpse of sea to the right as well. Gradually, over recent days, the land had tapered to the point I was standing now, where a solitary lighthouse puts an exclamation mark on Europe, and the oceans collide in rage.

There is something absolute about Cape St. Vincent: its lunar land-scape, the ceaseless pounding of the waves against nature's vast battle-ments, and even the black ravens circling majestically below as you look out to sea. Few things in life are so certain as these rocks. It isn't pretty, but it's real, with a meaning that everyone senses and perhaps no one can quite express.

People have always been drawn to this mysterious wasteland, which has been battered for thousands of years by the collision of the Atlantic and the Mediterranean seas. Bronze age tribes buried their dead here and erected standing stones. In 304 A.D., grieving monks brought the body of St. Vincent the martyr here, and according to legend, ravens guarded his bones. The place took on the martyr's name and became a place of Christian and Muslim pilgrimage for centuries to come. The Romans quite simply thought it was the end of the world. Here their maps ran out and their empire marched relentlessly into the endless sea. It would be centuries before Europeans "discovered" the Americas beyond the blue curve of that deadpan horizon.

But standing there that night, I knew none of this history. I only sensed something unfathomably sad and special about the place. Nick and I had pitched our little green tent right there on the cliffs, laughing that we were to be the most south-westerly people in all of Europe for a night. But, unable to sleep, I had climbed quietly out of the tent, leaving Nick gently snoring. A breathtaking sight had greeted me: the vast, glowering ocean glimmering under a shimmering eternity of stars; it was like being lost in the branches of some colossal Christmas tree. To the south, the next great landmass is Africa. To the west, it is America. I turned, and with my back to the ocean, I imagined Europe, rolling away from my feet for 10,000 miles. From where I stood, the continent began with a handful of rocks and a small green tent, but beyond that I could imagine Portugal and Spain, France, Switzerland, Italy, and Germany eventually becoming Russia, China, and the Indian sub-continent.

Visualizing nation after nation, I raised my hands and began to pray out loud for each one by name. And that was when it happened. First my scalp began to tingle and an electric current pulsed down my spine, again and again, physically shaking my body. Nothing like this had ever happened to me before, and it was years before the spiritual excitement associated with the Toronto Blessing would appear to plug millions into the mains. I could hear a buzzing, clicking sound overhead, as if an electric pylon was short-circuiting, and I seriously wondered if I was about to get fried. As these strange sensations continued, I received a vision. My eyes were open, but I could "see" with absolute clarity before me the different countries laid out like an atlas. From each one a faceless army of young people rose from the page, crowds of them in every nation awaiting orders.

I have no idea how long that vision lasted; it might have been a minute or as much as an hour, but eventually I climbed into my sleeping bag next to Nick who was quietly snoring, and with my head still spinning, I drifted into a deep sleep.

My life would never be the same.

---

Two years earlier, in the city of Leipzig in communist East Germany, a thirteen-year-old was looking around in amazement at all the candles and people crammed into the building to pray for peace. Markus Lägel felt like a small part of something very big—anonymous and special at the same time.

It was hard to be a Christian in one of the most repressive regimes in the world. The ever-present fear of conflict with the West weighed heavily on everyone, so the East German church began to mobilize prayers for peace. They started in 1979, and by 1989, the prayer rally at Leipzig attracted 300,000 people.

With so many people expressing their protest in prayer, the State was preparing for war. Markus remembers guns on the roofs of churches and tanks in the street. But when the Berlin Wall finally came down, one Communist official made an extraordinary admission to a journalist: "We were prepared for every eventuality, but not for candles and not for prayers."

Markus spent his formative years caught up in those extraordinary Peace Prayer Rallies in Leipzig. When the Communist regime finally fell, Markus became convinced that prayer has the power to undermine any ideology that oppresses. Watching consumerism usurp communism, one form of oppression for another, Markus began a spiritual journey that would one day make him an essential part of the 24-7 story.

---

As Nick and I hitch-hiked our way back across Europe, the vision of Cape St. Vincent kept replaying in my mind. "Where is the army, Lord?" I would wonder again and again as we traveled from Lisbon to Valladolid, Bilbao, Bordeaux, Paris, and London. "Where are the signs of such people in these streets, these tenements, these crowded places?" Maybe my vision had meant nothing at all.

It's a question I guess we all ask, looking around our towns and cities, looking at the classroom or the office or the campus, watching TV and even scanning the pews at church. Where are those "forceful" men and women rising up to lay hold of God's kingdom (Matthew 11:12)? Where are the people of God advancing the purposes of God with militancy and humility in the power of His Spirit today?

And why do we need such an army anyway when churches abound?
What is the urgency that compels us?

## TO DIE FOR

I still remember where I was when I heard the news that Kurt
Cobain had killed himself. Somehow it seemed momentous that a
world-famous musical genius had stuck a gun in his mouth and
pulled the trigger. In his suicide note, he simply claimed that he felt
"guilty beyond words." But, with hindsight, the rock star's suicide
wasn't momentous at all; it was just another death of another
depressed individual failing to find sufficient meaning in a messed
up world. After working twelve hours a day copying product numbers into account ledgers, a Japanese man called Wataru Tsurumi
wrote a book called *The Complete Manual of Suicide*, advising young
people on how to kill themselves. It has sold 1.3 million copies
since 1993.

*Der Spiegel* magazine estimates that in Germany alone there are at
least thirty Internet death forums where suicidal teenagers can discuss the best ways to kill themselves. A kid called Rizzo wrote on
one: "Hi people! I've bought a seven-meter long piece of cord. Can
someone tell me the height of drop to hang myself properly?" A
forum master called Markus "B" left his final message on November
11: "When you have a twelve-calibre shotgun in your hand, you
think differently about death. If you think there's something heroic
about shooting yourself, hold a gun in your hand." Three days later,
Markus' parents found him dead with the Beatle's song, "Let it Be,"
playing on repeat.

With suicide rates among young men soaring alongside self-harm and
eating disorders in women, we can say with some confidence that this
generation may well be hurting more profoundly than any other.
Amidst sparkling creativity, spectacular innovation, and unprecedented
wealth, growing up in the West means for many a sense of alienation, a
hunger for intimacy, authenticity, and hope.

That, surely, is a heart cry that moves the heart of God as His Spirit intercedes for us in groans beyond talking. It's why He anoints us to "preach good news to the poor and to bind up the broken-hearted" (Isaiah 61). It's why He is sounding the trumpet in our time, summoning His forces to wage war in heaven and peace on earth (Ephesians 6). The battle is real, but it's not just to save our souls from an epidemic of rock 'n' roll angst, and it's not simply to refill our lonely pews either. We need an army to arise because the poor and the oppressed are crying out to God for urgent intervention and some ray of hope. "Though I call for help," they say, "there is no justice" (Job 19:7).

## BLACK DEATH

We find ourselves living at the time of the worst epidemic in world history: AIDS has now killed more people than the Black Death. That's why in Africa tonight, 400,000 children will lie down to sleep without a mother or father to kiss them good night, innocently orphaned by AIDS. History will hold us accountable for our response to such suffering. And yet some countries, like Malawi, are being forced to spend more on debt repayment to countries like ours, than they are on preventing and treating HIV/AIDS or feeding their own people.[1] Our governments are effectively making things worse!

And in America, forty years after Martin Luther King's "I have a dream" speech, if you're black, you are nearly twice as likely to be fired from your job than your white co-workers.[2] What's more, the median income of black American families was 54 percent of the income of white families in 1992, which is significantly worse than it was back in 1969.[3]

---

1. *www.maketradefair.com*, August 2003
2. Even allowing for differences in age, education, job performance and a score of other factors, blacks in the U.S. are fired at nearly twice the rate of whites. (*Philadelphia Inquirer*, October 1994)
3. *Philadelphia Inquirer*, October 1994

## CHANGE

Something has to change, and Jesus says that something can change, promising that "the first shall be last and the last shall be first." In a world obsessed with celebrity sex and superficial appearance, He still chooses the lepers and the AIDS victims, the bullied kids from school, the "fools" of this world to confound the wise with hope and justice. In the company of Christ, the ugly become beautiful and classroom cowards become the bewildered heroes of His Kingdom. That, after all, is my story, and I suspect it is yours too:

> "Take a good look, friends, at who you were when you got called into this life. I don't see many of 'the brightest and the best' among you, not many influential, not many from high-society families. Isn't it obvious that God deliberately chose men and women that the culture overlooks and exploits and abuses, chose these 'nobodies' to expose the hollow pretensions of the 'somebodies'?" (1 Corinthians 1:26-28, The Message).

That is the Gospel as much today as it was when Paul was writing to the Corinthians. In fact, there may well be more outcasts in our modern industrialized society—slaves of the free market economy—than there were in the Roman Empire. When I worked in Hong Kong with heroin addicts as part of Jackie Pullinger's remarkable ministry, she would say, "If you want to see revival, plant your church in the gutter." Jesus warned us that the upwardly mobile middle classes would always find it extremely hard to receive Him. But among the losers, the freaks, and the apparent failures, what one preacher called the "shrimps and wimps and those with limps" … that is actually where the Gospel spreads quite easily.[4]

Revolutions always begin in the streets with the dispossessed—never in the corridors of power. Think of the early Church, the French Revolution, the Bolshevik revolution, and the American wars for

---

4. Gerald Coates

independence. Think of William Booth's Salvation Army and the birth of Pentecostalism in a back street of Los Angeles. Think of the roots of rock 'n' roll, of hip-hop and rap.

## THE CHURCH IN A TIME OF ANARCHY

Something must change. Something can change. But can the Church as we know her rise to the task? The respected researcher George Barna looks in the rearview mirror and concludes, "Recent decades have seen the impact of the Church wane to almost nothing;"[5] America is "a land where you may call yourself what you want, believe whatever you want, live however you wish and do what you will with religion, faith, and a spirituality." In short, he says, we are in a state of "spiritual anarchy."[6]

Teenagers and young adults are finding the Church increasingly irrelevant. Every Sunday thousands of our contemporaries leave the pew, never to return. But statistics mask the real story. A fifty-year time warp often separates Saturday night from Sunday morning. Faced with such alienation, some of our peers have simply retreated from the world, taking up residence in a protective Christian bubble. Others may send their bodies faithfully to church, but they keep their brains in a jar at home and their hearts at the Saturday night party, the bar, or the cinema. And of course many of our friends just avoid church altogether.

Right now, one in five American children is living in poverty, and yet, according to the Barna Research Group, "Half of all adults did nothing at all in the past year to help a poor person" and "few churches have a serious ministry to the poor."[7] With such crying needs and such self-absorption among God's people, surely things have never been worse?

---

5. *Boiling Point*, George Barna and Mark Hatch, Regal (Ventura) 2001, p. 311.
6. Ibid., p. 187.
7. Ibid., p. 41.

# CHRISTIANITY WILL BE FORGOTTEN IN 30 YEARS

J. Edwin Orr, a widely respected historian, in a message called "Prayer & Revival," described the situation in America in the 1780s.[8] Drunkenness was epidemic, and the streets were not judged to be safe after dark. What about the churches?

"The Methodists were losing more members than they were gaining. In a typical Congregational church, the Rev. Samuel Shepherd of Lennos, Massachusetts, in sixteen years had not taken one young person into fellowship. The Lutherans were so languishing that they discussed uniting with Episcopalians who were even worse off. The Protestant Episcopal Bishop of New York, Bishop Samuel Provost, quit functioning; he confirmed no one for so long that he decided he was out of work, so he took up other employment.

"The Chief Justice of the United States, John Marshall, wrote to the Bishop of Virginia, James Madison, that the Church 'was too far gone ever to be redeemed.' The great philosopher Voltaire averred and the author Tom Paine echoed, 'Christianity will be forgotten in thirty years.'"

The spiritual state of America's universities at the time concurred with such gloomy predictions, giving little or no hope for the future of the faith in that land:

"Take the liberal arts colleges at that time. A poll taken at Harvard had discovered not one believer in the whole student body. They took a poll at Princeton, a much more evangelical place, where they discovered only two believers in the student body, and only five that did not belong to the filthy speech movement of that day. Students rioted. They held a mock communion at Williams College, and they put on anti-Christian

---

8. International Revival Network: *www.openheaven.com*

plays at Dartmouth. They burned down the Nassau Hall at Princeton. They forced the resignation of the president of Harvard. They took a Bible out of a local Presbyterian church in New Jersey and burnt it in a public bonfire. Christians were so few on campus in the 1790s that they met in secret, like a communist cell, and kept their minutes in code so that no one would know."

It's hard to believe that this was taking place in America 200 years ago but then, Orr continues, God intervened, and He did so by mobilizing His people to pray.

"A prayer movement started in Britain through William Carey, Andrew Fuller, John Sutcliffe, and other leaders who began what the British called the Union of Prayer. Hence, the year after John Wesley died (1791), the second great awakening began and swept Great Britain.

"In New England, there was a man of prayer named Isaac Backus, a Baptist pastor, who in 1794, when conditions were at their worst, addressed an urgent plea for prayer for revival to pastors of every Christian denomination in the United States. Churches knew that their backs were to the wall. All the churches adopted the plan until America, like Britain, was interlaced with a network of prayer meetings, which set aside the first Monday of each month to pray. It was not long before revival came.

"There was a Scotch-Irish (sic.) Presbyterian minister named James McGready whose chief claim to fame was that he was so ugly that he attracted attention. McGready settled in Logan County, pastor of three little churches. He wrote in his diary that the winter of 1799 for the most part was 'weeping and mourning with the people of God.' Lawlessness prevailed everywhere.

"McGready was such a man of prayer that not only did he promote the concert of prayer every first Monday of the month, but he got his people to pray for him at sunset on Saturday evening and sunrise Sunday morning. Then in the summer of 1800 came the great Kentucky revival. Eleven thousand people came to a communion service. McGready hollered for help, regardless of denomination.

"Out of that second great awakening came the modern missionary movement and its societies. Out of it came the abolition of slavery, popular education, Bible Societies, Sunday schools, and many social benefits."

Utter hopelessness turned to renewal and restoration. Could it happen for a new generation?

## UCBONES

## "WHERE, LORD IS THE ARMY FOR TODAY?"

It was a question the people of Israel in captivity asked too. Then Ezekiel found himself in a valley of dry bones—as unpromising a place as any confronting us—only to witness a dramatic transformation. The bones became corpses, "breath entered them; they came to life and stood up on their feet—a vast army" (Ezekiel 37:10).

We may be tempted to look at youth culture around the world and echo the despair of the people of Israel: "Our bones are dried up and our hope is gone, we are cut off."

But could it be that as we declare the "Word of the Lord" in our time, the flesh will return, bones will reconnect, and the body will breathe again? Could an army arise in Silicon Valley or any other modern day valley of bones?

Years after Markus Lägel's experiences in Leipzig and mine in Portugal, we are friends from different countries walking the journey of faith together. These days you may find us on occasion wearing identical T-shirts: On the front they say "UCBONES" and on the back "ICANARMY." We're declaring to those cynics busy writing off our generation, "You see bones" but "I see an army"! We choose to believe that walls can still fall the way they did in Jericho and in Germany. We choose to believe that a heart cry can become a war cry for justice. We choose to believe that the army of the Lord can arise once again in the valley of dry bones.

*"Then [the Lord] said to me: 'Son of man, these bones are the whole house of Israel. They say, 'Our bones are dried up and our hope is gone; we are cut off.' Therefore prophesy and say to them: 'This is what the Sovereign LORD says: O my people, I am going to open your graves and bring you up from them; I will bring you back to the land of Israel ... I will put my Spirit in you and you will live'" (Ezekiel 37).*

## DEEPER

## VALLEY OF BONES

Consider for a moment some statistics. They're mainly from the U.K. and U.S.A., but with small variations they might represent any major Western nation. They could so easily be used to posture and condemn, accuse others and parade our virtue. But there is another way to view them. Think of them as the symptoms of a spiritually malnourished generation. Think of them as the evidence of loss, alienation and pain.

**Alcohol and Drugs**—Almost a third of U.K. teenagers have been drunk twenty times or more, and more than 35 percent have experimented with illegal drugs. Why?

**Bullying**—Nearly one-third of the middle school and high school students in one survey admitted to being a bully, being bullied, or both, according to a report published in the April 25, 2001 issue of the *Journal of the American Medical Association*.

**Priorities**—It currently costs $2.2 million to air a thirty-second commercial during the Super Bowl, while literally hundreds of millions of people are malnourished, homeless, and dying of curable diseases.[9] Where are the people crying for change?

**Sexually Transmitted Disease**—Every year 3 million young people—about 1 in 4 sexually experienced teens—acquire an STD. Why?[10]

**Self-Harm**—Children as young as six are cutting themselves. The average self-harmer is aged eleven, and 1 in 10 adolescents are thought to have cut themselves deliberately at least once. A typical sixteen-year-old girl says that most days she cuts into her arms until they bleed, explaining that "the pain proves your human." Why?[11]

There are never simple one-line answers to such questions. Maybe some people are merely rebellious. But for how many is sex a search for intimacy, drugs a way of escape, and self-harm a demonic self-loathing? Only a prophetic community can help people discover the wisdom that will heal these wounds.

## JOURNEY

## THE POWER OF STORIES

"How beautiful on the mountains are the feet of those who bring good news, who proclaim peace, who bring good tidings, who proclaim salvation, who say to Zion, 'Your God reigns!'" (Isaiah 52:7)
In New York City, a guy named John bought a Big Mac for a homeless man; it was the beginning of a life-long friendship. In Dublin, Lucy's heart felt like it was breaking as she prayed for friends who didn't know Jesus. In Tennessee, a prodigal stepped inside a prayer room and began the journey home.

The stories of Jesus are still being told. He is alive and moving powerfully in our generation, still comforting those who mourn, answer-

---

9. *Boiling Point*, George Barna and Mark Hatch, Regal (Ventura) 2001, p. 110.
10. Alan Guttmacher Institute
11. *http://my.webmd.com/content/article/12/1689_50857*

ing prayer, and making ordinary lives extraordinary.

Stories are powerful; they can evoke anger, ignite truth, inspire hope, or invade a person's loneliness with an empathetic hug. Jesus told stories, but He also was the story. Throughout this book in these "Journey" boxes, you'll find short quotes and personal accounts of God on the move. If life is a video, these are like snapshots capturing particular moments on peoples' spiritual journeys. Hopefully they will help you to understand God's character better. And when we get our heads around God's character, prayer, devotion, and discipleship ceases to be a technique and becomes an instinct. That's when we can take our place in an army that marches on its knees, fighting for the Prince of Peace.

# CHAPTER TWO

# SHIFTING **CULTURE**
[U.K.]

I'D BEEN IN TOWN JUST FORTY-EIGHT hours when the call came: "Pete, get down to the hospital quick. John's overdosed."

Leaving my Sunday lunch, I drove to the ER with my head spinning. Just two days earlier, I had arrived in the respectable cathedral city of Chichester, situated fifty miles south of London, by the sea, fresh from my tour of Europe and with that vision of the army still buzzing in my brain. I'd come in search of discipleship, relocating from the East End of London to a church community that was both exciting and challenging.

## DODGY HARI AND LOTS OF GOD

Revelation Church had begun in the '80s when a load of longhaired heavy metal freaks became Christians. Many of them had been involved in the occult. With all the naivety of new Christians, they simply assumed that God was more powerful than the devil and instinctively began praying for the sick, casting out demons, and yelling in tongues. This combined with the long hair, piercing, and raucous approach to life was just too much for the local Anglican Church, which had other problems at the time too. It became obvious that what God was doing could not be continued or supported there and that a new church would need to be started.

So the bewildered youth group began meeting in a nearby hall. Malc Garda was a white guy with an afro and more than a passing resemblance to Freddie Mercury. But because he was the only person in the group who could even remotely pretend to play the guitar, Malc was quickly appointed worship leader. The ringleader of the group was Roger Ellis, a blond-haired head banger still in his early twenties, with a croaky voice from too many gigs. Roger was taken aside by the group's first visiting speaker and told that they didn't have "even one fifth of what it takes to build a church." With these words of encouragement ringing in their ears, the group drew lots and found themselves named "Revelation." Roger leads the church to this day and has pioneered a number of very significant ministries such as Fusion, a campus cell movement. Meanwhile, the church has grown numerically and in maturity, planting a number of congregations in the south of England and even in Brooklyn, New York.

## WHATEVER THE WEATHER

It was really because of Roger that I was now here in Chichester, zooming down the road to the ER on a mission from God. Ever since that vision in Portugal, I'd been wondering what to do about it. All I knew for sure was that it had to begin with getting myself sorted. God had spoken to me clearly in a London park one day, pointing out a majestic oak tree before directing my attention to Jeremiah 17:7–8:

> *"Blessed is the man who trusts in the Lord,*
> *whose confidence is in him.*
> *He will be like a tree planted by the water*
> *that sends out its roots by the stream.*
> *It does not fear when heat comes;*

*its leaves are always green.*
*It has no worries in a year of drought*
*and never fails to bear fruit."*

I knew that God was telling me to put down roots by a stream. Like most people, I was relatively fruitful when the sun was shining: A few friends had become Christians, and I was even viewed as something of a leader by about half a dozen of my friends. I was the guy who did pretty much anything exciting he could think of for God. I had driven relief vans to Romanian orphanages, smuggled Bibles into China, worked in Hong Kong with heroin addicts and in London with the homeless. I was a full-on lone ranger for Jesus.

But I had to admit, I wasn't accountable to anyone for my actions and as a result, whenever the seasons of my life changed and the sun disappeared, so did my fruitfulness. Jeremiah was right. My girlfriend had recently finished with me and I'd been inconsolable. If I wanted to bear fruit supernaturally regardless of the climate, I knew I needed to draw water from an ongoing community that would challenge me, encourage me, and hold me accountable, whatever the weather. No more lone ranger.

## EMBARRASSING TEA

Finding that kind of support seemed impossible. I approached a godly older man who had an amazing grasp of scripture and asked him to disciple me. He said okay and invited me round for the most embarrassing cup of tea of either of our lives. I left with a reading list and was never invited to return. I'm not blaming this guy. He just didn't know how to do for me something that had never been done for him.

Then I met Roger Ellis, and he confused me. He and his friends were passionate about God yet gloriously and outrageously normal. Malc had long since shaved off the afro, Roger's hair was now tidily pulled into a ponytail, and I could imagine my non-Christian friends liking them a lot. Most of the really zealous Christians I'd known up until then seemed to live on a spiritual spaceship many miles from the real world. On the other hand, the Christians I knew who loved football and parties and could hold their own in a crowded bar were generally compromised in their commitment to God.

But Roger and the crew from Revelation were ordinary and extraordinary at the same time; they were in the world without being molded by it, and I was impressed. Roger offered to mentor me, and without a second thought, I quit the big city for rural Chichester by the sea.

## MORE HAIRCUTS ...

I arrived to discover a mini-revival among all the local Goths, punks, tree-hugging, tie-dyed crusties, and dreadlocked "alternatives" in town. Guys with chains from their ears to their noses, girls with mohawks, pretty much anyone with a weird haircut in town had recently become a Christian or firmly rejected Christ. There was manic worship led by a guy with "Sex Pistols" written on his bass guitar. There was deliverance, drugs, Satanists getting saved, spectacular backsliding, eating disorders, self abuse, and yes, there were evidently drug overdoses too.

So here I was, feeling totally out of my depth, speeding to the bedside of a new Christian who'd just overdosed. Arriving at the hospital feeling like an international man of ministry, I was relieved to find John conscious though white as a sheet, his stomach pumped and his eyes red with tears.

It was a fast learning curve. That great vision of an army of young people across Europe had suddenly shrunk to these people, in this place, with these profound pains and struggles. It often felt like one step forward and two steps back. Meanwhile, Revelation church was no longer a youth group. It had grown up, got married, and become family-oriented, which made the meetings less relevant to these wild new Christians. Gradually we realized that it wasn't enough simply to get these people saved. We needed to try to disciple them in their own context and to release them in ministry without requiring that they commit cultural suicide along the way. In short, we needed to plant some kind of youth congregation where the music could be thrash guitar or pounding decks and the teaching could be relevant to the everyday questions and struggles of this new flock.

## FALLING IN LOVE

We established the "Warehouse" youth congregation in the local student bar before, appropriately enough, moving to our own converted warehouse on the other side of town. Quite quickly there was an explosion of creativity with new bands, club promoters, and dancers developing their ministries alongside younger pastors and preachers. I had fallen in love with this crazy church where I was learning so much, and I'd also lost my heart to a girl named Samie with the most beautiful blue eyes I'd ever seen and a smile that could light up the room.

Samie's entire family had, it seemed, become Christians in the space of a few years, even her dad, the hardened policeman. Samie had been dating several different guys when she gave her life to Jesus and bravely ended the relationship with every single one. Her friends, who were used to Samie being the life and soul of every party couldn't cope with the change in her. At age seventeen, Samie found herself rejected and lonely, so she dropped out of school, landed a job, and poured herself into her newfound faith.

Samie and I were engaged on the Isle of Skye and married on a wet day in May, surrounded by friends, family, kids off the local estates in their father's ill-fitting suits, a couple of jugglers, and lots of laughter. Samie's band played cover versions of classic songs, and she sang her heart out dressed incongruously in her bridal gown.

We loved leading Warehouse, nurturing new Christians and trying to develop and disciple people. We wanted to build church around community rather than programs, platforms, and meetings. At this time we also began to connect as a church with other "youth churches," and the Cultural Shift Conference was born, where relatively unknown DJs like Andy Hunter could work with new bands Delirious? and wise older-heads Roger Ellis, Ray Goudie, and Billy Kennedy.

## DELIRIOUS RECALL

Around that time, the guys in Delirious?, who lived nearby, were discovering that many people wanted to worship more than they wanted to be entertained. Thousands would turn up for open-air worship gigs in their Littlehampton hometown. A couple of times at these events, I preached, petrified by the size of the crowd. Looking out over those worshiping crowds to the sea beyond, I recalled that moment, several years earlier, when a long-haired student on the cliffs of Portugal believed he saw a vision of an army of young people raised up by God. On those nights in Littlehampton, I could almost taste its fulfillment on the wind blowing in from the ocean. One time as the sun set, we baptized new Christians in a paddling pool and we prayed for the sick, and all around us the crowd sang and worshiped into the night. It was a night to remember, a night to rekindle old dreams.

Soon afterward, Samie and I sensed God moving us on. Warehouse was going well and leadership was maturing. It was time to pioneer again, and so we moved twenty miles into the city of Portsmouth, taking a team of twelve to plant a new congregation among students. It was great fun meeting in a room above a cafe and organizing DJ-led worship nights in the university bar with our friend Kenny Mitchell from New York. Unable to think of an imaginative name for these events, we simply called them "church," which the non-churchgoers thought was the coolest name ever!

Living in a cramped one-bed basement flat with "Wellie," our massive, boisterous black Alsatian shepherd dog, we became parents when Hudson was born. Having established the work in Portsmouth, we returned to Chichester. Everything was going well. We were busy but happy with a new child, a stream of lodgers, a growing ministry, and good friends. It was seven years since my move from London, and I now had my roots firmly planted by that stream Jeremiah described. Samie began to get migraines, but we thought little of it. Life was full and good.

So why, when things were so great, did I find myself awake, night after night, pacing the house in growing frustration? How could my diary be so full while my heart felt so empty? Why was a grown man with a great life secretly crying?

---

**Further Information:**

*www.culturalshift.net* began life as "Remix."
*www.revelation.org.uk* is part of the Pioneer network of churches.
*www.fusionuk.com* has information on work with students.

## DEEPER

## WHAT IS THE 'EMERGING CULTURE'?

"I have voluntarily become a servant to any and all in order to reach a wide range of people: religious, non-religious, meticulous moralists, loose-living immoralists, the defeated, the demoralized—whoever. I didn't take on their way of life. I kept my bearings in Christ—but I entered their world and tried to experience things from their point of view" (1 Corinthians 9:19-22, The Message).

This is an exciting time to be alive. The world is changing fast. We are thinking differently, approaching life with new expectations and a different set of questions. Sociologists call it a paradigm shift.

Author Leonard Sweet describes different reactions to this shift, distinguishing those who are native to the new worldview (generally younger people born into postmodernity) from those (generally older people) who find themselves immigrants, seeking to learn a new language of thought that will never be their mother tongue.

But whether you are a native or an immigrant, the challenges of relating what you believe to the world in which you find yourself remain the same. Graham Cray has noted that Western culture experiences major cultural shifts at least every 200 years. He argues that, just as the world changed forever with the invention of the printing press and the industrial revolution, so this generation stands at a time of profound social change. With the invention of the Internet, satellite communication, and low-cost air travel (not to mention global terrorism and the rise of tribalism), the Western worldview is becoming more complex and possibly less rationalistic.

We are, therefore, a vanguard generation with a responsibility to lead at a time of great opportunity and great danger. We are watching the world change, and we don't yet know what it is going to look like. This is what we mean when we talk about an emerging culture.

The challenges for the Church at such a time are profound. A generation that finds itself in the crux of such a change has a significant responsibility for shaping the new ways of thinking that will define its own age but also that of the coming era. When Christians get it right at such times, adapting themselves to the changing culture and finding new language for timeless truths, the Gospel spreads more easily for years to come because it makes sense to people. However, when the Church gets it wrong by resisting change and enshrining nostalgia, we risk apparent irrelevance and an upward struggle.

Will Jesus Christ be famous and favored in the coming age, or will He be a peripheral choice on the menu of social preference? You can call the culture "progressive," "emerging," or "postmodern." The challenge is the same: To reinvent the Church without changing the message, to reach this generation for the sake of the age to come.

**For further Reading:**
Leonard Sweet, *The Church in Emerging Culture: Five Perspectives* (Zondervan, 2003)
Brian McLaren, *The Story We Find Ourselves In: Further Adventures of a*

*New Kind of Christian* (Jossey–Bass, 2003)
Graham Cray, *Post-modern Culture and Youth Discipleship* (Grove Books Ltd., 1998)
Dave Roberts, *Following Jesus*, (Relevant Books, 2003)
Pete Greig, *Awakening Cry*, (Kingsway Publications, 2004)

### JOURNEY

## WHAT AM I BID?

Suddenly I find myself in a giant hall. Surrounding me are thousands of young people, battered, bruised, and broken. Then suddenly, I hear a voice: "What am I bid?"

A young girl stands out before the crowd of leering, sneering men. "What am I bid for this piece of flesh?"

The men start to cheer and shout figures: "Ten," "Twenty," "Fifty," "One hundred."

What can I do, God?

I start to bid. I have to save her. The cost becomes huge, and I begin to waiver. Can I afford this? What price will I pay?

The dream stops.

I'm alone again. But the faces are real enough: Sarah being sold into prostitution; Mike with a revolver in his mouth; Kat covered in cuts and bruises; John falling into crime; Laura alone and desperate; Steve, heroin needle bulging into his vein.

"What am I bid?"

The voice shatters the silence. The auction is on again. The bidding has begun. It continues day and night until the end. Most of the bidders desire only use and abuse. Satan drives them on.

And so I find myself in the auction. Will I watch or will I bid? The price of a single life is huge. The currency is prayer. The cost is massive, but the prize is glorious. A life for a life.

What am I bid?

*Written late one night in a Reading, U.K., Boiler Room*

# CHAPTER THREE

# TAKING **JERICHO**
[U.K.]

DESPITE THE HEALTHY STATE OF THE Church, invitations to preach all over the world, my growing family, and the fact that we lived in a really pleasant Southern English town, I was deeply restless. My journal entry on July 2, 1999, captures what was going through my mind and troubling my heart.

**July 2**
Okay, Lord, this is it. Here in the middle of the night, I've finally reached the end of a long road with nowhere left to turn but to prayer. It occurs to me that for maybe two years you've been trying to get my attention and I'm so incredibly slow-witted or perhaps hard-hearted that I've done most things other than really stop and listen to you for the next step in my life. Outwardly the course of my life is set. But inwardly I am profoundly restless and I feel far from you.

There is no risk left and I am scared of settling for this.

Trouble is, everything's going great! It would be easy to miss my life a day at a time. It's all become too easy, too predictable, too safe, too sensible, and I feel like I'm just dying spiritually. Everything is going really well on the surface. On this crazy Christian circuit I guess, I've got a job for life if I want it: Pastoring, speaking, planting churches, all the Yoda-for-Jesus stuff. But that was never what I wanted. What I wanted—what I want—is you. To know beyond doubt that I am seizing the moment, sucking the marrow from each day, right at the center of your plan. That was the dream of Cape St. Vincent. That was why I moved here from London. It was like jumping in the white water clinging to the raft for dear life. And yet somehow it's brought me to this slow, serene tributary. Why do I miss the white-knuckle ride? I guess those were the times I felt alive, clinging to you for dear life. So I've got nowhere left to go, but to get down on my knees and wait for you to speak.

The one thing that I do know is that if I don't learn to truly hear your voice for myself and follow it diligently regardless of what others say, I could feel like a fraud for the rest of my life.

"Nowhere left to turn but to prayer … white-water ride … all I want is you." Many of these comments are ironic, even funny, with hindsight. But these were important times; God was preparing my heart for the adventure that lay ahead. Augustine once said that God puts salt on our tongues that we may thirst for Him. Sometimes it is tears which carry the salt.

Finding answers in times of turmoil takes time. First we must find and formulate the questions. And before that we must simply face the pain. The godless philosopher Nietzsche wrote: "The essential thing in heaven and earth is … that there should be long obedience in the same direction; there thereby results, and has always resulted in the long run, something which has made life worth living."[12]

We're not good, I guess, at this "long obedience" thing. We want instant access everything—all our questions answered by return. But life is a journey with its own pace. There is often a process in God's dealings with us that goes something like this:

## 1. Numb, dumb heart

The passage of time brings to every disciple the pounding of pleasure, pain, and sin. These conditions can imperceptibly harden our hearts, slow the arteries, and make once lithe muscles grow inflexible. We are generally unaware of this aging process, but God sees and cannot look away. He loves us too much and has called us to too much to allow us to settle for less than full spiritual health. At such times, the writer of Hebrews says that God "disciplines us for our good, that we may share in his holiness" (Hebrews 12:10).

In order to call our independent minds and self-satisfied souls back to a place of spiritual intimacy and dependency, God must make our numb hearts begin to feel again. Through Scripture, circumstance—perhaps even through this book—He may begin to trouble and disturb your soul. Such feelings are not often associated with the Holy Spirit. They may be like the tingling ache in your mouth as the anaesthetic wears off after dental surgery or the howling pain of greater loss. But there can be no movement in our lives until we are confronted with the reality of our current state.

This is the first stage, and for me it took the form of sleepless nights troubled by something I couldn't define. This is a lonely time because you are feeling something you can't explain—even to God.

## 2. Wrestling

Next comes the wrestling, trying to make sense of this inner turmoil, looking for words to describe what you are feeling. You may study Scripture, splurge in your journal, read books, write songs, go for walks, and try to pray, wondering why you're weeping or wak-

---

12. Friedrich Nietzsche, *Beyond Good and Evil*

ing or wondering about taking some crazy, counter-intuitive step. Of course God is watching all this new activity with delight, biding His time.

## 3. Waiting

When eventually God gives you words for the things that are troubling your heart (and I'll say it again: this may take some time), things become easier. The internal storm calms, and you can talk at last with clarity to God and to others. The chaos has a pattern now. There may be no answers yet, but at least you have questions and you will throw these at the Almighty again and again. You no longer wrestle with yourself, but like Jacob, with God. This is the time of waiting and watching and can last years or mere minutes.

## 4. Blessing

Finally God steps in. The one who sowed those atomic seeds in your hard heart in the first place, the one who watched you cracking up and breaking down, the one who gently gave you the questions and waited and watched while you learned to pray, that same God now steps in to bless. A heart that was hard is now bruised and bleeding soft. An independent adult has become needy, humble, and poor in spirit. A self-sufficient child has succumbed to a hug. You have learned to need and to heed, to wait and to watch once again.

"And he said: 'I tell you the truth, unless you change and become like little children, you will never enter the kingdom of heaven'" (Matthew 18:3).

## AND GOD SAID NOTHING

As I poured out my heart to God that summer, I had no idea that I was embarking on such a journey; I was unaware that I was walking through the steps outlined above on this "long obedience in the same direction." All I knew for sure was that I was hungrier than ever for God, waiting for guidance, waiting for His fresh touch. Six days after that last journal entry, I was writing again:

## July 8

That night was incredibly significant (July 2). I realized that I had come to a point of desperation and that I can honestly say my greatest desire in life is to know that God is with me. I set my faith toward this great goal.

The truth of the matter is that I'd rather be unhappy and know that God is with me, than be happy, comfortable, and unsure of God's presence.

I remember times gone by of incredible fulfillment and others of great unhappiness, but the single thread that holds them together is that I knew that God was with me at the heart of it all. He was caught up in my decision-making on a daily basis and I felt truly alive. Right now by contrast I am technically happy but there is this underlying sense of dullness. I just spent a while in the mists of dawn on the Trundle [a local hill] looking for God, crying, trying to listen, being honest in a way that has to whisper.

Later Samie asked me what God had said to me, and I replied "nothing." God said nothing, and that's okay, because I'm starting to wrestle for His presence again, and I'm prepared to wait. I feel like God is waiting to see if I am waiting. If He just flooded in with answers and guidance right now, I would not have changed, I would not have learned to wait and trust without the answers, and without a road map for the future. So I'm kind of glad that God was silent, because I actually want to wait, I want to prove my metal to God; I don't necessarily want ease and instant anything anymore.

I want to be different before I do anything different. So I'm waiting for God, and God is waiting for me to see if I am really waiting for Him, and not just wanting things from Him. And as God and I eyeball each other in this way, I feel good. I feel alive and engaged with what matters, and I'm going to win this waiting game with God.

## CALL OF THE WILD

Looking objectively at the congregations Samie and I had poured ourselves into for the previous eight years, although they had grown, they were a million miles from the book of Acts. There had to be more to discover.

I also felt trapped in a life that was increasingly being dictated to me by a diary. I think there's a danger spiritually, for many of us, that if God packed up and left town today we might not notice until tomorrow, or worse. We have strategies and structures that can easily bypass the Holy Spirit, strategies for funding, strategic ways of prioritizing time and advancing the kingdom which were ignored completely by Jesus. He allowed the woman with the issue of blood to divert His 911 call to a dying girl's bedside. He never established a Bible school and never even thought of a name for His ministry. He prioritized people without influence, offended those with power, and apparently missed major ministry opportunities in order to picnic and pray.

I'm not saying that it's wrong to be organized. God gave us common sense and calls us to be good stewards of our resources. But if our techniques for time management, people management, and money management become automatic, we may well lose the dynamic leadership of the Spirit who is like fire and wind, a bird in flight, or a quiet whisper in the wake of calamities.

I just became sick of it, completely fed up with my own predictability. There was a lack of wildness, a lack of risk.

I was sitting up in the middle of the night reading books like Loren Cunningham's *Is that Really You, God?* It describes how Youth With A Mission began—the adventure and amazement of answered prayers, the sacrifices of pioneering faith, a bunch of friends simply daring to take God at His word. I ached to be part of a similar move, weeping and weeping in the middle of the night.

So I did it. I canceled all my upcoming appointments. I knew God had spoken to me about Europe that night in Southern Portugal and somehow I sensed that it was now or never. I'd served my apprenticeship. It was time for dry bones.

I took some radical steps. Samie and I passed on the leadership of the Warehouse congregation to two key people into whom we had poured ourselves over the proceeding years: Kerry Strotton and Dan Slatter. We trusted that these incredible people would soon outstrip us in their leadership, and we wanted to get out before becoming a cork in the bottle! As well as clearing space for them to lead, we were also clearing space for ourselves to hear from God and pioneer once again wherever He sent us. But letting go was only the first battle. Much of my sense of identity, I discovered, had been revolving around my leadership role, and without a title, I felt insecure. The personal questioning continued—what was I going to do with my life?

Faced with a vacuum, the part of my brain that is very strategic and that likes to plan and see goals achieved started to think about some amazing churches that have been planted in emerging youth cultures in Europe and America. Maybe, I rationalized, we should start to try and network these together?

But God had other plans and—more importantly—lessons He wanted to teach us about our dependency on Him. Whatever happened next would not be my idea, my plan, my achievement, for it is: "'Not by might nor by power, but by my Spirit,' says the LORD Almighty" (Zechariah 4:6).

## GOD'S WAY OF TAKING JERICHO

I'm not very good at hearing God's voice. I often get it wrong and have learned to cover myself to save embarrassment! When He does get through to me, it is often as I contemplate, write, and dialogue. For me there are times in discussion and even in writing, when my heart beats a little bit faster. It's like the PA system has been turned

up spiritually, and I just know that my words are mysteriously forming shapes around something God is saying.

He spoke to me one day as I meditated upon Proverbs 16:9: "In his
heart a man plans his course, but the Lord determines his steps." As
I explored the meaning of this verse, I found myself in dialogue
with God.

"Pete?" He said. "Congratulations! Your way of taking Jericho makes
perfect sense ..." There was an uneasy pause as I guessed the next
bit. "The only trouble is, son, it doesn't actually work." I knew it was
true—after eight years of hard work, and now these thoughts of networking new churches, no matter how hard we tried and planned,
our efforts were achieving a mere fraction of what we wanted to see.
"On the other hand," God continued with relish, "My way of taking
Jericho makes NO SENSE WHATSOEVER." He punctuated each
word, no doubt smiling with delight at the irony of it all: "And
yet"—and here was the killer—"MY WAY WORKS!"

Thanking God for this overwhelming vote of confidence, I began to
wonder what the Jericho metaphor might mean in practice. Was I
supposed to abandon common sense and go around yelling at walls?
I had to admit that had I been around when Joshua was sizing up
Jericho, I would have advised him to start making ladders. Maybe he
could build war machines or try besieging the fortress city—perhaps
with a prayer strategy alongside? I would almost certainly have
advised Joshua against yelling at the walls. As a military strategy,
shouting sucks. But the wild and strange voice of God told Joshua to
get the people moving and shouting—and of course the walls came
down. The power was not in the technique; the power was in
Joshua's ludicrous obedience. God is not a mindless dispenser of
demolition techniques; He is looking for relationship with those
who dare to trust Him against all other odds.

What, I wondered, was God's Jericho strategy for the emerging culture? What might it mean for the army of young people I'd envisaged in Portugal to advance not by might, nor by power, but in step

with the Holy Spirit? I knew there was something else for us to discover, but it would be a while before I detected the wild voice of God prompting me toward His strange strategy for breakthrough.

## WILD GOOSE CHASE

Waiting on God, according to Scripture, is not a passive, vacuous state, but rather an active process of asking, seeking, and engaging with His Spirit. Samie and I knew it was time to start waiting in this way; we also knew it was time to break a few rules. It's often said that the ancient Celtic church symbolized the Holy Spirit not as a domesticated dove but as a wild goose.[13] We decided therefore to embark upon a wild goose chase, following His leading around Europe, seeking simply to make friends, have fun, and all the while listen out for the still small voice of God.

As we boarded the ferry that would carry us across the English Channel, we had no idea what lay ahead. But years later we can see clearly that God had been preparing us for this moment. The very battles I had been fighting privately in my own heart—the growing desire to wait on God, to listen for His voice and to progress only in the power of His Spirit—these desires we now know were simultaneously growing in thousands of other hearts too. A generation with a great public cause was hearing the call to greater private spirituality, the call of God to pray.

Perhaps the atheists are right and God is a figment of our evolving imaginations. If this is the case, then in the words of Paul, we are to be "pitied more than all men" (1 Corinthians 15:19)! If there is no God, then the fact that we have now mobilized many tens of thousands of people to sacrifice sleep and talk to a wall in the middle of the night is the sum total of stupidity.

---

13. The Wild Goose motif is, however, challenged by the scholar Ian Bradley in his book *Celtic Christianity: Making Myths and Chasing Dreams* (Palgrave MacMillan, 2003). He finds no reference to the term "Wild Goose" as a representation of the Holy Spirit pre-dating George MacLeod, founder of the Iona Community in the twentieth century.

But if—just if—there is a God, we can be sure that we are connecting with the greatest power of the universe. And so, through these years of persevering, sacrificial prayer "we do not lose heart …"

> *Though outwardly we are wasting away, yet inwardly we are being renewed day by day. For our light and momentary troubles are achieving for us an eternal glory that far outweighs them all. So we fix our eyes not on what is seen, but on what is unseen. For what is seen is temporary, but what is unseen is eternal." —2 Corinthians 4:16-18*

## DEEPER

## THE FOUR MEN OF KELLS

The 1859 Revival In Ulster (Northern Ireland) profoundly touched the nine counties of the North. Sectarian violence slowed almost to a halt, and prostitution and drunkenness declined. A brewery had to close on account of the down turn in sales. One hundred thousand people made commitments to Christ. History suggests that the spark that lit this fire was a Friday night prayer meeting that started with four young men in the village of Kells in 1857. It was to be three months before it grew beyond the initial four, but by 1859 the parish of Ballymena was the scene of one hundred prayer meetings per week—sixteen a night.

God uses young people again and again to help restore nations and shape their destiny. It's not a hope statement or what Dietrich Bonhoeffer might have called a "wish dream." It's the inescapable reality of the witness of history. Young people stand at the heart of the salvation story.

Find out more on this subject in the "Even Deeper" section at *www.redmoonrisingbook.com.*

## JOURNEY

### HONEST TO GOD

"God thinks much more of your desires than of the words in which they are expressed. It may be natural for a scholar to consider the accuracy of your terms, but God especially notes the sincerity of your soul. There is no other place where the heart should be so free as before the mercy seat. There, you can talk out your very soul, for that is the best prayer that you can present. Do not ask for what some tell you that you should ask for, but for that which you feel the need of, that which the Holy Spirit has made you to hunger and to thirst for, you ask for that."

*C.H. Spurgeon, from a sermon entitled "Pray, Always Pray"*

# CHAPTER FOUR

# WILD GOOSE
# **CHASE**
## [GERMANY. KENYA.]

*"The wind blows wherever it pleases. You hear its sound,*
*but you cannot tell where it comes from or where it is*
*going. So it is with everyone born of the Spirit."*
*—John 3:8*

THE KID FROM LEIPZIG HAD GROWN UP,
died his hair blue, stuck a safety pin through his ear,
and moved to Dresden. That's where I first met him,
working in a restaurant in the Goth quarter of the
city. If Markus Lägel was a Christian, he was deeply
undercover. Back then I knew nothing of his experiences growing up in Leipzig with the Peace Prayer
Meetings. And in that German restaurant that night,
I also knew nothing of what God had in store for
me the next day and how it would connect my life
with that of the blue-haired guy and many more
like him.

Samie and I had been traveling for a number of days
now on our three thousand mile wild goose chase
around Europe with baby Hudson strapped patiently
in the back of the car. We had celebrated his first

birthday with a single candle on a Belgian bun at the home of a
South African pastor just outside Brussels. From there we had made
our way into the Netherlands, through Harlem and Amsterdam, and
down into Germany.

We were heading for Dresden because we knew of a radical community there called Kraftwerk (which means "powerhouse") made up of
many converted punks and pastored by a former medical doctor,
Karsten Wolff. It seemed like a good place to hang out.

Arriving in Dresden, a member of the church kindly allowed us to
sleep on his couch, but waking up the next morning, it became clear
that Samie was not well. With hindsight I know that the tumor that
would later nearly kill her was now growing in her head, lowering
her immunity and her energy level with each passing year.

But over a typically German breakfast of bread, cheese, sausage, and
strong coffee, our host happened to mention that Hernnhut, the
famous home of the Moravians, was just fifty miles to the east, and
asked if we would like to go and have a look. Although I was
familiar with the incredible story of the hundred-year prayer meeting which had taken place in Hernnhut in the eighteenth century, I
had been completely oblivious to its proximity. Samie, who needed
to rest in bed, encouraged us to go. Taking Hudson so that Samie
could be in peace back at the flat, we set off on a bright sunny day
to see Hernnhut. In many ways I left the apartment that morning
as a tourist and returned as a pilgrim. It was July 30, 1999.

## HERNNHUT

Hernnhut was established by Moravian refugees on Count
Zinzendorf's Berthelsdorf estate in 1722. Today it is a rural village
located at the juxtaposition of three nations: Germany, Poland, and
the Czech Republic. Zinzendorf's great ochre-colored chateau,
which had once hosted men like John Wesley, now stands sadly
derelict. We wandered around the immaculate streets, climbed the
prayer tower that overlooks the region, and studied the inscriptions

on the tombstones in the graveyard. It became clear that members of this sheltered, rural community had been shot out like rockets all over the world. Their tombstones spoke of the Americas, Greenland and many parts of Europe. Somehow the power of prayer had turned a very ordinary community into an extraordinary group of pioneers; from these quiet streets, basking in the summer sunshine, uneducated men and women had touched the ends of the known earth.

Next we went to the museum and saw Zinzendorf's original bowl from which the Moravians to this day select the Bible verses for their "Daily Texts" by lot. The Moravian Daily Texts are today the world's bestselling book of daily devotionals. Wanting to see the church where the prayer meeting had begun, we moved a mile or so down the road to Berthelsdorf. Here, in the picturesque, red-roofed church, with its fluted, two-tier spire, the community had gathered on the August 13, 1727. As they committed themselves to unity, the Holy Spirit had come so powerfully that some of the congregation—it is said—staggered from the building hardly able to stand.

That moment galvanized a profound vision for unity, for prayer, and for world mission. For the Moravians, it was both the culmination of a process of renewal (three months previously they had drawn up a "covenant for Christian living," something like a monastic "rule of life"), but it was also the beginning of a movement that would rewrite modern history. I knelt in a pew and said a little prayer, deeply conscious of the fact that an event in this building, almost exactly 272 years earlier, was somehow still impacting my life at the dawn of the third millennium. It would soon impact many more.

## THE POWER OF NORMAL

Some accounts of Hernnhut make it sound otherworldly and extraordinary. Some people seem to have had extraordinary experiences here, and God has spoken to them in powerful ways. But I was struck that day by how normal it was. There wasn't a radioactive glow around the village, and I didn't have any supernatural encounter. I was here out of interest, with my boy on my shoulders on a nice sunny day, partly because my wife was sick at home and wanted some space. I guess I'm not the most spiritually discerning guy in the world. When I get intense and try to hear God, I normally don't. When I do get the word of the Lord, it's often by mistake while I'm busy doing something else. And so, while simply wandering around Hernnhut, a simple thought occurred to me. There were no violins in the sky or bearded strangers muttering confirmation, just an idea that wouldn't go away.

Back home we knew that God was calling us to pray. We also knew that we were bad at it. Just a handful of worthy "intercessors" were diligently responding to the call while the majority of us struggled to even attend their weekly prayer meeting. We knew it was wrong whenever we thought about it. So we tried not to think about it. But the voice of the Spirit had been growing more insistent of late. I also had God's word about taking Jericho still ringing in my ears …

Maybe, I thought, there is something in this Moravian, nonstop prayer model that could help us back home to pray a bit more. Whatever the future held for Samie and me, I figured, it couldn't do any harm to get people praying a bit more. Walking into the Moravian chapel back in Hernnhut, with its plain, shaker-style interior, I calculated that it would only take twenty-four one-hour shifts to fill a day with prayer. Perhaps some people would enjoy praying through the small hours of the night. Surely, if this little community of thirty-two houses could pray nonstop for a hundred years, a church like ours could manage a month. And if God could touch the world from a place like Hernnhut, maybe He could even do it from an old English town like Chichester too!

The idea was not completely new. In some ways the visit to Hernnhut was confirming some earlier discussions.

## KENYA

Mike Brawan was orphaned at the age of eight when his mother and father were both killed in a car accident. With no one else willing to look after him, he was abandoned and simply left to survive by himself in the streets of Eldoret in Kenya, Africa. For the next six years, Mike slept under trucks and ate what he could scavenge from rubbish bins. The town's bus station often provided a place of warmth and shelter and was also a place he learned to steal from the waiting passengers.

At the age of fourteen, Mike's situation grew even worse: A friend who had lived on the streets with him was killed when the truck he was sleeping under moved. Grieving from loss once again, Mike got arrested for stealing. By the time Mike was released, he had already tried to kill himself. What hope was there for a street kid like him?

Desperate for hope, Mike attended an evangelistic rally at the city stadium. "It was as if the Lord Jesus was speaking directly to me," he recalled, and that night the orphaned street-kid quietly committed his life to Christ.

Mike continued to live on the streets and was eventually poisoned by some food he had scavenged. Taken into the hospital by some kind Christians, his condition became critical. The street kid was expected to die.

But God had different ideas, and that night, a "glowing doctor" (as Mike would later describe him) appeared at the foot of the dying boy's bed. In the morning, Mike woke to confound the doctors. He had been completely healed. Upon discharge, he was invited to live with a Christian family who taught him to read and write and encouraged Mike to go back to school. It was the first real care anyone had shown him since the day he had lost his parents.

Eight years later, I met Mike, now twenty-two. He was studying in England with a view of establishing a ministry for street kids like him back in Kenya. I was stunned by his testimony and amazed to hear that he had already started a church. His model of church planting impressed me, and with hindsight I realize that this young African understood far more about "God's strategy for taking Jericho" than we did with our cool music and our clever books.

Mike's instinctive approach to church planting had been simple. He gathered a dozen friends in a room, and they prayed nonstop for forty days. The two who didn't have jobs had to cover most of the night shifts by themselves, as well as ferry the others to their prayer slots in a beaten up old car. But they did it. They just assumed that this was the way you should plant a church.

After forty days they went out and began to preach. On the first day, "absolutely nothing happened," recalled Mike. "There was no crowd and no one got saved because I was just a former street kid and not a powerful white man in a stadium." But where we might have found this discouraging, especially after so much prayer, that was not in Mike's mindset. "We knew that we had broken through after all that prayer," he recalled with a typically African outlook, "we just had to keep going until it happened."

Going out again the next day, they began to preach once again. This time a crazy, homeless guy kept heckling them, until eventually he gave his life to the Lord. This was their first convert, and the transformation in him was so marked that many others followed. Mike's church, planted through prayer, grew quickly and now had several hundred members, including a local politician.

Mike's story had sown a seed in my mind. Even prior to this trip, we had been convicted about continual prayer by Mike's example in Kenya, and there had been some discussion about the feasibility of a similar forty-day stand. But now, finding myself in Hernnhut, the idea was making more sense than ever. Suddenly, continual prayer didn't seem so outrageous or ridiculous. In fact it was starting to seem like a perfectly natural thing for a church to do.

Just thirty-seven days later a candle would be lit that would unwittingly spark a new Moravian movement of prayer and mission. But first we had to drive south to Prague, and on the way, God would hijack us once again …

## DEEPER

### ZINZENDORF'S VOW

At school, Count Zinzendorf, leader of the Hernnhut community, founded a prayer group called the "Order of the Grain of the Mustard Seed." They made a solemn pledge that would shape the destiny of the rest of their lives, vowing to:

- Be kind to all men
- Be true to Christ
- Send the Gospel to the world

Each member of the order also wore a ring inscribed with the words, "No man liveth unto himself." For more about Zinzendorf, visit *www.redmoonrisingbook.com.*

## JOURNEY

### A PRAYER OF ZINZENDORF

"May there still be thousands of them who, in the plan and way assigned them, and in the orders into which you have called them, without leaving their way of worship and forming a new church for themselves, prove their identity as inward men of God, as members of your invisible and true body before all people, for your own sake. Amen."

*From Nine Public Lectures*

# CHAPTER FIVE

# FACING
# **FRONTIERS**
[THE CZECH REPUBLIC. AUSTRIA.
ROMANIA]

*"The King will reply, 'I tell you the truth, whatever you
did for one of the least of these brothers of mine, you did
for me'" —Matthew 25:40*

THE MORNING AFTER OUR VISIT TO
Hernnhut, Samie was slightly better, so we left
Dresden heading South, bound for the Czech capital Prague. But crossing the border an hour later, we
were totally unprepared for the shock that greeted
us.

Driving the winding forest road from the border
crossing, the sunlight fanned through the trees, and
we felt good. We were in the beautiful Czech
Republic at last, a secret land of fairy-tale castles and
delightful villages. As the forest road curved out of
the trees, we drew near to a town called Dubi. A tall,
slim girl dressed only in a bikini stood brazen with
her hands on her hips in the wooded rest area near a
few parked cars. Instantly a mental image was trig-
gered—like a flashback to the shop windows we'd
both seen a few days earlier in the red light district

of Amsterdam. It had been the same bikini, the same pose, but there the girl had been framed in a seedy shop window far away from pine forests and the Czech border. Driving on into Dubi, we saw more and more girls posturing by the roadside, offering cheap sex to truck drivers, loners, and German businessmen.

Some of the girls stood on their own; others clustered around the brothels and sex shops that lined the streets, smiling and strutting for the metal boxes speeding by. Samie and I were feeling dirty simply driving through this place, and Hudson just wouldn't stop crying. We had seen red light districts before. We had even been in one of the world's most infamous examples in Amsterdam just days before. But nothing had prepared us for the small, dirty border town of Dubi here in Czech. Every doorway, rest area, and shop-front seemed saturated with sex.

It's hard to convey the sense of lostness and dirt that hangs over Dubi. Nothing erotic, just hollow, gaudy, soulless, and sad echoes of what could be. Every bend in the road revealed a new assortment of girls for sale. And the eerie thing about the place was that there were no old people, and every girl, it seemed, was a prostitute. It took some time to work this out—like looking at a familiar room where something is missing. The only people around were prostitutes and young men: builders, boys on bikes, a few policemen, and pimps. To me, all the men looked guilty. I guess I despised them for even living there.

And as we drove on, hermetically sealed in our nice, shiny car, every instinct cried, "Get out of here!" The guy in the car in front of us was curb crawling; I just wanted to overtake, to accelerate smoothly away onto clean, fast highways that would take us to Prague, where a room waited with crisp white bed linen.

But as I pressed my foot down on the accelerator, the final fatal blow came—the blow that meant we could not leave Dubi just yet, the blow that makes Dubi more than a memory for Samie and me. A single figure was waiting by the side of the road and beyond her the countryside lay stretched out in the sunshine like a golden hallelujah.

Getting closer to this last, lonely figure, we could make out her tight white leggings, a white T-shirt and bleached blond hair. White like an angel. She was the last face to pass, the last eyes to ignore, the last bit of Dubi before the clean open road. But something wasn't right about her. Something was troubling me about this last, lone figure …

Her proportions were all wrong. The body was too small, the eyes were too big, the face too rounded. Speeding past, my eyes caught hers with a flash of recognition, and I realized I was looking at a child, not a woman—no more than twelve years old, hiding beneath heavy make up. Just a kid, pretending to be a woman for men who like it young.

Speeding past onto the open road, Samie and I sighed with relief and breathed again. Hudson stopped crying almost straight away. The air, it seemed, was cleaner. But then, a familiar small voice began to speak to my conscience, triggering an equally familiar wrestling match within me. If I could just ignore that voice another few miles …

"We need to go back," I said, remembering something Tony Campolo had said. "We need to buy that kid an ice-cream cone!" Samie looked at me incredulously: "Didn't you see that mean look-ing man in the car watching her? He was probably her pimp. It would be dangerous to park with a baby and all our luggage. And, anyway, Huddy needs feeding!"

Knowing she was right, we drove on and found a field for a picnic lunch. But sitting there in the grass we hardly talked. We were both troubled by the place we had been, just a few miles back toward the German border.

As we ate our picnic in silence, the conviction grew in me that this was a defining moment, a moment of truth, perhaps even a moment of judgment for Samie and me. Such moments generally cross our lives when we least expect them, but when they do, our actions and responses say everything about us for weeks, or months or years to come. They are tests, moments of divine crisis, which the Chinese call "dangerous opportunities." I knew that if we drove away from Dubi that day, a small irredeemable part of me would feel like a hypocrite forever, unable to guarantee a different response the next time round. How could we cruise from Hernnhut to Prague through Dubi, claiming to be listening to God, talking great concepts about an army of young people, yet ignoring the needs of the poor at our door? I knew that an apology to God later that night in Prague would be too late.

So we decided to go back to find that girl and buy her an ice cream cone and maybe let her be a kid for a minute before the next customer came along. It was a meaningless, pointless thing to do, but that is how all prayer and all worship appears to the rational mind. How hollow my prayers would be tomorrow if I did not do this today.

As we forced ourselves to head back up the road to Dubi, Samie and I discussed the best approach, agreeing in the end that I should go alone: A man, approaching a girl, with a simple gift of love instead of a payment for lust.

Stopping outside the town, I chose two ice creams, one for the girl and the other for her pimp. I also bought the biggest box of chocolates in the shop shaped like love hearts and the biggest bouquet of flowers they had too. The assistant winked as he took my money, "You must really be in love, my friend!"

But back at the rest area the girl had vanished. We waited for her, but she didn't re-appear. Was she with a man right now? Another prostitute had taken her place, an older woman pretending to be younger. We drove around looking for the kid in a daze, gutted to have missed her, praying for guidance.

Looking down at the flowers and the ice cream, which was beginning to melt, I parked the car feeling suddenly stupid. In my rearview mirror I could see one of the many brothels, and there were two women outside, leaning on the wall. Perhaps they would know where the girl was if I described her to them.

My heart was racing as I stepped out of the car and began to walk toward them. I whispered, "Help me, God, to look at them the way you looked at prostitutes: cleanly, in the eyes, and with love."

I felt clumsy and stupid approaching a couple of prostitutes in the Czech Republic clutching a big bunch of flowers and a heart-shaped box of chocolates. They were now watching my approach, no doubt amused by my contraband of confectionary and shifting themselves psychologically into business mode. I hesitated a split second, and, as if by reflex, they began to perform and to flirt right on cue. One of them had a Mediterranean tan and was wearing 1970s sunglasses.

I asked if they spoke English and they shook their heads. "Deutsch?" one enquired hopefully. It was going to be impossible now to ask them about the girl. But as I wondered what to do and scanned the faces of these two women, my heart began to melt like the ice creams in my hand. Up close they didn't seem soulless or dirty or even particularly sad. They just seemed like people living in a different world. It was no longer about the girl in the rest area. It was now about these two people in front of me. Grinning stupidly I handed one the bouquet of flowers and the other the large, heart-shaped box of chocolates. They laughed and took the ice cream too.

"Jesus liebe du," I stammered in terrible German. Seeing the look of confusion on their faces I repeated the phrase. "Aagh," said the Mediterranean girl knowingly. "Liebe. Liebe, ja?" and she began to move seductively toward me.

"Nein!" I exclaimed, a little too quickly. "Jesus." I pronounced it slowly, pointing to the sky. "Jesus, liebe ..." and I pointed to my heart, "du," and I indicated each of them.

The expression on their faces slowly changed. They pointed to the sky and then looked at their gifts and then back at me quizzically. The flirting had gone, and I thought they were smiling in a different way. I grinned back foolishly and Samie, who was watching from the car as I walked back down the road, saw the girls smell the flowers, exchange a few incredulous words, and just begin to laugh.

Driving away from this absurd encounter, Samie and I sensed that we had just prayed a prayer that pleased God. Our hearts were lighter, but still we think about Dubi. A year later *The New York Times* would carry a front-page article about the town and its trade in sex. Girls from Bulgaria, Belarus, Ukraine, and Russia, it reported, are lured there with the promise of work, but become prisoners of the vice trade, heavily in debt and without their passports to get home. The article goes on, "When you scratch the shiny facade which Dubi gives the sex industry you find a world of violence, hatred, sexually transmitted diseases, misery, and orphaned children which the prostitutes dump at the nearby Teplice orphanage."[14]

The article goes on to report that child prostitution can also be found.

We knew that Jesus would have done more than buy flowers. He made friends with prostitutes. He sat and ate with them and allowed one to massage His feet. He listened and dared to love in spite of what people would think. Giving them dignity, He refused to condemn them for their sin and even wrote their names in the very scriptures.

## PRAYER AND JUSTICE

In Luke 18:7, He said rhetorically, "Will not God bring about justice for his chosen ones, who cry out to him day and night?"

There is an essential link between justice and prayer—especially the continual prayer of those like the Moravians who "cry out ... day

---

14. *The New York Times*, September 19, 2000: "Czech Republic: Streets of Dubi Lined With Brothels And Prostitutes."

and night." As we drove on toward Prague, the pieces of the jigsaw were slowly coming together, though I didn't know it at the time. In Hernnhut the previous day, I had been brought face to face with the impact that people can have in persevering prayer. But today in Dubi, God had unexpectedly spoken about justice and compassion, about the fact that intercession is impossible until we allow the things that break God's heart to break our hearts as well.

This is exactly what the prophet Isaiah said to the people of Israel who had become "super-spiritual" and divorced their prayer life from the immediate issues of justice to the poor.

> *"If you are generous with the hungry*
> *and start giving yourselves to the down-and-out,*
> *Your lives will begin to glow in the darkness,*
> *your shadowed lives will be bathed in sunlight."*
> *(Isaiah 58:10, The Message)*

The prophet Amos confronted the hypocrisy of socially irrelevant spirituality with evident anger:

> *"I can't stand your religious meetings. I'm fed up with your conferences and conventions. I want nothing to do with your religion projects, your pretentious slogans and goals. I'm sick of your fund-raising schemes, your public relations and image making. I've had all I can take of your noisy ego-music. When was the last time you sang to me? Do you know what I want? I want justice—oceans of it. I want fairness—rivers of it. That's what I want. That's all I want." (Amos 5:21-24, The Message)*

As 24-7prayer developed, I would often have cause to reflect on the symmetry of those two days: the first in a peaceful village that was a place of prayer, the second so nearby, in a place of such pain and perversion. The marriage of prayer, mission, and justice was to be essential to our future, not least as our first Celtic prayer houses developed. But all of that was still a long way off.

## THE ARAB

"The Arab" was something of a legend. To all appearances she was just an ordinary, dark blue Ford Transit van driven around Eastern Europe, generally by three carefree young tourists from the West. In fact, she had been skillfully modified to carry up to a ton of Christian literature: Bibles, New Testaments, and tracts into countries suffering under Communist tyranny. Bibles were stashed secretly behind false walls, under a false floor, and even in special cavities behind the headlights. For eleven years The Arab had conducted two or three missions a month, breaching the iron curtain from Austria without discovery, carrying her illegal contraband to persecuted believers under constant fear of the secret police.

Freshly graduated from university, Ian Nicholson felt a thrill of excitement every time he was allowed to drive this legendary vehicle from the Operation Mobilization base in Vienna. It was an honor to be behind the wheel once again, bound for Romania on this cold, bright day, and he glanced across at his two accomplices who grinned nervously back. Linda was a red-haired missionary veteran who was full of the drive and focus that would later take her to pioneer a new work in Greece and Albania. And then there was Doreen from Ireland. Doreen must surely have been the only opera-singing Bible smuggler anywhere on planet Earth and seemed to spend most of the day in the cramped vehicle, practicing her scales. At times, Ian and Linda were able to laugh, but at others sharing the van with Doreen became intensely irritating. But all three of them often managed to see the funny side of their curious grouping, laughing about: Linda the red-headed human dynamo, Doreen like Madam Butterfly on a mission from God, and Ian who just three years earlier had been an eight-pint-a-night sports-mad atheist.

Signs on the road announced the immanent border crossing, and Ian glanced nervously back to check for the hundredth time that there was nothing suspicious lying around the van. Doreen volunteered a prayer in her lilting Irish accent. All three hearts were racing as The

Arab approached the Romanian border once again. Were they about to be discovered? After so many trips, the hiding places seemed so obvious to the team. Had a police informer finally called their bluff? Would The Arab finally be exposed and impounded? Would they spend tonight under interrogation or on the open road bound for the house of secret fellow believers?

That was the fear, more than any, which pumped adrenaline through their veins as the soldier waved them down: the believers, brothers and sisters in Christ facing imprisonment and terrible torture should their cover be blown or a certain blue transit van be followed. The believers, trapped behind the iron curtain, risking everything for their faith in Christ.

Pulling to a halt, Ian wiped his hands on his jeans and rolled down the window. The unshaven guard leaned in. The flaps of his regulation army cap were down over his ears, and a Russian kalashnikoff rifle hung menacingly from his shoulder. In broken English he began firing questions aggressively at Ian, his eyes scanning the van suspiciously as he spoke. His breath, which was steaming in the cold, smelled of cheap brandy and cigarettes. No other western vehicle would cross this checkpoint all day, and the Customs official fully intended to be thorough. His manner was threatening: full of anger, alcohol, and animosity toward these despised foreign visitors.

Retreating from the window, his predictable questions having received the predictable answers, the Customs guard began to scrutinize The Arab, banging his way down the panels, listening for any suspicious sound, and scanning the paint for any give-away marks. The banging reverberated around the inside of the van, and the team glanced nervously at each other. Unspoken prayers were offered by all three to "make seeing eyes blind" once again. The back doors of the van swung open, and a biting wind swept through the vehicle. Now the guard was searching the inside, shaking sleeping bags, banging the walls, rummaging through bags, boxes, and even Linda's wash kit. He was being extra severe, hoping for a "gift" to smooth things over. Disappointed after a while, he climbed out of the van muttering. There he paused before banging his way down the other side of the vehicle, stopping to examine the wheel arches and kicking the tires.

And then, suddenly, the mood changed, and a younger guard became animated and aggressive. He started shouting, calling another soldier who came running, carrying a box. "What's happening?" hissed Doreen in alarm, and Ian realized he was gripping the steering wheel so tight his knuckles were white. "It's okay," he assured the girls, "just a tool-kit." But he knew that this was not okay. This was not normal. All three tensed as the guards began to methodically unscrew the rear lights. Ian had been told the Arab was designed for this, but it was a journey into the unknown. Did they know something? What would happen if they started drilling?

Ian forced himself out of the van and wandered casually around to the back to express surprise. The soldier looked up at the tourist scowling and spat out an order in Romanian that needed no translation. Falling silent Ian watched the soldiers in slow motion. They had unscrewed the plastic cover and were removing the bulb, their hands close to The Arab's precious contraband. Ian wondered for a moment if they could hear the thudding of his heart pounding so loudly in his own ears. If they were this thorough with all the lamps, it would be extra brandy all round that night in the guardhouse, and the end of The Arab for sure.

Losing The Arab would be a tragedy but, other than that, Ian wasn't too worried about the prospect of arrest. Since joining Operation Mobilization's Eastern European team, he had been told that he must be prepared for at least two years in prison. It was just part of the job. They had also been trained to handle the inevitable interrogation. Nothing could be more vital than the protection of their brave Romanian contacts. Ian's mind wandered to the hand-written letter locked away in Vienna. If he disappeared today, he knew that it would soon arrive at his home in England, telling his non-Christian parents that he loved them, that he was okay, and that they should try not to worry.

Replacing the lens, the soldiers stood up and began to talk in Romanian. One of them laughed and offered the other a cigarette. Catching sight of the clean-shaven Englishman, he waved dismissively and simply barked: "Go!" Immediate relief flooded Ian's racing mind. Without hesitation the young Bible smuggler turned on his heels, ran to the front of the vehicle, and jumped in behind the wheel. "That," he told the girls, "was close," and then, as he turned the ignition and The Arab coughed to life, he grinned at the guard. "Hallelujah!" he whispered, and he had never meant it more in all his life.

Passports were quickly checked and stamped, the barrier swung open, and once again The Arab accelerated ahead into the Romanian countryside. A sense of elation and relief surged through Ian's heart. Everything was going to be okay. He was twenty-two years old, and while his friends were busy on the career conveyor belt at home, he was driving a ton of smuggled Bibles through the Transylvanian Alps on a bright, cold January day, certain beyond any doubt that this was the life Jesus had promised him.

## DEEPER

### NIGHT AND DAY ...

*"Praise the LORD, all you servants of the LORD, who minister by night in the house of the LORD." —Psalm 134:1*

*"O LORD, God of heaven, the great and awesome God, who keeps his covenant of love with those who love him and obey his commands, let your ear be attentive and your eyes open to hear the prayer your servant is praying before you day and night ..." —Nehemiah 1:5-6*

*"There was also a prophetess, Anna ... She never left the temple but worshiped night and day, fasting and praying." —Luke 2:36-37*

*"Be joyful always; pray continually; give thanks in all circumstances, for this is God's will for you in Christ Jesus." —1 Thessalonians 5:16-18*

**JOURNEY**

## DETOX AND A PLACE TO LIVE

"Chris came into the prayer room to find some shelter and to be in a safe place. He stayed for twenty-four hours and got a bit more than he'd bargained for. He was struggling with alcohol abuse and a whole lot of other problems, but he was desperate to receive help. A week later, thanks to the efforts of the Salvation Army he was registered with a detoxification program in London. Having successfully completed that, he underwent rehabilitation training. One year on he has a life, a job, a place to live, and he's still sober."

*Report from a Prayer Room, Southport, England*

# CHAPTER SIX

# WE HAVE **LIFT-OFF**
[U.K.]

*"Could you not keep watch with me
for one hour?"* — *Matthew 26:40*

AFTER OUR EXPERIENCES ON THE CZECH
border, Samie, Hudson, and I returned to Germany
via Prague, stopping in Nuremberg before traversing
the breathtaking landscape of Switzerland and crossing into France. As we traveled, we talked and prayed,
eventually returning to England with a conviction
that God was calling us into a season of continual
prayer night and day for a month.

And so, on Sunday, September 5, 1999, we launched
our Moravian experiment. The Warehouse congregation met as usual in Chichester, and I spoke about
Count Zinzendorf's model of continual prayer and
courageous mission, showing a shaky video I'd
filmed in Hernnhut. I also reminded the congregation about Mike Brawan's testimony from Kenya. If
he and just a few friends could plant a church by
praying nonstop for forty days, what might happen if
we did the same? The challenge seemed clear.

At 8 p.m. a tattooed wide-eyed boy named Lloyd, who had moved down from London to be nearer his beloved soccer team Portsmouth FC, lit a three-wick candle. It symbolized trinity as well as the flame of intercession that we were determined to keep alight for the whole of the coming month.

Just as the Moravians had divided themselves into "choirs" and watches, we devised a large chart breaking the month into weeks, days, and hours. On this, people were simply invited to sign their names in the hour slot they wanted to cover. The previous Sunday at church, we had taught on the power and privilege of prayer, concluding with a practical challenge to give ourselves to prayer in a disciplined way during the coming month. Many people had made pledges to God, promising to pray for anything from just an hour a week up to an hour a day, and we had encouraged them to make themselves accountable for these pledges by signing up for slots on the chart straight away. We also asked small-group leaders to consider taking on a twelve-hour slot, to share out between their members. Some groups planned "sleepovers" at the venue, in which group members would wake one another through the night to keep watch in shifts. In this way, we formed a bedrock of prayer so that the first few days of the first week were filled before we officially launched the prayer room that night. How long we could sustain it for, however, we had no idea.

## ROOM FOR GOD

There had been some debate as to whether we should base the prayer in a fixed location or whether to make the model more of a decentralized prayer chain where everyone could do it in the comfort of their own home. But remembering Mike Brawan's use of a prayer room in Kenya, and the way that the Hernnhut community was so close-knit geographically, we felt that perhaps there was something important about a dedicated location for prayer. Knowing our own frailty in prayer, we also figured that it would be a good discipline to have to turn up at a particular place at a particular time; making it far harder to hook off or sleep in! Unwittingly, in making this decision, we stumbled upon one of the keys to 24-7's impact: the biblical idea of "tabernacle" that seems to resonate powerfully with the postmodern mindset. As the apostle John wrote: "The Word became flesh and made his dwelling among us and we have seen his glory …" (John 1:14).

## KERRY

Having decided on the need for a fixed location, we selected a bare, white room adjoining our church offices that has a fire door out onto the parking lot. Kerry Dutton mobilized some of the congregation's artists to make the space as conducive as possible to intercession. I've never known anyone as gifted as Kerry at motivating people and making things happen. She's a natural leader, a born rebel, and a great friend.

When we first met Kerry, she was using her leadership gift to guide school friends into drugs and plenty of trouble. But with a little love and some straight talking from Samie, she dropped her hard, rebellious exterior, and the natural leader became a loyal follower of Christ.

"Please tell me I don't have to hang out with the Christians at school now," she begged, but was soon hatching plans to gather teens from across the town after school for worship and prayer. She came to ask my advice about these meetings one day, and I clearly sensed God saying, "Pete, if you touch this it will die!" I encouraged Kerry to go ahead and do it, but without any help from me. Several months later I ventured along to have a look at the resulting event—loads of teenagers in school uniforms milling around worshiping, chatting, and occasionally listening to whatever was being said by the person at the front. The music was terrible, the teaching was worse, the meeting was way too long, and people just kept becoming Christians. In fact, for about a year, every time they met, someone was healed or someone gave their life to Jesus. I knew that although I could have arranged better meetings, they would never have carried the indigenous impact of Kerry's extraordinary little gatherings.

A few years later, Kerry was to become a key pioneer of the 24-7 movement both locally, as we began in Chichester, and then internationally, by motivating, leading, and making things happen that others might consider impossible. With her infectious laugh and "can-do" mentality, she would mobilize many to pray like they'd never thought they could. And small decisions she made in those early days as we prepared to launch our first prayer room were to shape what would become an international movement. Little did she know that 24-7 would also trigger the succession of events that would lead her to the man she would marry. He wasn't a Christian yet but, as we gathered on September 5, 1999, many things were about to change.

## THE WHISPERING ROOM

The first time I stepped into the room, I was amazed. Kerry and her team had transformed a sterile, empty space into a place where prayer was going to be easy and exciting. By draping linen and placing lamps, they had divided the room into distinct areas with scatter cushions on the floor and paper covering the walls awaiting our clumsy graffiti. In one area they had laid out coffee facilities, and on the wall was a large local map. There was an altar built around the old pool table covered in tea lights, a Bedouin style tent made from white muslin sweeping down from the ceiling, and in one corner the branch of a tree studded with twinkling white lights. I noticed that the windows had been blacked out for privacy, and someone had already pinned a hand-written prayer to the branch of the tree. Even before the hours of prayer that would fill this room and before the walls were covered in artwork expressing people's heart cries to God, this was now a room that made you want to whisper.

This departure from "prayer as normal" was to be a key cause of the spiritual epidemic that this room would incubate. Thousands who were normally allergic to formal prayer meetings would discover that a solitary hour in a slightly chaotic looking small room could cure their prayer resistance, change their minds, and sometimes even change their lives.

## FIELD OF DREAMS, FIELD OF HARVEST

So, on the fifth of September, we gathered in the converted warehouse adjoining this twinkling, whispering, virgin space, lit a candle, and began to pray. To be honest, the first few hours until midnight were really hard, and I went home with a sense of apprehension about the prospect of returning at three in the morning for my first solo shift in the room.

But stumbling into the prayer room just three hours later, I blinked through bleary eyes in amazement. The only thing I can say is that the room was by now buzzing. It was quietly alive, and quite unexpectedly my heart began to race at the prospect of prayer. As soon as the previous person had left me alone, I found myself pouring over the things people had already written on the walls and thanking God with mounting excitement.

As I poured out my heart to God, the hour passed as if it was ten minutes, and I began to wish I had signed up for two. The very idea of praying for two hours would have seemed impossibly stupid just days earlier, but now it was exciting.

Word soon spread that the best slots were the ones in the middle of the night. In that timeless zone, between 2 and 4 a.m., there was often an electric sense that you were keeping watch alone with God, and these less civilized prayer shifts began to fill up as easily as any others. The momentum grew as people became more immersed in the reality of what meeting God in that room could mean. Word began to leak out to the other congregations of the church, and soon we had the full-on 24-7 rota covered.

## DÉJA VU

One guy stepped into the prayer room with a gasp of recognition. A year before he'd received a vision of people praying in a place where the walls were covered in spidery writing, a candle burned and a globe caught the eye. "I could never understand the writing. And now I'm here, standing in the middle of my vision," he whispered.

Kerry was seeing a change in her friends. "Two in particular absolutely loved it. They had never really liked praying or spending great amounts of time reading the Bible. And yet these were the ones that were now doing most of the graffiti and just spending hours and hours in there."

Stories about the prayer room were leaking out into other churches. One day Kerry encountered strangers in the prayer room. "I noticed someone I didn't know and found out that he'd been told about us by Paul Weston, a friend of ours at a church in Sidcup, sixty miles away. He had driven down after work and was planning to come back the next night, such was his excitement." Perhaps we might become a little matter-of-fact about such a visit in the light of the worldwide expansion that would soon take place, but in an ordinary, local church, it is extraordinary when people begin to travel many miles to see what you are doing—especially when it's not some big event, not even something you've publicized. It is the most private place of prayer.

## NATURAL AND MIRACULOUS

A bubbly eighteen-year-old with long dark hair named Sam became a Christian and the very next day did her first hour in the prayer room. We were amazed that such a new Christian was praying like this when so few of us had ever before prayed for an entire hour throughout years of salvation. Having never been an active church-goer, she had assumed that 24-7 prayer was exactly the sort of thing churches would do!

> *"Prayer itself is an art only the Holy Spirit can teach us. Pray for prayer. Pray until you can really pray." —C.H. Spurgeon*

In the prayer room, people really were learning to pray simply by praying. By locking ourselves alone in a room with God, we were encountering His presence night after night and learning to listen to the still, small voice of his Spirit. People were studying Scripture, writing poetry, carrying one another's burdens in prayer more than ever before, and talking to their friends about Jesus after praying for them hours earlier.

But as well as learning how to pray, we were discovering the power of prayer. Amidst many frustrations that required ongoing perseverance, we began to experience real answers to prayer. Some of these were dramatic and clearly miraculous …

## ANGEL FACE

Gareth was a good-looking sport student with mini dreadlocks and olive skin who had been attending church for a little while. He was supporting himself through college with a part-time job as a shelf stacker in a large home improvement store. As the spiritual tempo increased around him, he said, "God, if you're real, please speak to me at work today." Out of the blue that day, a frail old lady came up to him, and with a twinkle in her eye told Gareth that God loved him. She will probably have no idea, this side of eternity, the impact her words were to have.

Amazed that God had answered his prayer so clearly, Gareth came to the conclusion that this little old lady must in fact be a divine messenger—an angel of God. Full of bullish, newfound faith, he rushed home after work to tell his housemates that an angel, disguised as an old lady, had spoken to him as he was stacking shelves at work that day. Their response was predictably cynical, although one of them would soon have cause to think again later that night as she attended an end-of-season private party for staff of the local holiday resort where she worked.

She arrived at the venue and said hello to the security boys at the door who were checking people's passes to keep the party private. A while later as music blared out from the DJ and the room buzzed with laughter and attraction, a stranger approached the cluster of girls in which Gareth's friend was standing. Looking her straight in the eyes he said, "You look sad," paused, and then said, "A friend of yours has just become a Christian and it's time for you to do the same." How did he know, and who was this guy anyway, getting all intense at the staff party?

"What's your name?" she countered.

"You don't need to know that," he replied mysteriously.

The friends were starting to giggle; one mouthed "weirdo" behind the man's back. But for Gareth's friend, it was all suddenly making perfect sense. Gareth had obviously been right.

The guy had wandered off, and in a rush of excitement, she searched the room for him. He was nowhere to be found, and security hadn't seen anyone like that come in or go out. The girl's cynicism was shaken, but she chose not to respond to God on this occasion, unlike Gareth. That's the nature of our witness—not everyone responds, even when God sneaks up on them. But God seemed to be sneaking up on people more as we prayed.

When Gareth told me the story about his friend, I was fascinated. I'm pretty sure that the little old lady who had approached him at work was exactly that: a little old lady who simply loved Jesus enough to approach dreadlocked shelf-stackers in DIY stores and tell them they are loved. But what about his friend's strange encounter at the private party? Perhaps I am too cynical, but I also prefer to think that the mysterious man at the party was not an angel either. I would much rather imagine that there's a James Bond style evangelist out there who breaks into sealed buildings, has accurate words of knowledge for complete strangers, and then escapes without a trace.

But maybe I'm wrong and Gareth's right. Maybe the angels really are so desperate to share the Gospel and so frustrated by our human reticence to do the same that the occasional one manages to jump over the back wall of heaven, popping down to planet earth to blow a few fragile minds before being summoned back to paradise. Either way, it was amazing to see how God was moving even in the lives of non-Christians as we prayed.

## A THRESHOLD PLACE

The prayer room itself was becoming a place of witness as more and more non-churchgoers came to have a look and even to say a few words of prayer. This most private place was becoming a spiritual threshold, even for those who didn't know Jesus personally.

One night, as the prayer continued at the other end of the building, a local promoter rented out our converted warehouse to stage a club night with a couple of famous DJs: Fabio and Grooverider. We'd leased him the venue because we love our building to be filled with people, especially those who don't yet know Jesus. Kerry's sister Claire went to the gig with a friend and during the night took her to see the prayer room out of curiosity. Tottering into the tabernacle in her micro-skirt and party shoes, she looked around, announced to Claire that she could do with some prayer because "my head's messed up right now," and settled down for a two-hour stay while the beats pumped out of the PA at the other end of the building.

Another day, two serious-minded university students studying religious education came by to check out the room. Immersed in dry theory about religion, they found themselves in the midst of something totally alive and immanent and stayed for ages.

Vicky Ward had a visionary experience as she looked up toward a sky light near the prayer room. She reported seeing a huge angelic figure armed with a bazooka standing on top of the building. Vicky was so terrified that she fell trembling on her face. She stayed there for hours, too scared to look up again, and eventually crawled into an alcove where she fell asleep. Her vision was an assurance for us that in our spiritual warfare, though the battle is real, God's forces are with us protecting us.

Vicky's account interested me, partly because I've never understood why angels didn't move with the times in terms of their weaponry, and yet this one was carrying a twenty-first century bazooka instead of a first century sword. But Vicky's reaction to the vision also interested me, falling to the ground with the holy fear of God, which does seem to be the biblical precedent in such moments of epiphany.

## TIME TO QUIT?

At the end of our intended month of prayer, I presumed that we should simply stop. We had, after all, achieved our goal, and it had gone spectacularly well—far better than we had ever dared imagine. I knew that the momentum was, if anything, growing, as others heard about the prayer room and began to make use of it, but I figured we would be wise to "quit while we were ahead." Time to stop and find out what was next.

Kerry, however, was insistent that we should continue. "I just knew really clearly, I can't explain it, I just knew that we had to carry on," she recalled.

People have often tried to call me the founder of 24-7 prayer or other grand titles, but the embarrassing fact of the matter is that I only ever started one prayer room, and I tried to shut it down before the movement was even born. Thankfully, someone else didn't let me, and as a result many hundreds of other people around the world have now also started prayer rooms in which many thousands are meeting with God 24/7.

## TOLD YOU SO

The second month of continual prayer was amazing. Someone unearthed a prophetic word, which had been brought to the church by my friend Justin Blake back in February, predicting that God was going to bring us into a new intensity of prayer and that people would even rise at night to pray. Most remarkably, he predicted that this explosion would be focused around the period from September to December. His word had been diligently recorded and simply filed away. Now that it had been unearthed and stuck to the prayer room wall with certain passages highlighted, it was incredible to realize, once again, that God had somehow pre-empted this season of prayer long before we had planned it. For me it was humbling to concede completely that I had been wrong to try to snuff out that three-wick candle (we were now on our fourth!) We now knew that this was a season of prayer that should continue until December.

## RHYTHMS OF GRACE

As we moved into our second month of prayer, it would have been easy to assume that mass revival was only just around the corner. After all, we'd never prayed so hard in all our lives. But that was when God sent us two key men with clear messages from his heart.

The first messenger was John Dawson, a man who has written extensively on prayer and reconciliation and is actively involved in high-level peacemaking around the world. John spoke at church, and a single, simple phrase he used just exploded like a dum-dum bullet into our understanding of prayer. "Everyone prays," he pointed out. "Even non-Christians pray. The difference when Christians do it is that they are climbing into the lap of their heavenly Father."

A prayer room is not some giant spiritual vending machine: Just put in enough money and you're guaranteed a can of Coke. A prayer room is first and foremost a living room—a place where the Father waits for His children to come and climb into His loving arms. It's a place where we can experience peace so that we can make peace later; a place where we can accept forgiveness so that we can live our lives as priests at work; a place where we receive our Father's acceptance so that we can love even those who laugh at us later in the day. John Dawson is a man clearly "involved" in the nitty-gritty realities of human brokenness, and yet he was reminding us that we find our strength for involvement in "intimacy" with God.

Getting the balance right between intimacy and involvement is never easy, but if we are going to reach a generation, it will be the intimacy of the prayer room that keeps us involved.

## BECOMING THE PRAYER

The second messenger that God sent us at that time was the author Brennan Manning, whose life-message is God's grace for "ragamuffins." His writings had already been inspirational for many of us, and so when he happened to be in the neighborhood, I was keen to take him out for pizza and learn all I could.[15]

"How do you ever know when you've prayed enough?" he asked me good-naturedly as we ate Italian together. It was a good question— especially for someone so inspired by the Moravians! Gently but firmly Brennan answered the question by explaining some fundamental truths about prayer to me that have become truly foundational for us ever since.

In the contemplative traditions, he told me, prayer is not primarily about changing things somewhere out there. It is first and foremost about changing something "in here," and he patted his chest. The most powerful thing that can happen in the place of prayer is that you yourself become the prayer. You leave the prayer room able as Jesus' hands and feet on earth. This is what it means to pray continually, to see with the eyes of Jesus and to hear with His ears with every waking moment.

Henri Nouwen pointed out in his book, *The Way of the Heart*, the literal translation of the phrase "pray always" is "come to rest." The Greek word for rest is *hesychia* and so Nouwen wrote, "Hesychia, the rest which flows from unceasing prayer, needs to be sought at all costs, even when the flesh is itchy, the world alluring and the demons noisy."[16] As we prayed continually, God was speaking to us powerfully about grace. Prayer, we were reminded, was about climbing into the lap of our Father rather than triggering some vast spiritual machine. It was about

---

15. Brennan Manning is perhaps best known for his book *The Ragamuffin Gospel* although, in my opinion, *The Signature of Jesus* is even better.

coming to rest in constant awareness of God's presence in our unde-
serving lives, and we must never start striving and straining under the
false burdens of guilt.

## CHRISTMAS

By December 1999 it was clear that 24-7 was about to explode onto
a much bigger canvas. Aware of this and the prophecy about continuing until December, we sensed that we should stop for Christmas,
celebrate the millennium with our families, and rest as we prepared
for the year 2000. Looking back on a remarkable three months of
continual prayer, there was so much to thank God for. It had been a
season of incredible impact. As we had waited upon God, He had
moved powerfully and practically. Often this had been in our own
hearts calling us to greater levels of engagement when we left the
prayer room to get on with the rest of our lives. But people were
witnessing more, studying Scripture more, and caring for and com-
municating with one another at a deeper level.

I'm convinced that some churches would cease to exist if they were
to cancel the Sunday service, but we found ourselves functioning as a
real community in prayer and fellowship daily. Looking back on
those three months, I wrote in my journal: "In the Warehouse congregation there have been salvations and blessings in every direction.
We've seen new giftings of the Spirit and pastoral breakthroughs in
certain people that we've wanted to see literally for years. We've broken the 200 mark at meetings for the first time. We even have people
helping out with the administration now!"

## WATCHMEN ON THE WALLS

As we discovered all these things, the urgency of prayer was growing
in us. I had been struck by the words that someone had graffitied on
the wall early in the life of the prayer room: "We will give ourselves
no rest, and we will give God no rest ..."

---

16. Henry J.M. Nouwen, *The Way of the Heart* (Darton, Longman and Todd, 1999) London, p. 60.

I didn't recognize the phrase, but later found it in a passage from Isaiah. The chapter was like a description of all that we found ourselves doing, lending focus to our prayers for Zion and for a broken generation. It's a passage that has become a calling card for many prayer rooms since:

> *"For Zion's sake I will not keep silent,*
> *for Jerusalem's sake I will not remain quiet,*
> *till her righteousness shines out like the dawn,*
> *her salvation like a blazing torch …*
> *I have posted watchmen on your walls, O Jerusalem;*
> *they will never be silent day or night.*
> *You who call on the LORD, give yourselves no rest,*
> *and give him no rest till he establishes Jerusalem*
> *and makes her the praise of the earth." (Isaiah 62)*

## NEW GENERATION

Some other people were picking up the "no rest" baton. I had worked on a skate park project with a guy named Paul Weston, and we had since become good friends. Paul is a great chef and an excellent skier, well-built, with his trademark floppy hair and London accent; he now pastors a church that is one of the most creative and innovative communities I've ever seen. Paul took one look at our prayer room and decided to take the idea home to his church in Sidcup near London. And so, with a core team of just fifty people, New Generation Church went away and prayed nonstop for an incredible fifteen weeks.

They're a wild bunch, and as 24-7 began to spread, guys from Sidcup would often pile into cars and drive many miles just to encourage another group who were starting to pray. One time they even borrowed a van and drove it to Switzerland to bless, affirm, and just say hello to one of the first prayer rooms there.

By the end of October, the prayer momentum was unstoppable. People were becoming almost addicted to the presence of God.

There would have been an outcry if we had tried to stop the flow.

And then, in our third month of continual prayer, the whole thing just went crazy as we gathered in Southampton, U.K., for the annual Cultural Shift Conference.

**DEEPER**

## WHEN YOU PRAY, SAY 'OUR FATHER'

*"Whatever the Father does the Son also does."* —*John 5:19*

Prayer isn't easy. Even Jesus' first disciples had to ask Him for help, and in response He said that we should start by calling God Father. That's the key to prayer.

Jesus introduced a new depth of understanding about God the Father. Before Jesus, the Bible has just forty references to God as Father; but the New Testament has more than 260! And Jesus wasn't just pointing people to a distant, Freudian father figure in the sky; He dared to call God Abba (Mark 14:36), a word used by any normal kid at the time to express love for their Dad. The single key that explains everything Jesus did was this intimate relationship He shared with His Father. In prayer each day, He learned to listen to God, and then He lived His whole life simply speaking His Father's words and doing His works (John 5.19).

Prayer brings incredible answers to deep needs. It can lead to genuine breakthroughs in calling people, villages, and cities back to God. But the most important thing that any prayer, or prayer room, from Alaska to Australia can provide is a place where people can be alone with their eternal Father, a place where you and I can study His features, find comfort in His love, learn to recognize His quiet voice, seek His advice, and pour out our childish hearts to Him. In the prayer room, we pick up God's mannerisms; we grow in His likeness. We actually become the answer to many of our prayers. And of course that's the greatest miracle of all.

**For Further Reading:**

Richard N. Longenecker (ed.), *Into God's Presence* (Eerdmans, 2001)
Floyd McClung, *The Father Heart of God* (Harvest House, 1985)
Brennan Manning, *Abba's Child* (Navpress, 2002)

## JOURNEY

## WATCHMEN ON THE WALLS

*For Zion's sake I will not keep silent,*
*for Jerusalem's sake I will not remain quiet,*
*till her righteousness shines out like the dawn,*
*her salvation like a blazing torch ...*
*I have posted watchmen on your walls, O Jerusalem;*
*they will never be silent day or night.*
*You who call on the LORD,*
*give yourselves no rest,*
*and give him no rest till he establishes Jerusalem*
*and makes her the praise of the earth ...*
*Pass through, pass through the gates!*
*Prepare the way for the people.*
*Build up, build up the highway!*
*Remove the stones.*
*Raise a banner for the nations.*
*(Isaiah 62)*

# CHAPTER SEVEN

# A PRAYER ROOM
# EXPLODES
## [U.K. SWEDEN.]

*"It is too small a thing for you to be my servant to restore the tribes of Jacob and bring back those of Israel I have kept. I will also make you a light for the Gentiles, that you may bring my salvation to the ends of the earth."*
—Isaiah 49:6

BILLY GRAHAM DISEMBARKED FROM THE SS United States in Southampton docks in 1954 at the start of a crusade that would come close to triggering an English spiritual awakening. Amidst massive media controversy the thirty-five-year-old evangelist went straight to the city's Central Hall to preach the Gospel to a capacity congregation. Twenty-seven years earlier, revival had visited this same venue through the Pentecostal preaching of George Jeffries. In those days a banner hung at the entrance to Central Hall declaring "For Southampton and the world."

The crowd that gathered in the building that night in November 1999 looked nothing like those that had convened to hear George Jeffries and Billy

Graham, and there were no such giants of the faith preparing to preach. But although the Cultural Shift crowd dressed differently and perhaps even thought differently, our heart for the Gospel was entirely the same. And something was stirring that night in that building that would once again impact "Southampton and the world."

On October 26, 1966, twelve years after Billy Graham's visit to Southampton, he would address the Berlin Congress on World Evangelization with these stirring words:

> "The evangelistic harvest is always urgent. The destiny of men and of nations is always being decided. Every generation is crucial; every generation is strategic. But we cannot be held responsible for the past generation and we cannot bear full responsibility for the next one. However we do have our generation! God will hold us responsible at the judgment seat of Christ for how well we fulfilled our responsibilities and took advantage of our opportunities."[17]

The opportunities presenting themselves to us at the dawn of the third millennium are no longer those of the great, post-war stadium rallies. Our opportunities are those of the World Wide Web, budget travel, the rise of tribalism, and the postmodern desire for community, authentic spirituality, and social justice. With a passion to reach our generation, the annual Cultural Shift Conference gathers to wrestle with the challenge of expressing church in this brave new world. It's a context that God seems to enjoy and has been a hothouse for a number of significant new ministries over the years.

## DANGEROUS DOWNLOAD

As we gathered on that cold November night in 1999, Central Hall was heaving with people dancing to DJ Andy Hunter's mix of heavenly beats. So many people were being impacted by the prayer rooms in Sidcup and Chichester that we had decided to establish one for

---

17. Billy Graham, *Just As I Am* (Zondervan, 1997), p. 565.

the weekend here too. Suddenly Roger Ellis, leader of the church in Chichester, came bounding up to me looking extremely excited. In his usual croaky growl he said, "Pete, maybe we could fill a whole year with unbroken prayer." I looked nervous, but Roger was, by now, bouncing around with excitement like Winnie the Pooh's Tigger: "Maybe people want to try this 24-7 prayer thing back home for a week or more. If everyone did a week, we could link it all together and fill the year 2000! What do you think?"

It had taken Roger about ten seconds to download an idea that would take the rest of us about ten years (I suspect) to outwork …

On Sunday morning we moved the conference from Central Hall into the cavernous Icon nightclub. A matter of hours earlier, the place had been jammed with Saturday night party people, drinking, dancing, and flirting. And so, as we entered the building to worship and pray, the air was still stale from the night before.

As the morning progressed, I climbed onto a podium usually occupied by the best, or most scantily-clad, dancers. I didn't quite measure up to either of these criteria with my scruffy T-shirt and gangly frame, but right now the podium was a pulpit and I had a proposal to make.

"If anyone wants to pray nonstop for a week or more with your friends next year, let me know afterward," I said, looking dubiously down at the crowd on the circular dance floor. "Maybe we could fill the whole of next year with prayer." A cheer of approval rose from the congregation, and in a flush of enthusiasm I would soon regret, I added, "We'll try and link it all up on the Internet." Everyone cheered once again.

I jumped down from this unlikely vantage point to discover that we had, effectively, just launched a prayer movement in a stale and gaudy nightclub. People began to hand me their names, or those of their churches, indicating their intention to pray nonstop for a significant chunk of the year 2000.

And that is how I came to be sitting at my desk the following morning, stirring my coffee and staring blankly at a piece of paper which
listed twenty-three locations, all fully intending to pray 24-7 in the
coming year. Quite a way to start the millennium, I mused.

I could faintly hear music from our own prayer room directly below
my first floor desk. Somehow that room had given birth to twenty-
three others in a single weekend. Quite an achievement.

But staring at my piece of paper that morning, I had absolutely no
idea what to do about it. I groaned, remembering my impulsive
promise of a website. We didn't even have one for our church at that
time, and I didn't know anyone who would make one for us for free.
I decided to write everyone an encouraging letter saying "Go for it!"
and promising to keep them posted should we by any miracle manage to bag a patch of cyberspace.

That was Monday. First thing Tuesday morning I got an email from a
complete stranger named Pete. It said, "I've designed your website for
the prayer thing. Click here to see if you like it!"

"Wow!" I thought and then, as I eased my mouse onto the hyperlink
and clicked, "probably a nutter."

Two things were immediately obvious about the website on the
screen. The first was that this guy really knew how to design sites.
But the second was that it was not as visually hip as I might have
hoped. If we were going to mobilize young people to pray, I figured,
it was going to be the re-branding challenge of the century. Soft
focus photos of skipping lambs next to smiling worship leaders in
open-necked shirts might appeal to some people—but most of those
types were probably already into prayer! Such images just weren't
going to cause the average student to jump out of bed with a mysterious longing to intercede.

Yet this guy clearly knew a thing or two about programming, he was
unquestionably keen, and to cap it all, I was undoubtedly desperate.

## MEETING PETE

Sitting in the restaurant, I surreptitiously studied the face of the stranger opposite me. His fair hair was neatly shaved down to about grade three, I guessed, but seemed to be suffering the effects of a recent encounter with a bottle of bleach. A canary would have been perfectly camouflaged. He was speaking excitedly, his eyes smiling through round, John Lennon style spectacles. It was clear that Pete Worthington was clever, kind, gentle, quick to laugh, and had an absolute passion to serve God.

Thus far, there had been a number of defining moments, milestones on the 24-7 journey: the visit to Hernnhut, Paul Weston's involvement, and Cultural Shift. But the story that Pete proceeded to tell me that day in that pub was without doubt the moment I first felt the tinge of fear. It's frightening when you blink and discover that you're in a speeding car but no longer driving. It's scary to realize that God is moving and you are somehow caught up in something much bigger than you could possibly have known. 24-7 was about to take "one giant leap" forward as God brought about another key connection.

Just as God had been preparing me in Hernnhut, Kerry in Chichester, Ian Nicholson in Vienna, and Markus Lägel in Leipzig, so God had been preparing Pete Worthington here in Bristol near Wales for this meeting with me and the movement he would soon be helping to lead.

Two months earlier Pete had left his job at British Aerospace. He had won an award for being one of their most promising employees, but an inner voice was urging him to make space for something new. He had given three days to prayer, asking God what he should do now. He felt that it would involve Internet work because of an experience in June a few months prior to our meeting.

## MATRIX OF LIGHTS

"I was sitting in a plane flying over Europe on the way back from a business trip," Pete explained. "It was early evening and dark outside. I was thinking of nothing in particular when I suddenly had what I can only describe as a vision, which looked so real. From my window I could see a matrix, a web of lights, randomly criss-crossing the earth going in all directions as far as I could see.

"There were hubs of concentrated light, almost like powerhouses which were sending out pulses of light across the matrix. I didn't understand what it all meant, but the whole thing was accompanied by an intense excitement, and I knew that I had just seen something significant. It was just after this that I felt the urge to spend time seeking God as to what it all meant, and somehow this experience changed my life forever. It was only in the weeks and months that followed that I began to understand what it meant. I felt it had something to do with the Internet in some way, but I didn't know to what extent. It is now clear that this was a prophetic vision of the network of prayer rooms which were going to cover the earth connected by the Web."

And so, stirred by his vision, Pete had quit his job, convinced that God was calling him to use the Internet as a platform for ministry. This made sense, as it was his skill base; he had been running the intranet services for British Aerospace.

But as he prayed, he also got the strong impression that his vision had something to do with a place called Chichester. He didn't know very much at all about Chichester; I don't think he'd ever been there in his life. It's a small place with a population of 40,000 people. With a cheeky grin, he told me that he had checked our tourist information page on the Web and thought, "I don't want to go there!" And then, a few days later, he was driving somewhere and talking with God. "The Internet thing—I've got some great ideas. The Chichester thing—that was just my imagination, right?" He felt God say, "Pete, look in front of you." This is always good advice when driving, but to Pete's amazement he now saw that the truck in front of him was from Chichester; the name of the city 150 miles away was emblazoned across the back.

A truck from that small town in front of him at that very moment! God had Pete's attention. It was still a bit of a mystery to him nevertheless. He didn't know anyone in Chichester. He then arranged to meet his brother in-law in Southampton at some strange conference called Cultural Shift. It was there that he heard my notice on Sunday morning and discovered the fulfillment of his word from God. He went home, spent the next forty-eight hours designing a mock-up website, and has worked for us unpaid ever since.[18]

## WEB

Author Leonard Sweet said that the future belongs to "the storytellers and the connectors." The website that Pete and I designed on scraps of paper at my kitchen table was to become a key tool for telling stories and connecting people together around the world.

On the site we seek to link up all the prayer rooms that are on the go at any given moment, sharing answers to prayer as well as heartfelt prayer requests. It's also a tool that enables us to focus people's prayers on broader issues of justice and current affairs. Like our prayer room, it's become a nonstop community, currently receiving almost two million hits a month and growing. In the chat forums, you will find atheists, anonymous heart cries for help, and profound poetry.

Quite a number of people have become Christians through the site, and many others have been discipled in their faith. One woman wrote in to say that advice she had received on the 24-7 website had saved her life. She was seriously contemplating suicide, but had been advised to talk to a doctor and as a result had found help for her depression.

---

18. *www.worthers.com*

On a lighter note, a number of romances have blossomed thanks to the site that Pete Worthington dreamed up. Trish Miller was an all-American girl from Virginia who read the testimony of a young Romanian guy named Mari on our website. She had a heart for the country already, even having visited Mari's hometown of Timisoara several times on mission trips, so she emailed him to say hi. They began to correspond and eventually arranged to meet up in his homeland.

Mari thought that Trish was a boy's name. He would never have been so friendly and honest had he known he was sharing his heart with a member of the opposite sex! On his way to church in Timisoara one night, Mari bumped into a friend and a strange young woman who seemed to know far too much about him. Seeing the look of confusion on his face, Trish introduced herself, and soon the misunderstanding became clear. However, the friendship grew, and they eventually got married. An international romance and even a cross-cultural call for Trish catalyzed in cyberspace!

## OPERATION WORLD

Patrick Johnstone, pioneering author of *Operation World*, the best-selling prayer guide to every nation on earth, talked with friends at Dawn Ministries from Colorado about editing the book onto our site. We were stunned: This had in many ways been Patrick's life work and being offered permission to host it on our site felt a bit like being given Elvis' back-catalog. It took a Cambridge graduate working on a McDonald's wage more than a year to edit the book into a more youth-friendly format, adding pictures and special "youth facts" along the way and co-operating closely with Patrick's successor Jason Mandryk. Eventually in 2002, our version of *Operation World* was launched via the Internet to a generation that finds the words of the prophets written on the chat room walls, rather than in their church library.[19]

It was January 2000, and I was working with a church in sub-zero

Stockholm when I received an email from Pete announcing that the website was ready to be launched. "When shall we go live?"

I plucked a date in February off the top of my head and hit reply. Soon I received another email from Justin Blake, the prophet who had predicted all this in the first place: "I like the date you've chosen for the launch, Pete. Nice one!"

Bemused, I checked my diary for any possible spiritual, political, or personal significance but drew a blank.

"Eh?" I replied, once again revealing my complete insensitivity to the Spirit.

I had chosen, Justin informed me, to launch the website one year later, to the day, after he had released the prophecy about becoming a house of prayer to the nations. Maybe it was coincidence, but I was becoming increasingly aware of such spiritual symmetry in the growth of this little movement. The God who had hired Pete Worthington behind my back, the God who had predicted our prayer room before I had ever thought of it, this God was moving in mysterious and extraordinary ways, even in the details of all that was being born.

## DEEPER

### MY FIRST TV

My first TV (and I'll show my age here) was a portable black and white affair. Then I got color. Then I noticed that all the people on my color television were in fact orange, so I got a better color television. Next it was flat screen, then it had to have surround sound with interactive features.

---

19. *www.24-7prayer.com/ow*

These days I wouldn't even bother watching my favorite movies if they were on my original black and white set. God wants to take us on a progressive adventure in prayer, moving from monochrome spirituality to full color surround sound interactive! This may mean learning to open our eyes to pray instead of shutting them. It may mean noise as well as silence and harmony. It may mean movement as well as stillness.

Prayer rooms are workshops for five-dimensional interaction with the creator God. For more on this theme, visit *www.redmoonrising-book.com*.

**JOURNEY**

## HOLY GROUND IN IRAQ

Sometimes the heart overrules the head when we come to pray. Why did Moses keep bargaining with God over a sinful and perverse group of people, pleading with God to spare them? Jesus reminded the disciples that their enemies were their friends, challenging them with the idea that a Samaritan could be a good neighbor. A soldier came online during war with Iraq and hinted that maybe we should perhaps be praying for the peace of Baghdad.

*Dear 24-7 Brothers & Sisters,*

*I'm a soldier in Kuwait/Iraq and need your prayers … In one small town I caught the eyes of a peasant woman of about twenty-five and felt I was look-ing into the eyes of Jesus. I smiled at her. She smiled back, and the moment froze in time. I then turned and looked at a little girl about eight. She too smiled, and in her face I saw uncertainty and expectation all mixed up.*

*We moved on down the road past blown up trucks, tanks and cars. There was a Mig 21 still on the ground from the 1991 conflict. I saw a lot of things that I'm not at liberty to discuss, but the greatest thing I felt and what I can't seem to shake was the feeling that Jesus was saying: "I'm here and I love these people, so tread lightly, this is holy ground."*

*Mike, Iraq (May 2003)*

# HOLY
# SPACE

OVER THE LAST THIRTY YEARS, THE
Church has experienced something of a revolution
in the way we worship. The outrageously sacrile-
gious idea of bringing drums, guitars, and mixing
desks into "the house of God" is now the norm.
Fantastic new songs have taken their place in the
pantheon of classic hymns—the soundtrack to many
people's spiritual lives.

But while attention was being lavished upon our
corporate worship, corporate prayer remained largely
unchanged, defined by a row of plastic chairs and a
short list of topics in a drafty building on a Thursday
night. With just ninety verses in the Bible about
music and 375 about prayer, we are long overdue for
a cultural revolution in the way we pray—not just in
order to keep up with the changing times, but also,
as we shall see, to be truly biblical in the ways in
which we wait upon God.

As prayer rooms began to multiply around the
world, many wonderful stories started flooding in

by email and being posted on our website. Suddenly, it seemed, many people were, like us, learning to pray like never before: persistently and creatively in fixed locations. Come with me for a while as we explore one such mythical prayer room (a combination of several that I've seen).

## VIRTUAL TOUR

It's still dark as you arrive at 6 a.m. for an hour of prayer at the start of a busy day. Taking the key from a bleary-eyed thirtysomething, you pause while he prays for you (coffee on his breath) and emerge alone into an extraordinary room.

Stepping inside, a sign hinders your progress: "Take off your shoes for this is holy ground." Proceeding a little more slowly, now barefoot, into the room, the first thing you notice is a rough wooden cross and a crown of thorns made from the remains of a jagged-edged soda can and huge, rusty nails. A notice on the wall reminds you that Christ died so that your sins might be forgiven. You carefully pick the soda-can crown from the cross, fascinated by the way it's been made, and feel the sharpness of the torn aluminium and the weight of the nails. The thought of them plunging into skin and muscle causes a slight, involuntary recoil. They are cruel and heavy.

A jab of conscience tells you that by now you really should be praying, but of course you already are.

The first few sentences to God can often be the most formal, and you begin to thank Him for dying to forgive your sins and to cleanse you from unrighteousness.

Something about the soda can imagery keeps pulling your eyes back to that crown, and now you are thanking Him for the way He uses the garbage of life that everyone else just throws away. You find yourself thinking back to what you were like at school and who you have become. You thank Him for saving you and for bleeding for you. Noticing your shoes by the door, you diligently replay the day before in your head, the argument at work, the gossip, the thoughts last night, and you dare to admit them in a whisper lest anyone should hear.

There seems to be different "stations" or focal points around the room, and you move to a large bowl full of water. There's a rusty mark on your palm from holding the nail, and you wash your hands. Moving to dry them on a clean, white towel nearby, you notice a makeshift sign. It reads: "Let us draw near to God with a sincere heart in full assurance of faith, having our hearts sprinkled to cleanse us from a guilty conscience and having our bodies washed with pure water" (Hebrews 10:22). You notice that the mark of the nail has now vanished from your hands and reflect that so too have those embarrassing sins confessed in a whisper moments earlier.

As you turn, the silver foil that marks the edge of another prayer zone rustles. The room may be serene, but it glistens and whispers as you move from place to place.

Next you pause to put on a worship CD and offer thanksgiving to God for His care and compassion, for answered prayer, and for the gift of life. Big fat marker pen in hand, you advance to the graffiti wall and inscribe a pithy God is Good or draw a scene provoked by your prayer so far.

You find yourself reading another slogan, a bit of the Psalms carefully inscribed on the wall by a previous inhabitant of this space. It seems relevant and you look up the whole Psalm. As the music crescendos, you read out loud, enjoying the opportunity in a crowded world to have space to do so without others listening in. You are no longer just reading the words internally, you are declaring them to God, and as you do so, conviction is rising in your heart.

Noticing the "Answers to Prayer Book" hanging on a piece of string above the stereo, you begin to read the recent reports. Someone's friend has agreed to come to church on Sunday. A relative's cancer is in remission. One is anonymous, in spidery writing addressed directly to God: "Thanks for helping me finally get around to talking to someone about 'you-know-what.' Thanks that she didn't judge me and had good advice. Please, please God help me to change." You try to work out whose writing this might be and then figure you probably shouldn't.

The worship CD kicks in with an instrumental piece, and you start singing out your thanks to God. This gives you the idea of filling a piece of paper with a list of the things God has done for you in the last twenty-four hours, simple things like "coffee ... new CD ... the call with mom on the phone last night ... hot shower this morning ..."

## ANCIENT/FUTURE FAITH

Praying like this may seem new, but its rhythm stretches back through the centuries. It reflects an approach to prayer called "examen," which comes from the prayer traditions of St. Ignatius of Loyola. Examen involves a deliberate commitment to recollect events in the presence of God—the opposite of Eastern meditation, which is about emptying the mind. Just as God gave Abraham a covenant as a memorable landmark in their relationship, so He gives us landmarks and memories today. The Passover Meal helped the Israelite nation remember how God had delivered them. Examen asks people to look at the last twenty-four hours and take three steps:

1. Express gratitude
2. Reflect on how God's presence might have been made tangible in that time
3. Confess failure.

Richard Peace, writing in *Meditative Prayer*, describes examen like this: "In the end the prayer of examen is about noticing: noticing the good gifts God gives us, noticing the presence of God in our lives, and noticing the ways we fail God. When we notice, we become more conscious, when we become more conscious we grow."

## BACK TO OUR MYTHICAL ROOM

You've turned the corner now, and a variety of prayer ideas are arrayed before you. A pile of bricks artfully arranged reminds you of the stones Joshua erected as a symbol of deliverance at Gilgal. Perched on top of it are colorful cards—prayer request forms collected from some of the projects that your group is involved in around the community. They're heartfelt and poignant. Sometimes they're about sick children, drug-riddled young adults or widowed mothers. We've found that people will often ask appreciatively for prayer when they would rebuff our faith-sharing. You pick up just one card about a kid with leukemia and find it easy to pray for her healing and for her family and for her to somehow know joy amidst all the fear.

You hardly know what to pray for next. Should it be the big news stories of the day, your church's community projects (described in detail on special boards), the upcoming Alpha Course, or the twelve other churches in your locality? You pick up a stone on which someone has written with a marker pen the name of a friend of yours whose husband has just left her alone with a young child. You pray for her, slipping that stone into your pocket and determining to carry her in prayer until your next visit.

## THIS CITY, THESE STREETS

Your eyes fall on a wall-size map of the nearby streets covered in red dots marking the places people have prayed for—often where they live or work. They've asked God to bring peace to these specific locations and that they might be able to develop friendships there. They've asked for a chance to pray for people and to somehow demonstrate that God's kingdom is near and He loves them.

Someone has simply written "REVIVAL" on the map, across one of the local high schools. You pray a while for your street and determine to knock on your neighbor's door later that day and say, "Hi."

You're nearing the end now. A mock brick wall confronts you. In every brick is a name or names. It's the visual evidence of the heart-cry of others in the prayer room. They've asked God to speak to the hearts of their friends and relatives and to equip them to be a picture or symbol of God's goodness.

A box of Kleenex sits nearby, moved from a meditative table. You turn to that table and find a prayer journal, filled with texts, reflections, and prophetic insight. A liturgical prayer book sits nearby, together with a small bottle of communion wine and a small piece of wrapped bread. Two chairs are nearby. You stop, sit, and turn to the recommended passage: Philippians 2:6-11. You read it slowly, then you read it again, pausing after each verse to pray.

You stick on the phrase "humbled himself" as a white-hot streak of conviction interrupts your reverie. You know you were right and they were wrong, but suddenly Jesus is standing right in the middle of the conversation looking you right in the eyes: "Humble yourself," He says. And quietly you climb off your high horse and back down.

## LECTIO DIVINA

Once again you are drinking from a prayer well that has enriched God's people for millennia, not decades. Lectio Divina involves reading slowly and often aloud until a word or phrase begins to provoke you. You stay with that word and pray in response to it. This reflects biblical passages that encourage us to ponder or meditate God's works (Luke 2:19, 51).

John Wesley encouraged a similar practice and in his *Advice on Spiritual Reading* suggested, "Be sure to read …. with great attention, with proper pauses and intervals so that you may allow time for the enlightenings of divine grace."

Saint Cyprian told those in his care to "be constant as well in prayer as in reading; now speak with God, now let God speak with you."

Guigo II, a Carthusian, wrote that reading the Scripture is like putting food into our mouth, meditation chews it, and prayer extracts its flavor. Further reflection enriches us. Through this type of prayer, God's very self "breaks in upon the middle of our prayer, runs to meet us in all haste … and restores our weary soul."

You are nearly ready to leave the prayer room now. Standing by the pictorial flames next to the door, you ask for a fresh filling of the Holy Spirit. Someone is knocking on the door as the next shift arrives, and you welcome in a businessman in his suit clasping a Bible. You pass the baton of prayer to him with a few words of blessing and sign up for another hour later in the week. Behind you the businessman is removing his polished shoes.

Above the exit sign someone has written "Welcome Home." You step through the door to find that outside, while you have been praying, another day has dawned. Reaching into your pocket for your keys, you feel that cold, round stone, and a silent prayer escapes your lips as you turn the lock.

## BUT ...

Perhaps you've been in a prayer room like the one described in this chapter and battled the voice of your inner fundamentalist, a voice whispering to you: "Very nice, but is it biblical?" You can't help but feel that if your inner voice is whispering, the voice of your deacons, elders, pastor, or priest may well be talking quite loudly too— "What's wrong with the old style prayer meeting?"

Of course nothing is wrong with the old models. Prayer can't be straightjacketed into any one approach, and people should do whatever works best for them. But pragmatically, these prayer rooms are working in a surprising array of contexts: People are getting blessed/helped/saved/sanctified and filled with the Holy Spirit.

But the pragmatic argument isn't really the best response. Many things work, but are not entirely legitimate. Cannabis may relax you and help you feel peaceful, and Ecstasy can fill you with a sense of overwhelming love, but these things aren't in fact good! So rather than claiming, "It works," perhaps we should say, "It's the way we were designed to be." Biblical worship involves all five senses, the whole person loving God with all that is within them.

## GOD LOVES CREATIVITY

God does speak by His Spirit through our creativity. Bezalel was filled with the Spirit of God, with skill, ability, and knowledge in all kinds of crafts, and his call was to decorate the prayer room (Exodus 35:30-34). In the same way today, God has given creative leadership to those who have His Spirit. While some will use creativity for idolatrous purposes, we shouldn't be diverted from our proper use of it because of any form of guilt by association. No wonder we are beginning to see contemporary Christian artists: poets, painters, and rock stars filled with God's Spirit, influencing the broader culture as did Handel, Van Gogh, and Michelangelo.

A creative prayer room covered in artwork, with music pumping (for those who want it) and three-dimensional "prayer-provokers" dotted around, simply recognizes the fact that we are a diverse people with different ways of expressing ourselves at different times. Sometimes the creativity flows from you; sometimes the provocations to prayer are a creative invitation to you. Some like silence and a simple prayer book; some need to pace and proclaim. There is no best way to pray and no fixed method. If a prayer idea honors God, reflects the overall tenor of the Bible, and causes us to be able to talk to or hear from Him, then that's fine.

## TABERNACLE

As well as providing space for creativity, prayer rooms tune into an ancient biblical theme. The tabernacle was a mobile prayer room, accommodating the presence of God amidst the people of God as they traveled in the desert. People have established 24-7 prayer rooms in all sorts of crazy locations, from shops in Soho to a brewery in Missouri, perhaps without realizing that they are really establishing tabernacles for God's presence.

The tabernacle is a powerful motif for postmodern mission, resonating with a deep desire in the culture for "holy spaces," which may not always equate with a church service in a church building once a week. Jenny Robertson, in her book *Windows to Eternity* observed, "There is, in fact, a tremendous hunger now in the West to rediscover holy places. Places where tragic accidents happen are quickly turned into shrines, with flowers, candles, toys, photographs of the child struck down in a car accident, of the victim of a violent crime." In the wake of Princess Diana's death, high school shootings, and terrorist attacks on the World Trade Center in 2001, many candles were lit in meaningful locations other than churches. And why not, when "the earth is the Lord's and everything in it"?

It is the custom of certain gangs in New York to build a shrine for a fallen friend on the sidewalk where they died or in some other special place. Here they will gather around a picture of the deceased and get drunk on beer, piling the cans in a highly meaningful memorial to the former gang member. When Kenny and Sarah Mitchell with Lisa Carter were sent out from Revelation church in Chichester to establish a church called Tribe in Brooklyn, New York, one of the biggest compliments they received came in the form of some boys from the 'hood who wanted to build such a shrine to a friend in the team's large communal house. There was a sense in which Tribe's ordinary living space was to become for them a holy place.

Generally such shrines are not Christian. C.S. Lewis pointed out that in the absence of Christianity people will often return to an instinctive animism. However, prayer rooms can perhaps provide a truly biblical context for the unquenchable human desire to worship, to mourn, to wonder, and to wait. They help us to rediscover an unregimented theology of place and space as well as meetings and movements.

Colossians 4:2 encourages us to devote ourselves to prayer, being watchful and thankful. Ephesians 6:18 prompts us to "pray in the Spirit on all occasions, with all kinds of prayers and requests." Perhaps a creative prayer room simply allows for "all kinds of prayers" in all kinds of places, for all sorts of people all the time.

**For Further Reading:**
Norvene Vest, *Gathered in the Word* (Upper Room Books, 1996)
Richard Peace, *Meditative Prayer* (NavPress, 1998)
*24-7 Prayer—The Handbook* (Kingsway Publications, 2003)

*The 24-7 Prayer Manual* helps you do all the preparation for a week of prayer. This covers planning a prayer room, preparing the congregation, and establishing key principles and creative ideas. It also explores the history of tabernacle and holy space in greater depth. You can find out more about this resource and how to get it from *www.24-7prayer.com*.

### DEEPER

## ECCE HOMO

One of Zinzendorf's defining moments came when he was nineteen, as he stood before a picture called *Ecce Home* in a Dusseldorf art gallery. Domenico Feti's fine painting is a poignant image of a thorn-crowned Jesus, and at the foot of the picture, a Latin inscription reads: "This I have suffered for you, but what have you done for me?" Zinzendorf was challenged to the core of his being, reflecting that he had done little up to that point, and asked God to remind him of Christ's suffering whenever he might be inclined to wander away from his first love. (Visit *www.redmoonrisingbook.com* for more about this story.)

God loves beauty and creativity. He has made for us a world that is visually spectacular. We read in Genesis that we are made in God's image—He is an artist, a Creator! Similarly, the first man in the Bible to be described as being filled with the Holy Spirit is not some great king or prophet. It is a craftsman named Bezalel, anointed by God to decorate the prayer room—the tabernacle (Exodus 35:30-31).

## JOURNEY

# HEART TRANSPLANT

As we sit, pace, or reflect alone in a prayer room, it may be the first time for days, weeks, or even months that we have stopped and thought uncluttered thoughts. Jesus often retreated to a quiet place. Lucy from Dublin found that her life was very cluttered until she found time to be alone with God. And then He broke her heart ...

"Initially 24-7 was a lot of hard work. It wasn't easy persuading people to say they would come to the prayer room; prayer didn't really seem to be top of anyone's agenda! But when the week started, it just completely flowed—people came and people came back! Many people called in for an hour and ended up staying for three or four! It was incredible to see people's faces as they walked into this tiny room where the walls were plastered with heart cries and challenges and words—it inspired people to pray, and they finally understood why they needed to come to the prayer room and not stay at home and pray! God showed up, and we had people from so many different churches across the city come—one evening we had too many people to fit in the room so they had to take it to the streets!

"It wasn't until Thursday morning that I found myself in the prayer room alone. I was on my knees and just looked over at our wall covered in the names of family and friends—and God broke my heart. These weren't just random people, but people who were deeply loved, and someone was desperate for them to know Jesus. I was overwhelmed at the number of times 'Dad' or 'Mum' was written up there, and I thought, 'How much more do you love them, Lord, and want them to know you?' It was very significant for me!"

*Lucy, Dublin*

# CHAPTER NINE

# RED MOON
## RISING
[U.K. ROMANIA.]

DRIVING OUT OF TOWN, I WAS EXCITED
and nervous. This was the point of no return. The
previous few months had been a whirlwind of surprises. July had found me in Hernnhut. September
had seen the start of our first prayer room in
Chichester. In November at Cultural Shift, the
prayer rooms had begun to multiply across the
country. In December I had met Pete Worthington
and heard about his call to design our website. And
now it was February, six months after the launch of
that first prayer room, and we were about to kick
things off nationally with a name, a website, and
these ridiculous plans to pray without ceasing for
the rest of the year by passing the baton from location to location a month or a week at a time.

It was a wintry dusk as I drove across town to pick up
the others on my way to Guildford, near London
where the launch would take place. "What's this all
about?" I wondered aloud, making the most of the
empty car that would soon be jammed with passengers. "Lord, we really need you to be with us

tonight." In the twilight a giant full moon was rising above the rooftops of Chichester, luminous red and eerie against a watery sky. It's a sight that always moves me, but on this particular evening, something deeper stirred in my spirit. What was it the prophet Joel had said?

> *"'This is what was spoken by the prophet Joel:*
> *'In the last days, God says, I will pour out my Spirit on all people.*
> *Your sons and daughters will prophesy,*
> *your young men will see visions,*
> *your old men will dream dreams ...*
> *The sun will be turned to darkness*
> *and the moon to blood*
> *before the coming of the great and glorious day of the Lord.*
> *And everyone who calls on the name of the Lord will be saved.'"*
> *(Acts 2:16-21)*

I sensed God saying that this night, this launch, this movement was something to do with the last days. He was saying that 24-7 prayer springs up from an outpouring of His Spirit on the generations and would therefore be about the release of dreams and visions. Most of all, 24-7 prayer was to be outworked in the Great Commission, the message of salvation for "everyone who calls on the name of the Lord." The moon above us that night was red, but it was also full—a harvest moon. "I tell you," Jesus said, "open your eyes and look at the fields! They are ripe for harvest" (John 4:35) or as the Apostle Paul put it: "Now is the time of God's favor, now is the day of salvation" (2 Corinthians 6:2).

## BOJANGLEZ

An hour later, as we approached Guildford, the usual scene greeted us: On Stag hill, where Kings of England used to hunt, Guildford cathedral stands floodlit in mock gothic splendor, famous in many circles for its role in *The Omen* horror movies! Less auspiciously, Guildford town sprawls below the cathedral down to the River Wey, and tucked away in a back street is a rundown nightclub, inexplicably and incongruously named Bojanglez, presumably by an owner with some kind of commercial death wish.

It will surprise no one to learn that 24-7 was not launched in the cathedral on that royal hill, but in Bojanglez nightclub in a dimly lit back alley. More than 400 people from all over the British Isles converged on the gloomy venue that night, and, standing on its sticky beer-stained floor, bits hanging off the ceiling, we began to pray and worship. There was a band, a DJ, and a choreographed dance. By now I knew clearly the message I had to bring, and, standing to read Joel's prophecy, the image of the full-red moon branded on my mind. Concluding with the verse about salvation for "everyone who calls on the name of the Lord," I found myself convicted by my own words. Were there people in this crowd even tonight, I wondered, who had never called upon God's name and found salvation? It seemed unlikely; after all, this was the launch of an intensive prayer campaign, not a seeker-sensitive, bring-your-friends type event. But then again, I reasoned, what better way could there be of launching a prayer movement than with someone becoming a follower of Christ for the first time? Hesitantly, therefore, as something of an afterthought to my talk, I gave an opportunity for people to give their lives to Jesus. That night, as 24-7 was born, no fewer than thirteen young people committed their lives to Christ for the first time, and dozens more renewed their vows.

A time of passionate and prolonged prayer ensued, many kneeling, others crying out to God with their hands in the air. God, it seemed, was getting ready to do a new thing.

## VIENNA

Looking around the venue at so many young people giving themselves to prayer, Ian Nicholson, the former Bible-smuggler, found himself transported back more than twenty years to similar times of passionate prayer in Vienna, Austria. He was twenty-one, had been a Christian three years, and would spend every Wednesday night from 8 p.m. till midnight, sometimes much longer, with other young missionaries interceding for the nations and especially for the persecuted Church behind the iron curtain.

It had been easy enough back then, praying for people like the poor

Romanian family he had met in the town of Bacau that night—
seven of them in a simple, two bedroom house.

He remembered parking The Arab on the dirt road outside their home
at midnight and unloading the faithful vehicle's secret cargo of Bibles in
black garbage sacks into the believers' house. Anna, the mother, in her
typical, brightly colored headscarf, kept whispering "Hallelujah!
Hallelujah!" as she carried another bulging sack through the door.

This was hazardous work, to say the least, in a society where one in
every five was a suspected police informer, and Ian kept glancing across
at the windows of the apartment block overlooking their covert deliv-
ery. Just one suspicious neighbor or a single phone call was all it would
take to trigger a terrible chain of events.

Ian knew that for him it would mean arrest once again, with all the
ensuing psychological games and interrogation at the hands of the
police. That prospect didn't worry him too much. More distressing was
the prospect of losing The Arab. For eleven years the legendary Ford
Transit had been carrying Bibles into Eastern Europe, three tours a
month, and its loss would be sorely felt across the mission.

But of course the real fear was for Micur and Anna, this brave couple
who were already under surveillance by the secret police. Should this
contraband of Bibles be discovered in their hands, they would face certain imprisonment and torture at the hands of Ceausescu's sadistic
henchmen. And as for their five children ...

"Last one?" whispered Mircu, beaming happily, as his big rough hands
stretched out to receive the final sack. Inside the house a simple feast
awaited Ian and his team of unlikely smugglers. He knew that the steak
on their plates amounted to the family's supply of meat for the entire
month. An accordion was produced, and Mircu began to sing, praising
God for the gift of his precious Word. Doreen joined in the singing
heartily with her powerful, operatic falsetto, and for once Ian and Linda
accompanied her enthusiastically. Anna fussed around happily, smiling
from ear to ear and muttering "hallelujah" whenever she caught sight of

the garbage sacks still piled in the corner of the room.

As soon as they could, Ian pulled the team away from the cozy home, thanking them profusely for their hospitality. He knew that every moment they stayed endangered the family even more. Turning the key in the ignition, The Arab coughed into action, and in the still of the night, the sound seemed to echo down the street like rolling thunder. Instinctively Ian glanced up at the apartments and thought he saw a movement in one of the windows.

Without headlights the van pulled away down the dusty road as quickly and quietly as possible. In the rear view mirror Ian watched Mircu and Anna still waving and smiling as The Arab turned the corner and disappeared into the cover of night.

"Ian?" With a jolt he returned to the sticky floors of Bojanglez and found himself surrounded by people worshiping. It was a million miles from Bacau and the Romanian family, half a world away from those prayer nights in Vienna too. Now in his mid-forties, a seasoned pastor, Ian knew that he was no longer the angry young man, but looking around the room at that moment, something began to stir powerfully inside him. Watching this explosion of prayer, Ian knew that he was in at the birth of something new. And with every fiber of his being, he determined that the passion for prayer must someday soon become a passion for mission too.

Little did he know that just eleven weeks later this conviction would become reality in the form of an invitation from desperate Christians on the Spanish island of Ibiza: Would 24-7 come and pray through the party season in Europe's hedonistic party capital? It had taken the Moravians five years of continual prayer before launching out from Herrnhut in mission, but for us living in the global village, things were going to move much quicker.

## DEEPER

### LIVING ROOM

"I walked into the prayer room at 7:55 this morning," writes Phil Togwell, "and the air was still potent with prayer: That invisible fog of intercession that you can feel but cannot see—it hung there. It's the weirdest thing, but it felt like the room was actually 'alive' ... About twenty young people had been there all night—they'd arranged their own rota and had brought their sleeping bags to snatch bits of sleep in-between slots ... but for many those sleeping bags remained unused. For nine hours or so they'd poured it all out, before passing the prayer baton onto Julie at around 6 a.m."

*This is part of a weeklong journal from a prayer room near London. To read the entire journal, visit* www.redmoonrisingbook.com.

## JOURNEY

### PRAYING THE PRICE

Here in Taiwan, family is very important. Everyone lives together: mothers, fathers, grandfathers, and daughters. In China, people are supposed to burn sacrifices to the gods of their ancestors to keep everything good, so my parents hated it when I became a Christian. They're worried that because I've given my life to Jesus, I won't burn sacrifices for them when they've died.

I got beaten because I became a Christian. It's horrible when everyone—your mum, dad, grandfather—all beat you, mock you and laugh at you. I lead a cell group of twenty-five people. One of them was so badly beaten by her Dad when she became a Christian that I had to take her to hospital.

Twenty-four out of the twenty-five are first generation Christians. I have to fast for them because I worry about them. We're going to do

24-7 for a month. For each of us to pray for one hour a day is a small price to pay. Becoming a Christian costs a lot more.

*Ian, Taiwan*

# CHAPTER TEN

# OUT OF
# **CONTROL**
## [SWITZERLAND. SPAIN.]

EVERYTHING SEEMED TO BE GOING
really well. More and more people were hearing
about 24-7 and joining the flow of continual prayer.
This was already far bigger than just the core
Cultural Shift churches that had gathered in
Southampton six months before. But (and there is
always a "but"), I had a confession to make to the
visitors to the 24-7 prayer website:

> "Okay—time to confess: Since 24-7 started I've
> had a worry nagging at the back of my mind:
> 'Surely people aren't really praying nonstop,
> sacrificing sleep to do 24-7?' I've thought.
> 'Perhaps everyone is exaggerating! There just
> can't be people praying at every single moment
> of every day and night?'"

About that time, Samie and I found ourselves driving home late one night, past a city where a prayer
room was allegedly on the go. And so, nervously
with this doubt nagging at the back of our minds,
we decided to pay an unannounced visit, hardly dar-

ing to hope that people might actually be in the building praying well after midnight. Pulling up at the church, that niggling worry became worse: 'Would we even find anyone here? Surely it was ridiculous to expect it at this time of night?'

My heart sank to see the parking lot deserted and the building locked and dark. Perhaps someone had fallen asleep and missed a shift? I couldn't blame them. I almost didn't bother knocking on the door, but as soon as I did, a light went on, and we found ourselves ushered down a corridor and into a room that looked strangely familiar. Stepping into the prayer room, I suppressed a gasp. No fewer than eight people, mostly in their teens, were lying on the floor, praying passionately and fervently to God. Matt Redman was on the stereo: "Let our prayers to you be as incense," he sang, "Let our prayers to you be as pillars of your throne." I could hardly believe what I was seeing. Could it really be true, that all around the world, God is mobilizing such people to pray through the night and day: watchmen on the walls of Jerusalem crying out continually for her salvation?

## NEXT STOP: THUN

Two months after the launch in Guildford, the Cultural Shift leadership team went to the beautiful town of Thun in the Swiss Alps to connect with similar networks around Europe. In a stunning house, built into the side of a mountain with a glass wall looking out over the valley to snow capped mountains beyond, we met with other leaders from Spain, Sweden, Switzerland, and Germany. We all represented networks struggling to make sense of church in the emerging culture, and we were conspiring together about the possibility of gathering young church planters in Frankfurt the following year.

For me it was a significant and exciting time. I felt closer than ever to the fulfillment of my Portuguese vision, as we planned the event (which would be called E.merge) and as I shared with these leaders about the spread of 24-7. Perhaps an army of young people really was rising up across Europe as I had envisaged so many years before.

I remember sitting in the hot tub as a sunset tinted the distant mountains pink and thanking God with all my heart for the incredible ways in which He had moved since my last time in Thun, with Samie and Hudson on our wild goose chase around the continent. I thanked Him for allowing someone like me to be part of something as awesome and out of control as this.

## MARKUS

Among the German delegates was Markus Lägel, the guy I'd met briefly in Dresden on the eve of my visit to Hernnhut. His blue hair had gone, and he was now wearing a cowboy hat, big sideburns, and a Hawaiian shirt. Sitting in that exquisite house, the boy from Leipzig and I became friends as we talked into the night. Markus, it emerged, was at seminary near Cologne—his stint in Dresden had been part of a placement with Kraftwerk, the only youth church in Germany at that time. As I shared with Markus about my recent experiences, he became more and more excited. "This is what I saw in Leipzig," he said, his eyes wide with excitement. "24-7 could be our generation's equivalent of those Peace Prayer Meetings. I don't know what this means, but I want to be involved."

Markus returned to seminary and straight away set about organizing a 24-7 prayer room. It was the first one in Germany and was met with a great deal of apathy from the other young theologians at the college who were apparently more interested in talking about God than talking to Him. Undaunted, Markus poured out his heart to God for Germany in that room, he interceded for the generation, and most passionately of all he prayed that a girl called Andrea might agree to marry him. For a while they had been friends, and he had inevitably fallen hopelessly in love with her cute smile, blonde hair, crazy clothes, and big green eyes. But she, it seemed, was blind to the hidden charms of the guy in the cowboy hat. "Make her love me the way I love her," he beseeched the Almighty night after night, who was doubtless smiling at the time.

Not long afterward, Markus and Andrea were sitting together emailing a mutual friend. Glancing across at the beautiful girl, giggling as she typed another message, Markus could contain himself no longer. "Close your eyes," he said with a big grin. On the computer screen he typed four words that made his heart almost explode with trepidation and joy: "WILL YOU MARRY ME?"

Andrea opened her eyes and stared in disbelief at the monitor. She started shaking and laughing in disbelief: "But you haven't even asked me out yet!"

But Markus was learning to persevere in every area of his life—even his love life! He asked Andrea three more times for her hand in marriage, and on June 16, 2000, she finally succumbed. The boy from Leipzig had finally found his bride.

After graduation Markus and Andrea relocated to Dresden to be part of Kraftwerk. They knew they wanted to learn how to plant churches for people like themselves, and they had a sense by then that 24-7 prayer was going to be an essential part of that plan. At the meeting in Thun, Karsten Wolf, the inimitable leader of Kraftwerk, had also captured a vision to see 24-7 grow in Germany. When Markus and Andrea arrived in Dresden, Karsten asked them straight away to open a German-speaking base for 24-7, sending the newlyweds over to England to get some training from us (by this stage we had developed a few fairly primitive resources, including a manual advising people how to run a prayer room).[20]

## SUSANNA

Back in Thun we were being hosted by a young Swiss leader named Susanna Rychiger in whose parents' incredible house we were staying. Susanna, who lived a while in Canada and has suffered terminal wanderlust ever since, was running a Christian skate park called Rollorama in downtown Thun for local street kids. It was attracting up to a hundred inline skaters every day and having a significant

---

20. *The 24-7 Prayer Manual* (Kingsway, 2003).

impact on the local scene. Rollorama had two large halls covered in graffiti housing an eight by six meter half pipe, a twin pipe, quarters, and a DJ booth.

A fourteen-year-old named Sarah turned up at Rollorama one day. She enjoyed skating almost as much as she enjoyed hanging out on the streets with her friends and doing drugs like acid. She began to visit the skate park more and more, and when she was invited to join their summer camp to the South of France, she readily agreed. In France she sat in on one of the leaders' meetings, listening intently to them praying for each kid by name. She was amazed by how much they seemed to know about God and amused by how little they seemed to know about the kids at the camp—most of whom were smoking dope like crazy behind their backs.

Two weeks later, Sarah became a follower of Jesus, and her life changed around completely. Almost straight away the teenage tear-away stopped doing drugs and started being friendly and respectful at home. The change in Sarah was so dramatic that her mother began her own spiritual journey, secretly pouring over her daughter's Bible when she was away at school. Sarah complained to Susanna one day that her mother was really annoying her. When Susanna asked why, Sarah said it was because her mother kept stealing her Bible and not putting it back! Before long Sarah's mother had her own Bible and her own relationship with Jesus Christ, too.

By the time of our meeting in Thun, Sarah was one of Susanna's key young leaders in Rollorama. At the time of writing, she is traveling around Switzerland preaching the Gospel. In one week in the Swiss town of Altdorf, Sarah led three people to Jesus and connected them to local Christians who now plan to plant a little church. Susanna spends a great deal of time mentoring people like Sarah and mobilizing prayer.

The following year the churches of the region combined forces in an unprecedented way: For forty days they prayed nonstop, joyfully culminating on Easter day in 2001. Through all this, Susanna was herself being raised up as a significant prayer warrior, embarking on a forty-day food fast. Through this period of intense focus, God began to lay an almost unbearable burden upon Susanna's heart for the young people of Switzerland. The girl with terminal wanderlust was being called back home. She remembers just crying out to God in the prayer room, feeling as though her heart would break. The following year another such fast would bear fruit in an even more extraordinary way …

## BACK TO VALLADOLID

The Spanish contingency in Thun represented a youth movement called Contracorriente ("against the flow"), which gathers more than a thousand young people every year. This is an extraordinary number in the Spanish culture where the evangelical wing of the Church is so small, and even the Pope has said that the Catholic Church needs renewal. Spain has never experienced an outpouring of the Holy Spirit in revival and yet has changed remarkably over the last thirty years and seems ripe for harvest.

I was looking forward to visiting Contracorriente the following month, and in Thun I happily agreed to do an interview about 24-7 for their conference magazine.

Arriving at Contracorriente, the first clue that something unusual was taking place came when a guy named Aitor thanked me for my interview in the magazine. It had been his job, I learned, to translate the piece, but he had kept crying as he tried to type. I cast my mind back to the interview, wondering what I had said that might have had such an impact. I remembered dunking my biscuit in a cup of tea, sitting on the floor, and chatting into a tape recorder. All I had done was told the usual story: the stuff about the army, the red moon rising, and the prayer room explosion. Aitor had eventually emailed the text to his brother at work, who had himself been so moved that he had left his desk then and there and driven into the mountains to pray for the rest of the day.

I knew that my words couldn't make stuff like this happen. Clearly the Holy Spirit was up to something. That night they asked me to speak to the conference, and I shared stories with some confidence, preaching from Isaiah 62.

## VENGA!

I led the group in a corporate act that was becoming our war cry: "C'mon!" (or "Venga!" in Spanish). This is yelled really loudly, and as I watched a thousand people jumping up and down crying out to God in unison, I remember seeing two older people in Salvation Army uniform with their white shirts standing out against all the scruffy clothes, and they were yelling with equal passion. At the end there was an incredible response as people began to pray for their friends and for their nation. Technically it was dinnertime, but most people couldn't have cared less about food—they stayed and prayed.

Arriving back at the venue the next morning, I was greeted by a wild-eyed older man: "What's happening?" he asked. "The young people are still praying—fifty of them didn't stop all night! For years I've been trying to impart a heart for prayer and for the lost, and now it's suddenly just happening."

Much as I wanted to take the credit and claim that my talk had been particularly good, I had to admit that this was evidence of God's work and not mine. Only the Spirit can make fifty people pray all night. One leader said: "This is exactly what we need right now in Spain—a prayer movement for the young people that can mobilize them to make history." Sitting in the prayer room a little later, I emailed the growing band of 24-7 people around the globe:

> "I'm sitting in a basement in Valladolid, Spain, tapping away on my laptop. The sense of God's presence is strong. Fifty Spanish young people just prayed and wept their way through the night here. The scene is by now familiar ... a candle flickering, artwork every-where, coffee cups, and assorted CDs scattered on the floor, maps and stuff on the wall. In the corner a girl is kneeling and praying

silently. Last night felt momentous. Watching a thousand young Spaniards doing a war cry with extraordinary passion, God suddenly reminded me of something. As far as I knew, this was my first ever visit to Valladolid. But at that precise moment, God reminded me that I had in fact come here nine years ago as a longhaired student hitching my way home from Portugal. Suddenly I remembered sitting on a bench in Valladolid, knowing no one, looking around and praying, 'Lord where is the army, where are your people here in Spain?' And then, nine years later, I find myself back in the same city, but this time standing in front of a thousand young people yelling a war cry to God with every fiber of their beings. 'Here they are,' God seemed to be saying, 'Here is my army!' Isn't that incredible?

"This revelation took a matter of seconds, and with it I just crumpled on the platform. Lying there in front of all those people God showed me one more astonishing thing: "Pete," He seemed to say, "even though you forget most of the prayers you pray to me, I never forget a single thing you ask." That revelation finished me off, and I lay there a long time just stunned by the goodness of God, trying to get my head around the idea that He has treasured every little prayer I've ever prayed and is still weaving fulfillments. It's a concept almost beyond comprehension; there must be answered prayers most days that I never even recognize as such.

As I concluded my bulletin to the 24-7 tribes, there was one more amazing piece of news to report. I wrote:

"So many groups are now planning to pray 24-7 here in Spain that a group of pastors came to see me wondering how we were going to support them. Of course the truth was that I didn't have a clue. But as I looked blankly at the circle of pastors, my translator—a YWAM missionary named Jonah Bailey—leaned over and whispered in my ear. God had spoken to him and his wife, he informed me, prior to the weekend about giving their time to work for 24-7 in Spain, supporting churches and translating resources. Without missing a beat, I turned to the inquisitive pastors and told them as if it had been carefully planned for months, that Jonah and Heather Bailey were going to help develop Spanish 24-7 resources to help them!"

## SEVILLE

Once again, God was hiring people behind my back. Jonah and Heather Bailey have since become key players in 24-7 and great friends too. Originally from California, God called them to the gorgeous city of Seville where more than a million people live today. Seville boasts the second largest cathedral in the world, built on the site of five previous religious temples: Roman, Visigoth, Jewish, Muslim, and Christian. It was from Seville that the Spanish Inquisition was launched and ships from all over the Spanish empire would come and go. Today Seville has one of the largest universities in southern Europe, with eighty thousand students, and yet they are like sheep without a shepherd; few churches are making any impact whatsoever upon these young lives.

This is the mission field to which God has called Jonah and Heather, and from which Jonah now also travels extensively for 24-7, mentoring and caring for our Base Leaders around the world.

The Contracorriente Conference had both energized and scared me. It was there that I suddenly realized how much this 24-7 prayer idea was capturing people's imaginations around the world. Not just in Spain, but also in Switzerland, Germany, and many other nations, this thing seemed to be spiraling out of control. But the weekend in Valladolid still had one more major surprise in store …

## DEEPER

### THE POWER OF PERSEVERANCE

Jesus told the parable of the persistent widow (Luke 18:1-8) to emphasize that we "should always pray and not give up." The disciples probably remembered and re-told the story as they passed the long hours in the upper room, reeling from the trauma and the wonder of recent events and patiently anticipating His promise of "another helper."

Daniel, we are told, would get down on his knees and pray three times a day. One day, as he read the book of Jeremiah, God showed him that the exile would come to an end after seventy years. Taking God at His word, he "turned to the Lord God and pleaded with him in prayer and petition, in fasting and in sackcloth and ashes" (Daniel 9:3). Daniel humbled himself and took it upon himself to confess the sins of his nation, interceding for mercy and forgiveness. He prayed passionately and with perseverance because he believed the firm promise of God. Three weeks later we find Daniel still persevering in prayer, fasting meat, wine and even body lotion! Eventually an angel appeared and told him, "Since the first day that you set your mind to gain understanding and to humble yourself before your God, your words were heard, and I have come in response to them. But the prince of the Persian Kingdom resisted me twenty-one days" (Daniel 10:12-13).

## PERSEVERE IN SPIRITUAL WARFARE

Here we have a glimpse of the spiritual dimension that explains the need for persistence in prayer. It is not that God is slow to act, or that we are trying to persuade God (for prayer is laying hold of His highest willingness). Prayer requires persistence because it is also an act of warfare against "the spiritual forces of evil in the heavenly realms" (Ephesians 6:12). Such prayer reverses the fall in which Adam asserted his independence. In it we say, "not my will, but yours be done." We fight with God to liberate enemy-occupied territory, knowing that while the victory is certain, the length of the battle is not.

## JOURNEY

## HOLY OF HOLIES

The most exciting thing about 24-7 in Canada has to be the stories of lives changed in the prayer rooms, the people being healed, and the way that the emerging generation of youth have embraced the movement:

> A seventeen-year-old girl in Alberta called the students of her city to a week of nonstop prayer that turned into two and had the mayor of the city calling with prayer requests.

> A group of students in New Brunswick prayed nonstop for a week and have continued to meet for a twenty-four-hour block of sustained prayer every Saturday since.

> A senior pastor wrote, "I was not completely prepared for what met me when I walked into the 24-7 room for my first one-hour segment of prayer. It felt like walking into the holy of holies, and I was immediately brought to the point of confession where I spent much of my time on my knees before the cross pouring out my inadequacies, failures, weaknesses, and unholiness before a God of immense holiness."

> People traveled to a Saskatchewan prayer room in the middle of the coldest night of the winter (minus 35 degrees).

> *Dan King*

# THE **VISION**
[SPAIN. U.K. U.S.A. CHINA. SWEDEN.]

IN VALLADOLID, SPAIN, I SAT IN A WHITE plastic garden chair with a thousand others watching some guys from Tulsa doing a very cool contemporary dance routine on stage as a DJ played and someone spoke passionately in Spanish into the microphone. This was big-booted, muscular, athletic dance, and it was working well with the big, fat beats and the strangely rhythmic Spanish voice-over. I'm not a big dance fan, but this I kinda liked.

Something about the routine and the syntax of the Spanish seemed strangely familiar—like when you recognize an actor in a movie but you just can't figure out what else they've been in. And then, suddenly, I recognized a word: "Venga! C'mon!" and it began to dawn on me that sitting in Valladolid I was watching an American dance group perform a choreographed version in Spanish of a poem I had written six months ago in England. Those words, written quietly on the prayer room wall one night and christened "The Vision," seemed to have taken on a life of their own, inexplicably spreading around the world at an unbelievable rate, completely and bewilderingly out of control.

## CHICHESTER

Of course there's always the possibility that we're all crazy.

It was about 3:15 a.m., and I'd taken a middle-of-the-night slot in the Chichester prayer room where we'd been praying now without a break for several weeks. I wandered around the room, reading what was on the walls, trying to pray. I think Moby was on the stereo as I sipped a Red Bull energy drink and tried to shake off the sleep that was hovering nearby, waiting to return if I wasn't vigilant.

"Why am I here in the middle of the night anyway when sane people are all tucked up in bed?" I wondered, trying to make sense of the events of the previous weeks: the wrestling with God, the wild goose chase around Europe, Hernnhut, and Dubi, and now this crazy prayer room. Wasn't it all a bit extreme?

I grabbed hold of a big blue marker pen, sat down on the floor with some sheets of paper and began to write: "So this guy comes up to me and says, 'What's the vision? What's the big idea?'" I wanted to explain the dreams and visions that were causing so many of us to pray like never before. I guess, when you're going against the flow of what the culture around you expects—and often against the flow of what the church expects, too—you need to be able to explain yourself.

The words that tumbled out onto the paper reflected conversations, thoughts, and prayers from previous weeks, previous months, and sometimes even previous decades. I soon lost track of the time, scrawling a stream of consciousness, a succession of word-pictures onto the paper as Moby's soulful gospel samples filled the room. I was formulating a declaration of spiritual intent that would reach far beyond the walls of that converted warehouse in Chichester— although it never occurred to me at the time. If I'd known what would happen with my poem-prayer, I would have seized up, unable to write, but at that moment in the middle of the night, I was intimately alone with my Master, and the world outside was forgotten as I scribbled my fervent thoughts onto paper, lost in a place somewhere outside of time.

I taped the sheets of paper to a large piece of linen separating the room and went home to bed still buzzing. This is what I had written:

## THE VISION [20]

*So this guy comes up to me and says, "What's the vision? What's the big idea?" I open my mouth and words come out like this …*

The vision?
The vision is JESUS—obsessively, dangerously, undeniably Jesus.
The vision is an army of young people. You see bones? I see an army.
And they are FREE from materialism.
They laugh at 9-5 little prisons.
They could eat caviar on Monday and crusts on Tuesday.
They wouldn't even notice.
They know the meaning of the Matrix, the way the West was won.
They are mobile like the wind, they belong to the nations. They need no passport. People write their addresses in pencil and wonder at their strange existence.
They are free yet they are slaves of the hurting and dirty and dying.

What is the vision?

The vision is holiness that hurts the eyes. It makes children laugh and adults angry. It gave up the game of minimum integrity long ago to reach for the stars. It scorns the good and strains for the best. It is dangerously pure.

---

20. In a reflective volume simply called *The Vision*, I'm going to explore the biblical imagery that informs the piece I wrote that night. In this book, to be published in 2004 by Relevant Media (USA) and Kingsway Publications (U.K.), I try to get my brain and heart around what radical Christian discipleship in the third millennium might mean.

Light flickers from every secret motive, every private conversation.
It loves people away from their suicide leaps, their Satan games.
This is an army that will lay down its life for the cause.
A million times a day its soldiers
choose to lose
that they might one day win
the great 'Well done' of faithful sons and daughters.
Such heroes are as radical on Monday morning as Sunday night.
They don't need fame from names. Instead they grin quietly upwards
and hear the crowds chanting again and again: "COME ON!"
And this is the sound of the underground
The whisper of history in the making
Foundations shaking
Revolutionaries dreaming once again
Mystery is scheming in whispers
Conspiracy is breathing …
This is the sound of the underground
And the army is discipl(in)ed.
Young people who beat their bodies into submission.
Every soldier would take a bullet for his comrade at arms.
The tattoo on their back boasts "For me to live is Christ and to die
is gain."
Sacrifice fuels the fire of victory in their upward eyes.
Winners.
Martyrs.
Who can stop them?
Can hormones hold them back?
Can failure succeed?
Can fear scare them or death kill them?
And the generation prays
like a dying man
with groans beyond talking,
with warrior cries, sulphuric tears and
with great barrow loads of laughter!
Waiting. Watching: 24-7-365.
Whatever it takes they will give:
Breaking the rules.

Shaking mediocrity from its cosy little hide.

Laying down their rights and their precious little wrongs,

laughing at labels, fasting essentials.

The advertisers cannot mold them.

Hollywood cannot hold them.

Peer-pressure is powerless to shake their resolve at late night parties before the cockerel cries.

They are incredibly cool, dangerously attractive inside.

On the outside? They hardly care.

They wear clothes like costumes to communicate and celebrate but never to hide.

Would they surrender their image or their popularity?

They would lay down their very lives—swap seats with the man on death row—guilty as hell.

A throne for an electric chair.

With blood and sweat and many tears, with sleepless nights and fruitless days, they pray as if it all depends on God and live as if it all depends on them.

Their DNA chooses JESUS. (He breathes out, they breathe in.)

Their subconscious sings. They had a blood transfusion with Jesus.

Their words make demons scream in shopping centers.

Don't you hear them coming?

Herald the weirdos!

Summon the losers and the freaks.

Here come the frightened and forgotten with fire in their eyes.

They walk tall and trees applaud, skyscrapers bow, mountains are dwarfed by these children of another dimension.

Their prayers summon the hounds of heaven and invoke the ancient dream of Eden.

And this vision will be. It will come to pass; it will come easily; it will come soon.

How do I know? Because this is the longing of creation itself, the groaning of the Spirit, the very dream of God.

My tomorrow is his today.

My distant hope is his 3-D.

And my feeble, whispered, faithless prayer invokes a thunderous, resounding, bone-shaking great "Amen!" from countless angels, from heroes of the faith, from Christ himself. And He is the original dreamer, the ultimate winner.

Guaranteed.

## NEW SYMBOLS

Little is new in "The Vision." Instead of talking about the blood of the Lamb, I use the phrase "a blood transfusion with Jesus," but it isn't new revelation, just a contemporary image for a timeless truth. Some of the imagery may seem a bit obscure, but to me it makes sense! It often cross-fertilizes the iconography of popular culture and biblical truth.

When I worked in Hong Kong, many of the Triad gang members had ornate tattoos of Buddhist gods on their backs or chests. Way too big for removal. When they became Christians, a few were able to somehow redeem the imagery, but there was no escaping the fact that such things are for life. Many of the German Jesus Freaks—an awesome movement of punks and alternatives—have a word like "salvation" emblazoned on their chests when they become followers of Christ. This, they know, is for life, and they are not ashamed.

I guess I was thinking about Chinese Triads and German Jesus Freaks as I wrote the line in "The Vision": "The tattoo on their back boasts, 'for me to live is Christ, to die is gain.'" The back is a strong place, and this is one of Paul's strongest lines. It could easily have come from a swaggering East Coast rap star. Such artists, from 50 Cent to deceased Tupac Shakur, seem to carry their strongest tattoos splayed between their shoulder blades and down their spines. David Beckham had a figure that looked like Christ on the cross tattooed on his back. Then he added wings and it became an angel. Next he wrote the names of his two children: Brooklyn at the base of his spine and Romeo on the nape of his neck. The back is a place of strength, and this verse is an incredible life goal for anyone.

# CRUSTS ON MONDAY

Most of the imagery springs from Scripture. The description of "Crusts on Monday, caviar on Tuesday" is a direct reference to Paul's words in Philippians 4:12: "I know what it is to be in need, and I know what it is to have plenty. I have learned the secret of being content in any and every situation, whether well fed or hungry, whether living in plenty or in want."

Working in Hong Kong with Jackie Pullinger-To's extraordinary ministry to the poor, I saw this amazing polarity repeatedly. On one hand I met barristers—very wealthy ex-pats in their penthouse suites who were coming to Christ through Jackie's ministry to the poor and were now getting involved themselves. On the other hand, my daily reality was amongst poor heroin addicts. On Lantau Island I slept in a dormitory without air conditioning—you have to live there to understand how humid it is in the summer. There were no flush toilets. I guess we lived a pretty simple lifestyle, but I came to love it.

But there were a couple of times I got invited to a wealthy lawyer's air-conditioned apartment, where we sat and looked through the French windows at the glittering lights of Hong Kong harbor as the sun set. A family friend took me out on his company yacht around the islands of the South China Sea. A waiter brought us food so rich that I found it hard to digest after months of mostly rice, noodles, and watermelon. Another member of the staff drove the speedboat so that I could try water-skiing.

It was most definitely "crusts on Monday, caviar on Tuesday," and for me that was the very adventure of following Christ at that time.

Although the imagery of "The Vision" had such personal resonance for me, its biblical underbelly meant that it seemed to resonate with everyone who read it. At this stage no one knew who had written these words, and it didn't really matter. In a way we all had.

## WALKABOUT

I began to realize that "The Vision" had left the building one after-noon as I worked in my office, hemmed in by desks, other people's football posters, and a life-size picture of Kurt Cobain. I checked my email and discovered one from Kim Unrau, a Canadian friend. Kim had found "The Vision" on the Internet and thought it was the kind of thing that I might like. It was really weird because the prayer room was still going on downstairs, and it was still taped to the wall down there, but somehow it had walked.

It continued to walk, hitchhiking its way all around the world. Eventually a particular organization started claiming they'd written "The Vision," even inserting the name of their own ministry into the text. This was when we realized that it was time to go public, and I finally asserted my right to be known as the author. We were beginning to realize that there was something prophetic in the words and that we had a responsibility to prevent this "word" getting abused and distorted. We also wanted people to realize that this wasn't just some new youth resource, it had come from a place of prayer and belonged to the emerging generation, wherever you might find them.

---

In Valladolid the dance group was coming off the stage, and as soon as I could, I grabbed the guy on the microphone. Bob Jobe is one of the funniest, most passionate and creative lovers of life you can imag-ine. Just an hour with Bob can leave you exhausted for a week. Beaming, he grabbed me, and with his fine features and intense blue eyes about an inch from my face, he said, "So what did you think, bro? Did you like the dance?"

I told him truthfully that I had loved it but that it had also totally freaked me out to see something I'd written in Chichester choreo-graphed by Americans, translated into Spanish, and performed here in Valladolid to a thousand people screaming "Venga!"

"Well, get this, bro," Bob said, flinging one arm around my shoulder and starting to walk. "Get this ..."

Bob told me that he had been invited to a presentation by John Phillips, the uncle of Rachel Joy Scott, who was killed in the Columbine High School shootings. The investigating team have since attested that Rachel was singled out to be killed for her faith, making her a modern-day martyr. From the pain of bereavement, John's life had been turned upside-down as he was inundated with requests from schools to come and share his niece's testimony. Almost overnight, he found he had a ministry traveling around schools with amazing opportunities to share Jesus.

John Phillips had called together some Christian leaders, including Bob, to present to them what he was doing and to ask them to endorse his newfound ministry. But how do you put into words what's happening to you? Your niece has been shot, and somehow out of sharing that story, your whole life has changed. A strange mixture of emotions swirling in his mind, John cleared his throat and began to speak: "It's hard for me to explain to you what has happened in my life since my niece died in Columbine," he ventured. "The only way I can even begin to make sense of the last year or communicate what the Lord is doing is this ..." He reached into his pocket and pulled out a few sheets of rather crumpled paper. Glancing around at the silent audience, John Phillips began to read a thing he'd come across on the Internet that somehow made sense of the pain and the passion of recent months. His voice cracking, he began to read "The Vision," words written anonymously on a prayer room wall more than a thousand miles away, just weeping his way through each line.

By August "The Vision" was truly touching the extremes of the earth. That month it was translated into Mandarin and published in *The Way*, which is the newspaper of 100,000 Chinese underground churches, read by literally millions of persecuted believers. And then on the second of September, it was used by the organizers of The Call, a gathering of 200,000 people in The Capitol mall of

Washington, D.C. They didn't use all of the subversive stanzas, but many went home with the call to a life that was "obsessively, dangerously Jesus" ringing in their ears.

## SOUND OF THE UNDERGROUND

In January I had been in Umea in the far north of Sweden. This lonely city is the "Straight Edge" capital of Europe, full of vegan Goths and techno-freaks deprived of sufficient natural light all winter and wasted on perpetual daylight in the summer. I was staying with a DJ named Simon Johnsson, who is part of a hip-hop collective called The Zealots. At about two in the morning, Simon forced me into a recording studio. Outside it was way below zero, and the streets were walled with snow piled as high as people. In the studio that night, my friend Elvis placed his hands on my shoulders and prayed silently while I spoke—again and again—into the microphone as Simon tried to get a good recording. By the time I climbed into my sleeping bag on Simon's couch that night, my voice was shot, and I could barely croak "Goodnight."

That recording began to travel the way the text had done. DJs in Britain, Scandinavia, and New York remixed and sampled my Swedish croaking onto dance tracks far cooler than anything I could ever have imagined.

A newly converted TV filmmaker in London, Jez Higham, listened to one of these mixes on his personal stereo on a train journey one day and just began physically shaking as the Holy Spirit touched him right there. He would later film "The Vision" and make major documentaries about the 24-7 movement.

From China to Washington, D.C. via Spain and Sweden, these 743 words written quietly one night in a prayer room were touching the ends of the earth, expressing some kind of longing in an emerging culture.

The spread of "The Vision" mirrored the extraordinary way in which the prayer rooms were also multiplying, and we began to talk in terms of a spiritual "epidemic." Looking at Chinese "bird-flu" and the SARS virus, it was clear that just a few people carrying something dangerous could quickly affect entire nations. A handful of people in close proximity in a solitary prayer room were watching words they had written, ideas they had shared, somehow touch the ends of the earth.

A few months later I'd get a glimpse of just how fast, how far, and how deeply the virus was spreading on the breath of God.

## JOURNEY

## HISTORY BELONGS TO THE INTERCESSORS[21]

> Hey fre@k,
> you're an alien on planet earth
> a million miles from home.
> You hear voices
> (the call of the wild).
> And deep down you know
> you are more than you have become:
> (Tomorrow exists in you today)
> History belongs to the intercessors.
> So do you dare to be alone with God?
> Do you dare to share
> the prayer burden for an entire generation?
> Light the fire and watch it spread:
> nonstop prayer
> across the nations
> for a generation lost in space.
> "Pray continually" (Jesus)
> Simple as that.

---

21. Walter Wink, *Engaging the Powers* (Fortress Press, 1992).

# CHAPTER TWELVE

# GOD OF THE
# SMALL PLACES
[CALIFORNIA. AUSTRALIA. PRAGUE.]

IT WAS TO BE A SUMMER OF WANDERING to obscure destinations with glorious names. First Samie and I went to a place called Eurcka, about 200 miles north of San Francisco in the heart of California's giant Redwood Forest. Then I would travel alone to the exquisitely titled Tumbi Umbi on the Central Coast of New South Wales, north of Sydney, Australia. In both of these remote locations, I was stunned to discover first-hand the impact that 24-7 prayer was already having.

## EUREKA!

Samie was three months pregnant, and we were both jet-lagged but excited to be landing in San Francisco on a beautiful evening in July. After a call home to Hudson who was almost two and staying with his grandparents, we picked up a car and were soon crossing the Golden Gate Bridge in rush-hour traffic, admiring the view of Alcatraz sitting majestically in the misty bay below. We were heading north on Highway 101 through vast redwood forests bound for a remote town on the "Forgotten Coast."

We arrived in Eureka to speak at a weeklong discipleship course and were thrilled to see that a 24-7 prayer room had already been set up at the back of the church hall, full of the usual graffiti and holy mess. One night in that room, a sixteen-year-old boy from Oregon named Brian had a profound experience of God. He testified, "I've always known that God was my Father, but it was in the prayer room this week that I really understood it for the first time." He had listened to talks and even read books on the father heart of God, but it took a moment alone in prayer for God to finally bypass his brain and touch Brian's teenage heart. Remembering John Dawson's word about prayer as the act of climbing into the Father's lap, we thought this was awesome. More and more we were discovering that God is fond of turning the mundane commitments of our heart into moments when He can reveal His mercy.

Prayer rooms are places of direct encounter with God. So much of our faith, if we are not very careful, can be second-hand experience. We listen to talks that tell us what to think. We read books that inspire us with other peoples' experiences of God. But alone with God in a prayer room, it's time to get the Bible open for yourself, going straight to the source. It's time to dialogue directly with God face to face without a middleman. In such a context, God often is able to speak to us and touch us in a way that no ministry session could ever achieve. For Brian it had been a revelation of God's fatherly love. For people on the other side of the world in Tumbi Umbi, God was doing other things as people dared to enter His presence unaccompanied.

## TUMBI UMBI

Jesus spent His childhood not in Jerusalem but in a nowhere place called Nazareth. "Can anything good come from there?" enquired Nathanael in disbelief when he heard of the Messiah's humble home. The cities are important in God's strategy for human history, but he also has a clear agenda for nowhere places to this day. Places like

Chichester outside London, Eureka north of San Francisco, and Tumbi Umbi north of Sydney.

I arrived in Australia at an exciting time as Sydney prepared to host the Millennial Olympics. The harbor was sparkling and the city was immaculate as we drove north through the peripheral bush and gum trees to Tumbi Umbi on the Central Coast near Newcastle. I had been invited to speak at another discipleship camp by a youth pastor named Simon Forsythe who had evidently connected with 24-7 through the Internet.

Simon had just returned from a snowboarding trip when I arrived, and we immediately "clicked." Simon is cheeky, irreverent, and gently besotted with Jesus. The thing that impressed me most about him from the start was the way he talked about the guys and girls in his youth congregation; you could tell that he really, really loved them and that alongside his family, they were the most important focus of his life.

Simon was the youth pastor of Bayside Christian Life Center, where he and his wife Mel had built a significant youth congregation of about two hundred people from scratch, and more than 90 percent of these young people had become Christians from completely unchurched backgrounds. Many of these first-generation believers had been discipled so well that they were now taking on leadership responsibilities. I've seen plenty of bigger youth congregations and events, but in such contexts, you generally find out that the vast majority of the people are from Christian backgrounds, no matter how wild they may appear on the outside. Anyone who's ever been involved in real, pioneer missionary work among unchurched, cynical, Western teenagers will know how tough such a mission field can be, and how significant people like Simon and Mel are. "It all began," Simon told me, "when the church sent us out to plant a totally separate congregation for young people," and they quickly grew to about eighty, even though their Sunday meeting at the time was a carbon copy of the adult service.

"It took us a few years," chuckled Simon, "to realize that most teenagers are asleep on a Sunday morning and that our style of worship wasn't necessarily relevant to the young people we wanted to reach." The service was moved to a Friday night with screaming guitars, slam dancing, and a strongly relational approach, and they also began to reach out into the local high schools. As they did so, numbers quickly grew to almost 200.

English friends encouraged Simon to check out the 24-7 prayer website. "I thought that this crazy idea of praying nonstop for a week was totally outrageous and therefore exactly where we were headed as a youth ministry!" he recalled.

"Our first prayer room was unorganized, unstructured, messed up, but honestly one of the most intimate and refreshing weeks of my Christian life. The adults in the church had been somewhat skeptical, but my young people were totally changed.

"Our senior pastor Chris Gleeson thought we were crazy, but agreed to pray at home, instead of coming into the prayer room. However, on Tuesday morning I came into the room around 9 a.m. and found him sobbing as he read the prayers and poetry and prophetic words of our young people pinned on the wall of our dirty, messy prayer room.

"We love to worship, so on our first week a tradition was born: Every Wednesday night of a 24-7 prayer week, the band plays and the whole youth ministry just worships and cries out to God. These meetings became famous and an event not to be missed. Another tradition that was born that first week was the Crazy Crew, a group of young men who loved to pray together and specialized in Early Hour prayer between one and six in the morning.

"It wasn't uncommon to see six young men sleeping on makeshift beds in the church during office hours, after praying through the night. The smell was ungodly, trust me!"

## SANCTUARY

During my visit to Simon's church, they were running another season of 24-7 prayer which would trigger loads more amazing occurrences in this unlikely location more than 10,000 miles from where it had all begun. One night a man being chased by a gang ran terrified into the church to hide. What he didn't expect to find was forty young people praying and crying out to God. The impact shook him, and he gave his life to Jesus.

There were plenty of lighter moments, too. Simon described a guy named Jay so passionate about prayer that he would march around the 24-7 room like a soldier. One night, while Jay marched for Jesus around that room and Simon prayed more sedately in the middle, there was a sudden loud crash. Simon opened his eyes in time to see Jay sliding to the floor like something out of a Tom and Jerry cartoon, having marched, eyes closed, face-first into one of the walls. Apparently undeterred, Jay hauled himself to his feet and, as if nothing had happened, continued marching round the room—this time with his eyes open!

Another of Simon's friends, Ricky, is an Australian square-jawed "Occa": a good sport, a good laugh and a good bloke—as real as they come—not the kind of guy who goes around seeing angels. "There were eight of us in the prayer room at about 3 a.m.," Simon recalled, "and Ricky was reading some of the prayers on the wall when he just suddenly freaked out and started to cry. We looked across, and he just kept whispering, 'There's an angel, there's an angel.' He had sensed someone standing next to him, but turning to see who it was, the figure had stayed a moment before just fading away. White as a sheet, Ricky told us what had happened, and we too began crying, all eight of us, just generally freaking out! All I can say for sure is that there was an awesome sense of the holy presence of God."

One young Christian was lying on a sleeping bag quietly praying when he had a vision of himself standing in a city in Venezuela.

The streets were chaotic, and there was broken glass everywhere. Suddenly he found himself looking down on the city from the sky and saw a banner proclaiming, "I will protect you." There in that prayer room in Tumbi Umbi, he felt sure that God was calling him to Venezuela on another continent. This is a kid with no church background who, before that night, had never even heard of Venezuela, let alone of visions.

## ETERNAL FLAME

Hearing these stories was almost too much to take. The Olympic flame had just that week passed through Tumbi Umbi on the final leg of its marathon from Athens to Sydney. More than 13,000 people had helped to carry it thus far by foot, canoe, bus, motorcycle, and even by camel. Almost a hundred days earlier, the torch had been lit in Athens with a prayer to the Greek sun god Apollo: "Send your rays and light this holy torch for the hospitable city of Sydney."

The "Eternal Olympic Flame" was a powerful picture for me at the time. In another age, the Moravian flame of continual intercession to the one true God (not some mythical sun-god) had traveled many thousands of miles from Hernnhut to the ends of the earth. In a smaller way, the flame of our little prayer room on an industrial estate in England had crossed time zones, oceans, and continents to ignite hundreds of places like Eureka and Tumbi Umbi, where unsuspecting young men and women might be touched by the Father's heart or called to countries they couldn't even pronounce.

The time in Tumbi Umbi was an extraordinary confirmation. It was also a steep learning curve for me as I tried to puzzle out how to make sense of this movement without constraining or controlling it. I knew by now that if we simply wanted 24-7 to become a big, global brand, it wouldn't be hard to do. In some ways the logical next step seemed to be to approach the biggest youth ministries in any country where prayer rooms were starting to multiply and ask them to take it on. In this way the movement might be sustainable, accountable, and indigenous, and 24-7 would quickly become massive over night.

But I also knew that our call was to surf waves and not to make waves. This movement was unquestionably God's idea. He had hired Markus, Jonah, Pete Worthington, and me. This thing was holy, and I knew that we must never touch it without humility. Time and time again we would say—and continue to say—that the moment God stops, we will too.

During my time in Australia, I had arranged to meet one of the leaders of a very big and exciting youth organization with a view to ask his ministry to take on 24-7 nationally. I knew that if they did so, the number of prayer rooms down under would simply explode. He kindly drove a long way to see me, and we sat talking, but as the evening progressed, God placed a strong impression on my heart: "Don't give it to him, Pete." The evening became increasingly embarrassing as it became less and less clear to the poor guy why I had been so desperate to see him. I asked about his family, about his hobbies, about his ministry, and his pets. I asked everything I could think of asking until about two in the morning when he finally said a perplexed goodbye and headed home.

I sat on my bed that night feeling really stupid. Knowing my track record, it was highly possible that I hadn't heard God right anyway and as a result had missed a massive opportunity as well as wasting the man's time. I called Samie who was just getting up in England: "I think I might just have done something really stupid." But the next morning God gave me part two of my instructions. "Give it to Simon, Pete. I want you to give 24-7 in Australia to Simon."

My heart just leapt with excitement and relief. Working with Simon would be fun! He had the same heart for what Mike Yaconelli calls "messy spirituality." I knew that, if Simon agreed to take it on, 24-7 might not grow so large in Australia. But I also knew that the prayer rooms would have our vision and values.

It was a key moment. We could choose to partner with large organizations all round the world and create a strategy to be the biggest prayer ministry ever, or we could choose to be a group of friends dreaming together. And so, at the airport I asked Simon if he would take on 24-7 prayer for Australia. He was almost in tears and said: "You don't want to give it to me, Pete, I'm a nobody."

I knew in my heart that this was exactly the reason Jesus wanted to give it to him and others like him. Once a year everyone involved in 24-7 anywhere in the world gets together at our "roundtable." This is where all the big decisions are made for the coming year, but it is also always a time for friendship and fun. Simon, who now lives with his family in America, laid the foundations for 24-7 in Australia. He sums up the sense of friendship and vision at the heart of this strange, organic movement: "I feel so attached to the 24-7 family; the two roundtables I attended will be remembered as two of the best weeks of my life."

## PRAGUE

My summer on the road had also included a return to Prague. Between Eureka and Tumbi Umbi, I found myself in the historic capital of Bohemia, speaking at a gathering of the International Charismatic Consultation on World Evangelization (ICCOWE). I was way out of my league addressing Orthodox priests, a Catholic Cardinal, and Pentecostal preachers from the States. But this conference was to provide another extraordinary twist in the 24-7 tale.

One of the other speakers was Mike Bickle, author and instigator of the International House of Prayer (IHOP) in Kansas City. Since 24-7 had started, people had been asking me if I knew about this other nonstop prayer ministry, and I had always assumed that, when the time was right, God would fix up some kind of meeting between Mike and me; Prague was clearly "it."

Another speaker at the conference was a remarkable Texan nun named Kim Catherine Marie Kollins. Kim, I discovered, had established a 24-7 prayer ministry among the world's 100 million renewed Catholics called Burning Bush International. So the three of us thought we probably ought to go for a drink ...

The locals looked up and blinked as we walked in. I don't suppose they had ever seen a nun in their seedy basement bar, let alone such an elegant one in a long, flowing white habit with silvery hair, followed by a guy who looked like a street fighter and rather a gangly Englishman with scruffy hair.

As we swapped stories about Burning Bush, IHOP, and 24-7, it became evident once again that God was doing something far bigger than any of us and that we all had a part to play. It was also extraordinary to discover that IHOP and 24-7 had started simultaneously in September 1999. It was clearer than ever that something was happening with prayer worldwide, and each one of us had a part to play. As Kim Catherine Marie Kollins wrote:

> "Everywhere I turn I seem to hear this same call to prayer being proclaimed—prayer for cities, prayer for nations. Everywhere I look I see writings calling the people of God to intense worship and adoration and intercession. Many new prayer initiatives are being called forth—houses of prayer are springing up, prayer mountains and prayer vigils are being held in response to this prompting of the Holy Spirit. Now is the time and the trumpet is being sounded to the whole people of God. We are being called to awaken from slumber and be empowered anew by the Holy Spirit. We must become once again passionate adorers of the Lord and powerful instruments of intercession for the Church and the world."[22]

### DEEPER

## JESUS—PRAYING EVERYWHERE

*"But Jesus often withdrew to lonely places and prayed." —Luke 5:16*

---

22. *Good News*, Issue 164, March/April 2003: *http://www.ccr.org.uk/gn0303/goodnews.htm.*

Jesus wouldn't have been phased by a 3 a.m. prayer slot and was known to rise while it was still dark to find a solitary place and pray. He is recorded as having spent a night in prayer prior to appointing twelve of His disciples as apostles. Another solitary time of prayer preceded His wider preaching ministry.

Jesus was familiar too with the liturgical prayers of the day, which involved reciting key Old Testament passages. Challenged by an expert as to how he might inherit eternal life, Jesus asked him what he thought. The expert replied, "Love the Lord your God with all your heart and with all your soul and with all your strength and with all your mind, and love your neighbor as yourself." These were the opening and closing lines of the *schema* prayer recited daily by many throughout Israel.

Jesus embarked on His public ministry after a prolonged time of prayer and fasting, but had to help His disciples as they sought to know how to pray. His response was not to quote the eighteen-part prayer that was part of the temple and synagogue worship. But what He did pray had a similar structure and included:

**Reverence and awe**—Hallowed be your name
**Hope**—Your kingdom come
**Request**—Give us each day our daily bread
**Confession**—Forgive us our sins
**Protection**—Lead us not into temptation, but deliver us from the evil one

Many prayer rooms seek to cover these different aspects of prayer during the one-hour experience of being alone with God.

**For Further Reading:**
Larry Richards, *Every Prayer in the Bible* (Thomas Nelson, 1998)
Richard N. Longenecker, *Into God's Presence* (Eerdmans, 2001)

## JOURNEY

## SOLDIERS OF CHRIST

God's whole impulse is toward the good and pleasant. He loves harmony and respect. It's kind of spiritually ironic that He would portray that in the context of military academy, uniting men who are trained to fight in the "bonds of peace."

We've dreamed of 24-7 here at the U.S. Naval Academy for a while, but it always seemed to be a monumental task in this institution ... Well, we jumped in full force on Friday, February 8, and it has been quite a ride ... I have seen the prayers of the students shift as the time has gone by. At first, most of the prayer dealt with personal deliverance from sinful habits as they sought to get right with God. Then it generally shifted to the salvation of the lost and a holy movement of God on the Academy. In fact they have posted the names of every student at the school (about 4,400) and are praying over each of them by name ...

I am excited about what I see happening here. A school such as this presents some unreal opportunities to touch the world. I tend to think of it as making missionaries and sending them out to every corner of the globe. If they are Christians they should be acting as ambassadors for Christ in the uniform of a sailor or soldier. God-willing 24-7 will become a permanent fixture of how we operate here at the Naval Academy.

*Captain Todd Ferry, United Sates Marine Corps*

# CHAPTER THIRTEEN

# SIGNS, WONDERS, AND RED BULL
[GERMANY]

IT WAS A SURREAL MOMENT. A CONVOY of twenty had traveled from England, arriving in Dresden's gothic center under the cover of darkness. Tanked up on Red Bull energy drink, we had navigated the cobbled streets and found ourselves standing on the site of a disused Communist-era power station next to a pyramid.

The pyramid had three sides. One said, "Father," the second "Son," and the third "Spirit." A Soviet-era car sat inexplicably on top of a nearby outhouse, covered in graffiti about Jesus. A guy in a camouflage jacket was talking in animated German to a girl. Buses, vans, and cars that looked like they'd been hijacked from the local breakers' yard were parked outside. After many hours of traveling, we'd made it to the extraordinary headquarters of Kraftwerk, and this was the building in which 24-7 Germany would be launched later that night.

## HERALD THE WEIRDOS ...

I had absolutely no idea what to expect. How many people would there be? Was there a plan for the weekend? What color would Markus Lägel's hair be this time? The thing I did know beyond any doubt was that this weekend would be historic, and we simply had to be here to support our German friends.

Stepping into the dimly lit, semi-derelict building, I could hardly believe the sight that greeted me. The cavernous venue was buzzing with people, some of the strangest-looking people I had ever seen. Like entering the underground vaults of Zion (the last free city in *The Matrix* movies) I found myself among tattooed punks, dark Goths, and people who looked homeless, ragamuffins. A number of respectable-looking older people milled happily among guys with dreadlocks and girls with skinhead haircuts and dogs on pieces of string. These people had gathered from Austria, Poland, Switzerland, and all over Germany, and now from England too. But this, I reminded myself, was not for some great rave. We had gathered to launch a German-speaking prayer movement. It seemed hard to imagine that we could be some of the successors of those Moravian refugees as we convened here in Count Zinzendorf's home city on the 300th anniversary of his birth.

People were sitting on dirty old sofas, on boxes, a few chairs and on the floor. A band was playing, and I remember the worship leader's dog jumping on and off the stage. Markus came over smiling to greet us, and I presented him with a bottle of his favorite: Dr. Pepper—hard to get in Germany. We settled down to absorb the atmosphere, feeling a little self-conscious in our more conventional clothes and haircuts. But it soon became clear that no one really cared what anyone else looked like. In fact, the gray-haired couple in matching overcoats with a large black Bible seemed like the wildest people in the room right then. They were clearly loving it, grinning and hugging and occasionally closing their eyes in prayer. Gradually we acclimated ourselves and began to join in with the raucous worship in another tongue.

After a while Karsten Wolf clambered onto the platform, Bible in hand, to speak. Looking as serious as ever in his usual sleeveless hoodie and camo pants, he opened the Bible and began to read. Someone kindly began to whisper a translation for us, and we smiled in recognition. Karsten was reading Joel 2, unwittingly using the very same passage with which we had launched in England nine months earlier. He too was talking about the army of the red moon, the outpouring of the Spirit, the release of vision, and the call of the Gospel.

## DARK WAVE

The coincidence of Karsten's message that weekend was the first of a succession of confirmations that God was with us. The building next to Kraftwerk belonged to a Dark Wave club—this was the venue for a lot of very dark and occasionally anti-Christian Goth music. While some of the clubbers simply liked the drama of the Goth scene and its sounds, many of the clientele were also being drawn into the destructive spiritual underbelly of Satanism and the occult.

Ironically, this club had announced plans for an extensive Dark Wave Festival on the very same weekend as we were launching 24-7. A number of very famous Goth bands had been booked, and the organizers, we learned, were expecting two to three thousand people to convene. Quite aside from the logistics of so many people converging on the same place at the same time, the spiritual encounter was also going to be interesting to say the least! This had been a cause for some prayer as we prepared for the weekend.

But much to everyone's surprise, the Dark Wave Festival had, at the very last moment, been thrown into confusion and cancelled. The city's authorities, it emerged, had refused them permission to hold the event over a technicality. To us it felt like a spiritual victory. Somehow, just by turning up, the opposition had been overcome. As the apostle James wrote two thousand years earlier:

"Submit yourselves, then, to God. Resist the devil, and he will flee from you" (James 4:7).

James then continued with the positive: "Come near to God and he will come near to you ..." (v. 8). We had no idea just how near God in His grace would come as we visited Hernnhut together the following day.

## HERNNHUT

My heart was full as we drove to Hernnhut through lashing rain the next morning. It was hard to comprehend all that had happened in the sixteen months since my previous visit. In many ways my life had changed. The Moravian model of prayer had been mobilized once again and was spreading like wildfire around the world. And I was returning now in convoy with a couple hundred weird-looking people to launch the movement in Germany. The very thought sent shivers down my spine.

For old friends like Kerry, Paul Weston, and Susanna Rychiger, this would be the first time they had ever seen Hernnhut, a place that had already shaped their lives. I had tried to demystify the location, telling them again and again that it was just a normal, neat, and quiet village in the German countryside. In many ways that was the whole point—if they could do it here, then so could we. In the gray rain that day as people in parkas splashed through the puddles, the place seemed more ordinary than ever.

And yet God, who loves to shatter expectations and hijack ordinary lives, was planning something extraordinary: a moment that would be significant for years to come; in many ways for us it would be a modern day sign and wonder.

## ZINZENDORF'S LEGACY

The pastor of the Moravian church in Hernnhut had kindly agreed to speak to us, and so we parked our cars outside the church and entered the building excitedly. A TV crew was waiting inside to film the lecture for a documentary on Zinzendorf and his influence today. The pastor, respectably dressed and focused on his lecture, was about to be joined by the weirdest congregation he had ever seen. We trooped in, dogs in tow, some with great big afro hats perched on their heads. The TV crew, realizing that they had just missed a highly visual moment, asked us to go out and come in again with the cameras rolling!

The pastor, blinking nervously from behind his notes, gave a brilliant summary of the Moravian renewal that had visited his parish almost three centuries ago. We realized how many parallels there were between our evolving model of prayer and that of Zinzendorf.

In a quiet voice, reading directly from his notes, the pastor described the way in which Zinzendorf had organized twenty-four women and twenty-four men into prayer "choirs," each one taking turns to pray for one hour every two days. Of course this prayer chain was to continue for one hundred years. Every man between the ages of sixteen and sixty was called upon to cover the night watches, prayer-walking around the village. A quiet murmur of approval rose from the girls in the congregation at the idea of the men having to cover all the night shifts in this way. Zinzendorf wrote a hymn that captures what it was like to be on one of these night vigils, an experience that was becoming a familiar part of our lives too (both men and women!):

> *"The hour is come: though darkness steals the day;*
> *Shines in your hearts the morning star's first ray?*
> *The clock is two! who comes to meet the day,*
> *And to the Lord of days his homage pay?*
> *The clock is five! while five away were sent,*
> *Five other virgins to the marriage went!*
> *The clock is six, and from the watch I'm free,*
> *And everyone may his own watchman be!"*[23]

---

23. A.J. Lewis, *Zinzendorf the Ecumenical Pioneer* (SCM Press Ltd., 1962), p. 54.

Next the pastor described the way in which Zinzendorf had organized the community into single-sex cell groups called bands, which provided a context for radical accountability. Zinzendorf described them like this: "The societies called bands, consist of a few individuals met together in the name of Jesus ... who converse together in a particularly cordial and childlike manner, on the whole state of their hearts, and conceal nothing from each other, but who have wholly committed themselves to each other's care in the Lord."[24]

Such concepts of discipleship are perhaps familiar to us, but in other respects, the Moravian model was far more radical than ours. For instance, they would meet three times a day: at four in the morning (five o'clock in the winter), eight in the morning, and eight at night. In these corporate gatherings, they would worship and receive teaching (though please remember that this was an agricultural community where people tended to rise with the lark and turn in at dusk, so such an early start would not have seemed quite so painful to them!).

It would be a while before our first 24-7 Boiler Room (tagged as a "Millennium Three Monastery") would be established to explore similar ideas of ongoing community centered on strict rhythms of prayer.

Occasionally the community would gather to hear letters read aloud from their family members in far distant lands bringing reports of the Lord's work and heart-rending requests for urgent prayer. As the pastor quietly described these letter-reading days in the very place that we were sitting, my mind flashed to the 24-7 website and the way it was disseminating similar reports and requests from the ends of the earth to our modern community.

The pastor seemed to be enjoying this opportunity to teach the firm facts about his predecessors. So many people come to his hometown

---

24. Rev. August Gottlieb Spangenberg, *The Life of Nicholas Lewis Count Zinzendorf* (London: Samuel Holdsworth, 1838), p. 87.

in order to impose their own theology or eschatology upon the history of the place. It's easy to exaggerate or to distort the stories or romanticize the realities, but in the long run, this doesn't help anyone, and it certainly doesn't reflect the heart of Zinzendorf, who so loved the traditions of the Moravian church and sought to serve them and renew them, not use them to serve his ambitions.

In particular, people often over-romanticize the famous gathering in Berthelsdorf on August 13, 1727. Undoubtedly, this meeting was the great Moravian "Pentecost," as Spangenburg, one of their later Bishops, would describe it. Undoubtedly, God moved in an extraordinary way on that day. But that Sunday service was part of an ongoing process of renewal in the community. Initiatives like the nonstop prayer meeting were much more planned and less explosive in their origins than many preachers today suggest. It was exactly two weeks after this famous service that the prayer schedule began. And it was five years later that the missions thrust commenced.

Gazing down at his strange congregation, the pastor seemed to be warming up to us as he was warming up to his theme. He described Sundays in Hernnhut, when you could hear music all day long as the villagers sang continually (presumably in shifts), worshiping God from five in the morning to nine at night, at which point all the young men would complete the day by marching around the village with a final song. On these days the congregation might also break bread and practice foot washing. Visitors were drawn to Hernnhut, coming to see this extraordinary community for themselves. Zinzendorf therefore made Sunday afternoon an open day in which people could interact with members of the community. Many were so impressed by what they saw that they moved to Hernnhut to be part of this community of prayer before being shot out to the ends of the earth as ambassadors of Christ and emissaries of a truly radical community.

## UNITY

The Moravian pastor was coming to the end of his lecture and had saved one of his most passionate points for now. The Moravian church, which had become, under Zinzendorf's renewal, a powerhouse of prayer and mission, had from the beginning held its highest allegiance to the ideal of Christian unity. To this day the denomination is known as "The Unitas Fratrum": the united brethren. It was a passion reflected in Zinzendorf's brilliant motto:

> *"In essentials, unity;*
> *in non-essentials, liberty;*
> *and in all things, love."*

What a great guideline for us today. 24-7 Prayer is not a new organization or an alternative church. We are not part of the Moravian denomination or any other tradition. We are a renewal movement, rather than a replacement for existing expressions of faith. Our sense of identity is generational rather than denominational, and it is a generation more concerned with finding common ground and celebrating diversity than with dividing over religious tags.

This is not to say that we are unaware of where we have come from, nor that we are ungrateful for the ways in which our predecessors have pioneered. But as we learn from the past, we find heroes and villains in every tradition, and as we look to the future, we know that Jesus is still praying that His broken body might be one. It's time to widen the gene pool, to learn from each other, and to come together in love without losing our sense of tribal or personal identity along the way. And if the tribes of Israel can't come together in prayer and mission, there is little hope for an immanent "Amen" to the Lord's last longing before the cross.

Hernnhut had been a powerhouse of renewal in Anglican and Lutheran contexts as well as the Moravian denomination. In a similar way, we are thrilled to see the way that 24-7 prayer is uniting different denominations in many areas as they work together to set up citywide prayer rooms. Catholics, Pentecostals, Baptists, Anglicans, Salvationists, and Presbyterians: every shade of faith coming together to seek God's face. Such endeavors are not without their challenges and disagreements, but Zinzendorf's motto will help us to love one another, release one another, and combine our forces for the sole purpose Christ's pleasure.

Glancing around the room, I realized that even this unlikely gathering of people from so many nations and such diverse cultures was perhaps an exercise in love and liberty, united together around the essence that is prayer.

## THE FEAR OF THE LORD

As the pastor drew to a close and gathered up his papers, a spontaneous round of applause went up from the congregation, making the godly teacher look distinctly uncomfortable. Karsten Wolf, the Jesus Freak pastor, jumped from his pew and strode up the steps onto the dais at the front of the church. "Would you pray for us?" he asked the pastor, adding, "and we would like to pray for you." The pastor seemed happy for this and moved into position next to the man in the camouflage pants. Karsten was gripping *The Lösung*, the Moravian book of Daily Texts, which is the best-selling daily devotional in the world.[25] First published in 1731 by Zinzendorf himself here in Hernnhut, today it has a staggering 1.5 million users in over fifty languages and dialects.

"But before we pray," Karsten said, "Let's just see what the Moravian text for today is." He thumbed the pages quickly stopping on Saturday, November 25. I remember thinking that he was about to kill the moment, because whenever I need an instant word and try playing pot-luck with the Bible, I end up getting some totally irrelevant verse about goats' milk from Leviticus. But it was too late to object, and slowly Karsten began to read.

The first gasp came from the Germans, another one, a second later, from those receiving the English translation. Of all the verses it might have been, it was the most appropriate one it could possibly

---

25. You can get the Moravian Daily Texts emailed to you from: *http://www.moravian.org/daily_texts/*

have been: "And afterward," he read slowly, "I will pour out my Spirit on all people. Your sons and daughters will prophesy, your old men will dream dreams, your young men will see visions …"

The Moravian text for that day, read in fifty languages by more than a million people, was Joel 2:28-32, the passage with which we had launched in Guildford under a blood red moon and the passage from which Karsten had spoken the night before in Dresden.

What statistical chance could there be that on the one and only day we happened to convene in Hernnhut, and out of all the texts in Scripture, that this particular verse would be the one awaiting us in the Moravian church as we launched 24-7 Germany? Many members of the crowd were just shaking their heads in amazement, and an atmosphere settled in the room that was hard to define. It took me quite a few minutes to identify the feeling as fear: The fear of an Almighty God. Probably more than any other instant on the 24-7 journey thus far, that single moment in that simple place was when we knew beyond all doubt that this was not just something we were doing for God, but that God was allowing us to be involved in with him. And with that realization came a sobriety: the absolute certainty that this great wave of God's Spirit could crush us. It was an awesome moment, in the truest sense of that word.

## MORE POSSIBLE THAN EVER

Seeing the impact of the text upon the congregation, the Moravian pastor pointed out that it would have been selected at least a year before, by lot, from Zinzendorf's original bowl. Once again it seemed that before we had envisaged 24-7, God had been dreaming of this day. For many of us, such concepts didn't fit with our theology, but God didn't seem too bothered about that.

Just as Justin had predicted our call to prayer six months before 24-7 had begun, as another member of the church had "seen" our prayer room before it existed in reality, as Pete Worthington and Jonah Bailey had been hired before we ever met, so now, more than ever, we had a sense of being caught up in the purposes of God. We suddenly felt very, very small.

## WESLEY

I was invited to stand and teach the second lecture of the day in a building next door. There was only one thing to do, and I expounded Joel 2 once again.

Here in Hernnhut, I reminded them, a fourteen-year-old girl named Anna Nitschman was appointed an elder and became one of their most dynamic leaders. I pointed out that, according to Joel, we should expect such things today as the Spirit is poured out on all flesh: young as well as old, women as well as men.

I talked about the way that the Spirit releases dreams and fresh vision and talked about the extraordinary way in which the words of The Vision had spread.

I talked about the red moon that rises over every generation and the call to take the Gospel of mercy to every tribe and tongue, here in the place that sent out such radical evangelists to the very ends of the earth. I mentioned the fact that John Wesley had come here to Hernnhut for instruction and the part the Moravians had played in taking the message of salvation to every corner of the United Kingdom, profoundly influencing the church in the West to this day.

And finally, I talked about the fact that such things are the signs of the last days and reminded the congregation of the earliest recorded prayer of the First Century Church: "Maranatha—Come quickly, Lord Jesus." We have been living, I reminded them, in "the last days" for 2,000 years, living with the possibility that a generation could arise to take the Gospel to all nations and usher in the return of Jesus. We are called to live like the earliest believers with expectancy, with a naive sense that anything is possible and a longing for the bridegroom to come.

There was still an intense sense of God's presence, and I noticed a few people quietly crying. Looking around the room, I remembered something I had been told by German friends: Many young Germans don't like being German because they still carry an undermining sense of national shame about the Second World War. It can be hard for other nations to understand what it is like growing up with the knowledge that your grandparents' generation served under Hitler, but many ordinary German young people still seem to carry this gnawing sense of surrogate guilt for something they didn't do and therefore can't ever rectify. It's a sense that "nothing good can come out of" Germany. And so, as an Englishman, I thanked the Germans for their great redemptive gift to the body of Christ: Count Nicholas Ludwig Von Zinzendorf. And as I did so, a German member of the congregation let out what can only be described as a howl of pain, falling to his knees in the aisle. As God mobilizes a different army, a fighting force that will wage peace on earth, it must begin with healing and hope for those soldiers crushed by the past.

Waking up the next morning, I realized it was my thirty-first birthday. But as I began the journey home I felt drained and exhausted, like I'd been on the road too many months, in America, Australia, the Czech Republic, and now Germany. All I wanted, more than anything else, was simply to get home to my family, my own bed, and my beautiful wife Samie.

**DEEPER**

## ALEXANDER THE SLEEPLESS

Alexander came from a well-to-do Greek family. While studying in Constantinople around 375-380 A.D., he discovered a new direction in life when faced with the challenge of Matthew 19:21—"If you want to be perfect, go, sell your possessions and give to the poor." He joined a monastery, but convinced that his fellow monks weren't taking the Bible seriously, he left and for seven years wandered around the edge of a desert. When his time of reflection was over, he established a monastery and began a 24-7-365 prayer cycle that was to last twenty years.

Romans, Greeks, Syrians, and Egyptians sought him out and formed distinct groups according to language. He organized them into teams of fifty so that they could meditate on the law of the Lord day and night (Psalm 1:2). They sang the Psalms and prostrated themselves in prayer, singing hymns and doxologies in liturgical shifts.

He then formed a mission team of seventy zealots and traveled down the Euphrates singing psalms day and night. It seems that the monks didn't always keep their prayer vigils in secluded rooms. Described by one historian as a "mobile house of prayer," they went out onto the streets, swaying, sometimes prostrate, and always singing psalms. Alexander's intercessors were met with a hostile reception in Constantinople, but he managed to sneak back into the city, settled into an ancient bathhouse, and became "a tutor and teacher of all" through his preaching and care for the city's poor. To find out more about Alexander the Sleepless and many like him, go to the Even Deeper section at *www.redmoonrisingbook.com*.

## JOURNEY

### PRODIGAL RETURNS

A young man, Doug, stood in front of our whole church and told how God led him to the prayer room. He was a prodigal, living in sin. He tearfully told how he gave his heart and life back to Jesus in the prayer room. He has been faithfully attending the prayer room since that night to pray for others!

*Ann Burns, Johnson City, Tennessee*

# CHAPTER FOURTEEN

# PAIN
[U.K.]

"PETE, WAKE UP!" SAMIE SOUNDED SCARED as I rolled over bleary-eyed and turned on the bed-side light. Instinctively I checked the Moses basket at the end of our bed, but Danny lay peacefully, just seven weeks old and fast asleep.

Samie, however, was sitting up in bed white as a sheet and holding her right leg. "I can't move it," she whispered, "I can't move my leg." At that moment the fingers on her right hand began to contort like an arthritic fist and Samie gasped in excruciating pain. "What's happening to me?" Cold terror glazed her eyes as we watched that first epileptic seizure march relentlessly up her arm. I called the ambulance, quite sure I was watching my beautiful bride dying. I had never felt so powerless in all my life.

Everything was unreal, impossible, and suddenly silent. In his sleep, Danny's lips were pouting contentedly for milk while his mum lay nearby, unconscious and waiting for the paramedics.

Hours later a doctor would sit down next to me in the hospital corridor, his voice rumbling from some other reality: A large tumor had been discovered in Samantha's brain. It would be a while before they knew if it was possible to operate. "Shall we go and break the news to your wife?"

I begged him to wait, at least until she woke from her sleep. I wanted her to stay in a world where everything was still going to be all right. Too soon she would wake to this nightmare that wouldn't go away. "Besides," I said, "she's going to need all her strength for the battle ahead," hoping desperately that there was at least a battle to be fought.

People began to pray for us, and we were grateful beyond any possible words. Paul Weston texted me: "PETE, WORDS DON'T CUT IT RIGHT NOW BUT WE R PRAYIN 4U." Messages like that meant a lot. Prayer was suddenly the most practical thing anyone, anywhere could do.

A bunch of people—complete strangers—from a prayer room in Reading (pronounced "Redding") sixty miles away jumped in a car one night, turned up at our hospital, and prayed right through the night for Samie in the chapel near our ward, leaving in the morning without a word. That was the first night Samie managed to sleep without the help of pills. More importantly, the story of their unconditional love helped us grasp the reality of God's heart for us even in the valley of the shadow of death.

The good news came eventually: Surgeons were prepared to operate, but waiting a month for Samie's life and death encounter with the surgeon's knife seemed an eternity. During that time, we found ourselves clinging to Scripture like never before. It was a source of unspeakable comfort. Samie memorized Psalm 91 and would recite it to herself at night and as she lay utterly alone in the MRI scanner tube:

> "Because [she] loves me," says the Lord, "I will rescue her;
> I will protect her, for she acknowledges my name.

*She will call upon me, and I will answer her;*
*I will be with her in trouble,*
*I will deliver her and honor her.*
*With long life will I satisfy her*
*and show her my salvation."*

We would go to sleep most nights reciting Philippians 4:6-7:

"Do not be anxious about anything, but in everything, by prayer and petition, with thanksgiving, present your requests to God. And the peace of God, which transcends all understanding, will guard your hearts and your minds in Christ Jesus."

One of the hardest things for me was putting the kids to bed each evening. Unbearable possibilities choked in my throat as I kissed the boys good night.

## STRONGER WEAK

On March 30, 2001, Samie came round from successful surgery. A growth the size of an orange had been removed from her head, and she was alive, with full mobility and speech. Without doubt we had experienced a miracle of God's love. The recovery, however, has been excruciatingly slow and difficult. Samie continues to suffer from regular debilitating seizures that have often escorted her back into hospital.

All this has had a profound effect on us personally and on the 24-7 movement. At a time when we might have become triumphalistic, intoxicated with the excitement of miracles and movements, we were suddenly confronted with the stark reality of suffering, unanswered prayer, and even death. Samie and I were beginning to understand Paul's experience of a "thorn in the flesh," allowed by God to keep him "from becoming conceited" because of his incredible experiences (2 Corinthians 12:7). Like him, we pleaded with God to take our suffering away, and yet in the midst of it all, we were discovering that His promises are true: "'My grace is sufficient for you, for my power is made perfect in weakness" (2 Corinthians 12:9).

Of course Samie and I are not the only ones to suffer. Many of the key leaders within 24-7 have found themselves struggling with enormous difficulties too. Some have been bereaved; one guy's wife walked out on him; another woman found her diabetes getting steadily worse; and many face real financial challenges as they seek to follow the call on their lives. Whatever the "thorn," these things keep us feeling weak, dependent on God, and painfully aware that all the amazing stuff we've experienced as a movement is entirely thanks to Him. "That is why," Paul said, "for Christ's sake, I delight in weaknesses for when I am weak, then I am strong." (2 Corinthians 12:10).

## DAY OF GOD'S FAVOR

In November 2001 I posted this message entitled "Where Angels Fear to Tread" on our website:

> What a mess! Members of the 24-7 team got together in the U.K. recently, and it was incredible to realize how much stuff we are all struggling with. Amidst fantastic blessing and monstrous answers to prayer, we are contending with sickness, family problems, near-exhaustion, lack of money, and even bereavement … We laughed, realizing we're not a very "victorious" bunch to be leading a prayer movement! (Sorry if that disillusions anyone.)

> Just the situation with my wife Samie's brain tumor—the operation and long, slow recovery—that alone would have been enough to wipe us out. But looking around the room today at all these gifted people, I realized that almost every one of them is going through extreme and challenging times.

> And I know from emails, postings on the website, and chats on the phone that many of you are facing massive struggles too. Then, today, Billy Kennedy brought us a bit from the Bible that just summed up the whole thing with such power …

> "I tell you, now is the time of God's favor, now is the day of

salvation. We put no stumbling block in anyone's path, so that our ministry will not be discredited. Rather, as servants of God we commend ourselves in every way: in great endurance; in troubles, hardships and distresses ... in hard work, sleepless nights and hunger; in purity, understanding, patience and kindness; in the Holy Spirit and in sincere love; in truthful speech and in the power of God; with weapons of righteousness in the right hand and the left; through glory and dishonor, bad report and good report; genuine, yet regarded as impostors; known, yet regarded as unknown; dying, and yet we live on; beaten, and yet not killed; sorrowful, yet always rejoicing; poor, yet making many rich; having nothing, yet possessing everything" (2 Corinthians 6:2-10).

For many of us, that passage is pretty much a checklist of our lives right now! It's the best of times and the worst of times all at once.

## THE BEST OF TIMES ...

In many ways, we find ourselves living in a time of "God's favor ... the day of salvation." Most weeks people just walk into prayer rooms and meet Jesus—that in itself is just amazing!! God's favor is upon us as 24-7 continues to grow in so many countries, with dramatic answers to prayer, new artwork, fresh missions movements, new monasteries, and history being made in so many situations. This really is a day of God's favor. He is doing "immeasurably more than all we could ask or imagine." It's just, we never thought it would feel like this, did we?

## THE WORST OF TIMES ...

In spite of all the blessings, it often takes "great endurance" just to make it through the day.
  • "Troubles, hardships and distresses" (v. 4) may surround us as

they did Paul.
- We have to work hard (v. 5) as did Paul, who even sacrificed sleep at times (v. 5).
- We are being called to greater purity and kindness just when we could so easily get ratty and short-tempered!
- While some people speak well of us, others don't, saying unkind and untrue things about us as they did of Paul. God knows our hearts are "genuine," but some people seem to think we've got hidden agendas.
- Like Paul, we find ourselves "poor" and yet "making many rich."

Paul's experience is something we can all relate to right now (aside from a few beatings, a couple of riots, and a spot of imprisonment, that is). So, I've been asking God why being blessed is proving such a pain! I may be wrong, but here's what I've come up with ...
- Attack: Maybe some of the stuff we're dealing with right now has to do with the enemy challenging and resisting us as we make advances into his domain.
- Weakness: But most of all I'm coming to the conclusion that, to be used by God, we must be weak and foolish rather than all-conquering heroes. I reckon God is sick and tired of people posing as "overcomers" with permanent grins as if they some how avoided "The Fall" and went hang-gliding instead. He needs us weak and childish to be used by Him. Let's face it— any glory from 24-7 has got to go to God because no one else can realistically take credit for it!

*"For the foolishness of God is wiser than man's wisdom, and the weakness of God is stronger than man's strength." —1 Corinthians 1:25*

Ultimately, in the words of the song, we may get knocked down, but we get up again ... Or, in the slightly more spiritual words of Paul, we are "more than conquerors in Christ." Perhaps through our trials we are discovering that all things really do work together for good for those who love God. What an amazing assurance.

## LEARNING TO INTERCEDE

A guy named Paul with long matted hair and massive flares stood up
rather hesitantly to speak at one particular 24-7 gathering. He began
with a confession, but we were soon to discover he was carrying a
powerful message from the Lord.

"My sister has anorexia," he confided, brushing the hair from his
face. "She's 26 years old and weighs just seventy pounds. The anorexia is so bad that she's now developed arthritis so she can't even dress
herself or straighten her hands. She also seems to have diabetes and is
going through menopause twenty years too early. She isn't a
Christian; she just seems to have been robbed of everything: her
womanhood, her future, her dignity, her life."

The crowd had grown totally silent, hanging on every tortured
word: "I'm here to confess something to you ..." Looking up at his
audience, Paul paused: "I don't even pray for her. I've been asking
myself, 'Why not? Don't I care? Yes, I care! Do I believe in prayer?
Yes, of course!' The reason I don't pray for my sister is because it's
just too painful. To pray for her is to think about her situation. It
means identifying with her and feeling her pain. So I find it easier
just to forget the whole thing and pretend it's not happening.

"But God's been challenging me to feel my sister's pain, because
that's actually what it means to truly intercede. I also believe God is
challenging us as a movement of young people to dare to feel the
pain all around us. To move from praying 'for' people from the comfort of our own salvation to interceding 'with' them from a position
of need." He grew in confidence as he sensed the Holy Spirit putting words in his mouth: "Here's the question: 'Will we allow the
things that break God's heart to break our hearts too?' It'll mean
more tears, more listening. It may even be the reason why so many
of us struggle with our own personal burdens and heartaches—God
is allowing us to feel the pain, to be weak and broken so that our
prayers have power.

"Intercession means weeping for the earthquake victims in the news right now, and for the anorexics, the drug abusers, the sexually abused, the friends who don't know Jesus. And God says that if we will stand in the gap in this way, bridging the ravine between a hurting generation and a healing God—we will see breakthrough, a new level of effectiveness in prayer. In short, there will be very great power in our pain, or, in the words of The Vision, we will weep 'sulphuric tears.'"

Paul scanned the crowd for a moment and noticed the way some were avoiding his gaze: "This is a tough word isn't it? We're so often told to trust Jesus for a problem-free existence. But what if the call to pray is a call to bleed as well as to receive blessing? Maybe we'll run out of words in the prayer room and just join the Spirit in praying with 'groans that words cannot express.' Maybe our passion will consume us until we actually live out our prayers in practical action? Will you carry this cross? Can you receive it?"

## I'LL FIGHT ...

His humble challenge was timely and sobering, and it made perfect sense. God is mobilizing an army, but it is a broken army that marches on its knees. As Christians, we are not immune from the pain of the world around us, and in addition to these trials, we find ourselves engaged in a spiritual battle against temptation and demonic attack. As our commander in chief inspects the ranks of His wounded, weeping soldiers, He speaks to you and He speaks to me saying, "Blessed are the poor in spirit, for theirs is the kingdom of heaven. Blessed are those who mourn, for they will be comforted. Blessed are the meek, for they will inherit the earth" (Matthew 5).

When things are tough, it would be easy to back off. Samie and I continue to wrestle with the profound challenges of her illness, and it would be easy to make excuses and do anything to settle for an easy life. But when I am feeling weak and weary, strength comes from clinging to the promises of God in prayer:

*"Why do you say, O Jacob,*
*and complain, O Israel,*
*'My way is hidden from the Lord;*
*my cause is disregarded by my God'? ...*
*Even youths grow tired and weary,*
*and young men stumble and fall;*
*but those who hope in the LORD*
*will renew their strength.*
*They will soar on wings like eagles;*
*they will run and not grow weary,*
*they will walk and not be faint."*
—*Isaiah 40:27, 30-31*

At such times William Booth's famous war cry inspires me to persevere, to fight on for a Kingdom where there will be no more crying, no more dying and no more sin. Booth wrote:

*"While women weep as they do now, I'll fight; while little children go*
*hungry as they do now, I'll fight; while men go to prison, in and out, in*
*and out, I'll fight; while there is a poor little lost girl upon the street, I'll*
*fight; while there yet remains one dark soul without the light of God, I'll*
*fight—I'll fight to the very end!"[26]*

William Booth did exactly that, fighting for justice to the very end of his life. And his legacy in the Salvation Army was to provide one of the most exciting and unexpected new twists in the 24-7 tale so far.

### JOURNEY

## WITH OR WITHOUT YOU

Raw honesty in prayer is like a volatile liquid, powerful if used right, destructive if dropped or shaken. Trapped in our belief that we can never say what is really on our heart, we can be polite to God and

---

26. Richard Collier, *The General Next To God* (Collins, 1965).

submerge our real emotions and real issues. Prayer rooms seem to give permission for honesty even when the angry one is drunk.

A girl who was angry with God ended up in our prayer room. She had been blaming God for her dad's cancer and didn't want to have any more to do with Him. She got drunk and in that state came to our prayer room where she started weeping before God. As she did so, her heart was recaptured by Him again. She wanted His love even though she was hurting so badly about her dad. Kids in church the next day heard the girl's story and prayed for her dad. That same night the girl got a phone call to say that the doctors couldn't find the cancer anymore but only a cyst in its place!

*Cardiff, Wales*

# CHAPTER FIFTEEN

# THREESIXFIVE
[WESTERN EUROPE. SWEDEN.
EASTERN AUSTRALIA.]

IN A SALVATION ARMY SOCIAL CENTER IN
the north of England, the Anglican Bishop of
Bradford knelt to pray next to a homeless man. He
later said that it was one of the most moving experiences of his life. Together they were launching a
week of 24-7 prayer in which many of the prayer
shifts would be filled—remarkably—by people who
were not yet Christians. Lawley House takes in men
who are homeless and often have an addiction of
some kind, and because most of the residents are not
Christians, no one had been quite sure how well a
"week of prayer" would be received.

But the Territorial Commander, Alex Hughes,
described what happened next: "As the week went
on, the staff and residents (Christian and non-
Christian alike) spent hours and hours in the prayer
room, enjoying God and pouring out their hearts to
Him. Many of the men met God for the first time
in their lives."

The way that 24-7 has spread through the ranks of the Salvation Army around the world has been one of the most extraordinary and wonderful surprises in the story of this accidental prayer movement so far.

## UP AND DOWN

In many ways we are a grassroots movement: Little churches in unlikely places and groups of students simply get hold of the 24-7 idea and establish lo-tech, nonstop prayer rooms, often in surprising places. But larger bodies have also seen the strategic potential of this groundswell to impact their entire organizations. Here, they realize is a prayer model that can unite people nationally and even internationally in global community, while being outworked locally, focused on real schools, real streets, real people: a model for global/local prayer. Suddenly it was possible to call entire denominations to pray like never before, connecting local prayer rooms nationally or even internationally to fill an entire year with unbroken intercession.

The book of Hebrews describes a great "cloud of witnesses" cheering us on. I like to imagine Count Zinzendorf in that heavenly throng alongside his friend John Wesley and their big-bearded spiritual son William Booth, the three great eccentrics chuckling together and nodding sagely as the Moravian model of prayer came home to roost in the Salvation Army.

## RADICAL HEARTS

This shambolic prayer movement, inspired by the Moravians, launched in a run-down nightclub in England and among wild-eyed punks in Germany, was about to encounter the crisp white shirts, gleaming brass bands, and immaculate military uniforms of the Salvation Army. Outwardly, it may have seemed a strange marriage, but beneath our clothes, an identical heart was beating: a call to the poor and marginalized, a theological pragmatism, and above all our sworn allegiance to the same Commander in Chief. Of course, "radical" is not about the clothes we wear or the music we listen to. Some of the least radical, most predictable people on planet earth have pierced skin and wild hair. But the real radicals are rooted in the Gospel of Christ, living sacrificially for others. And we would soon discover that some of the most sacrificial servants of the savior Jesus Christ on planet Earth right now iron their shirts, play in Brass bands, and wear the uniform of William Booth's Salvation Army.

- The Salvation Army in the U.K. was the first to pioneer 24/7/365, and other groups have been quick to follow.
- A network of Swedish Free Churches (Evangeliska Frikyrkan) filled every minute of the 2002 with intercession for their land, an achievement unprecedented since the days of the Vikings.
- The Salvation Army year was having such an impact in the U.K. that the idea of nonstop Moravian prayer soon spread to their Eastern Australian Territory.
- Next to join the party was an entire Youth With a Mission region: Western Europe. In 2003 YWAM bases began to pray nonstop, passing the baton of intercession from Italian villas to Scottish castles and from Portugal in the West to countries like Belgium in the East.
- So too did the Pioneer network of churches in England, of which Revelation in Chichester is a part.

Many extraordinary stories continue to surface from all these networks of prayer as testimonies to a God who hears the heart cries of the humble and can transform communities and even nations today as surely as He can transform individual lives. Through recent years of such great international turmoil—with the AIDS pandemic ravaging Africa, 9/11, Afghanistan, Iraq and Palestine, sexual scandals in the Catholic church, and the gay debate threatening to split the Anglican Communion—many organizations have found themselves praying like never before.

---

As all these surprising developments took place, I found that Samie's illness had thrust me into the role of primary caregiver for Hudson and Daniel, and it was no longer possible for me to travel and minister the way I had done during the first eighteen months of the movement's growth. But amid the trials of our situation at home, there were also many blessings, not least this opportunity to bond deeply with my children at a time when I could so easily have become a distant figure to them traveling the world. I nursed them both through chicken pox and woke with Daniel night after night. Meanwhile, Samie's quiet courage and under-girding faith throughout this time were amazing to watch in spite of repeated traumas. During this protracted period of helplessness, our family and friends supported us incredibly, and we quickly learned to receive people's kindness with a simple "thanks."

Suddenly all our grand dreams seemed faintly ridiculous. Sitting in hospital wards and changing diapers, I now knew beyond any doubt that it wasn't my job to save the planet and felt so grateful to be just a small part of God's great, global purposes. An army was being mobilized, but it was God's army led not by might, nor by power, but by His Spirit. And God's Spirit, like the wind, is unstoppable, uncontrollable, and wild.

And so, as I eased back on my schedule, others were putting their feet firmly to the floor, speeding ahead with 24-7 in ways and down avenues I could never have imagined. In God's economy it was clear that 24-7 was not and could never be about me and my ministry. This was God's movement, not built on personality or platform, and He was raising up all sorts of people, often in surprising places, to take a lead. Offices had opened by now in Canada, Spain, Germany, Sweden, and Australia, with developments afoot in Mexico, Switzerland, Indonesia, Japan, and the United States. In all these locations, people were pioneering, catalyzing, and resourcing a fresh wave of prayer. We were learning new things almost weekly and had begun to be able to answer the huge variety of questions that arose from prayer rooms around the world.

In many ways the challenge as we grew was to get organized without becoming an organization in the restrictive sense of that word. We were so grateful to God when a brilliant young American

Express executive, Carl Barkey, consolidated his hours at work to free up every Friday to work as an unpaid consultant for 24-7. It was a radical step for an upwardly mobile young businessman whose time was already highly pressurized in a stressful job, but it has been a massive blessing to us. With Carl's careful insights, we were able to bring a bit more structure and accountability to the movement and, rather than restricting the wildness of what God is doing, this seems to have released it even more.

## CLONE FREE ZONE

We weren't trying to provide a cookie cutter, one-size-fits-all prayer room concept. 24-7 prayer rooms aren't prescriptive; they're deliberately and delightfully diverse. There's no blueprint that you should adhere to or rules to follow, just minimal principles. Instead we try to pump out ideas and circulate those of others. People visit prayer rooms or the website and hopefully go home to their own church, student group, or mission inspired with new ideas.

There was, by now, a website to run in a dozen different languages and cultures, there were articles to write, resources to post, missions to co-ordinate, plans afoot for our first Prayer House, staff to support, and a hundred other tasks. We were trying to email and phone every single prayer room with encouragement, sending them free resources, wanting every place of prayer to be a life-changing experience for every person who stepped inside. Our priority was not all the big stuff of structure, numbers, partnerships, or hits; it was the person praying right then, and the fourteen-year-old boy who stumbled into a prayer room the night before and wondered what to do.

With so much activity, one of the most exciting and encouraging dimensions of 24-7 has been the supernatural ways in which God has provided for our needs again and again as we have sought to live by faith. From week to week finances were, and continue to be, a major prayer focus as we try to keep up with all that the Spirit is doing, but we have never yet gone without a single meal or been unable to pay a single bill. Many times, money has come in miraculously at the last moment from unexpected sources, just like it does in the books! At others we have been frustrated, unable to develop things the way we would like, but this has kept us dependent on God to drive us forward—using the brake pedal at times as well as the accelerator.

## PHIL'S STORY

Back in Chichester my frequent absences from the office were being covered by the ever-faithful Kerry and a guy who had quickly become one of the great unsung heroes of 24-7: Phil Baldwin.

Phil is a likable, funny, gentle guy whose quiet character belies his love of loud music—the weirder the better—and our Chichester office will often be filled with the surreal sounds of his latest obscure CD. For quite a long time, Phil was the only full-time member of staff we had anywhere on planet earth. At twenty-three, he was, in effect, the guy who kept the whole 24-7 show on the road.

The amazing thing about this is that, in our first prayer room, Phil Baldwin's name had been inscribed on the wall as a non-Christian who we all needed to pray for! Night after night, from September to December, people prayed for him without apparent success. And then, in January, Phil finally relented to "the hound of heaven," gave his life to Jesus, got baptized in July, and started working for us two months later in September. Having been in debt, resulting from a lifestyle that revolved around alcohol and casual drug use, and feeling trapped in a job that was unspeakably boring, Jesus has made an extraordinary difference to his life. Here's how he described it at the time of his conversion:

> "Last night someone prayed for me, and for the first time in my life, I really felt God enter into me, and it was an incredible feeling (almost like I was a child again). It's impossible to say what it felt like; sort of sad and really happy all at once, like a fairground ride—only a million times better!

"I love being a Christian and I love God. Last night as I read my Bible, I was overcome, and I cried and prayed, asking God to look after me. And then God actually talked to me (something I didn't think could ever happen). His exact words were 'You are my son, I will never leave you,' and He said it over and over again and I could hear music. I literally wanted to shout out to Jesus. I looked at my Bible notes, and they told me that God is holding my hand.

"This is the most amazing time of my life, and I want everyone to know. I want all my friends and the people I work with to know. Also on Saturday my sister phoned to say that she has been going to a church in London for about two weeks and has just become a Christian too. What a coincidence!"

Phil's sister is now in India, working for Jesus in the slums of Delhi, and Phil continues to serve 24-7 behind the scenes with plenty of patience, laughter, and terrible music. What a difference Jesus makes in people's lives! Soon after his conversion, Phil began to pray for his best friend Gavin to come to Christ, but he didn't have much faith that it could happen. Gavin is a great guy with the gift of gab, a natural salesman, a gifted soccer player—the kind of person everyone likes, but not the sort who seems primed to "get religion." But Gavin too became a "non-Christian name" on the prayer room wall, and within a year, he too had met Jesus and joined the church. And in meeting him there one day, Kerry, the girl who had persuaded me to keep the prayer room going in the first place, met the man she would soon marry. It was amazing to see the way that prayer was shaping people's destinies as we all progressed on this adventure together.

## AN ARMY ON ITS KNEES

It was one in the morning, and the wind was biting cold, but people were still waiting to get onto a bus parked near the Atlantic Ocean in Southport, England. Prayer rooms have opened in loads of crazy locations over the years: a tee-pee at a new age festival, a police station in London, a brewery in Missouri, and even at the U.S. Naval

Academy, but here in the north of England, the Salvation Army was praying nonstop in a double decker bus at their annual Roots Conference. The hunger for prayer was unmistakable and would soon be spreading fast through the ranks of William Booth's Army.

It had all begun a few months earlier over coffee with my good friend Russell Rook in a café opposite Chichester cathedral. As I shared with him about the bewildering way 24-7 was exploding, I could tell that his razor sharp mind was whirring even faster than I was speaking, and sure enough, by the end of the conversation, a ridiculously wonderful plan had been hatched. Within a matter of weeks, the senior leadership of the Salvation Army in the U.K. had approved Russ' proposal for an entire year of 24-7 prayer within their ranks. It was to be an historic undertaking not just for the Salvation Army, but also for 24-7.

But no one could have predicted the way in which this Moravian prayer model would capture the hearts of the Salvation Army around the world. The initial plan had been to find fifty-two corps (congregations to the rest of us) that would take a week each, thus covering twelve months with prayer. But when the year was officially launched in May 2001, "it blew apart our highest expectations and our wildest dreams." Lyndall Bywater, who is employed by the Salvation Army to coordinate 24-7, could hardly believe it when "over 200 corps and centers got involved, four times the number we had originally hoped for, bringing an estimated 10,000 people into prayer rooms right across the country."

But the year was more about depth than such numbers. At the launch of the Salvation Army's first year of prayer, Johnny Smith described the scene:

> "It's just after midnight, and I am sitting in the 24-7/SA prayer room at the Roots Conference with approximately 140 other people. There is a real sense of the presence of God in here.

> "Currently a group of twenty-five young people is standing in

the overflow part of the prayer room, huddled in a group, praying for each other. Next to me, two girls sit praying, supporting and encouraging each other. There are people painting their prayers or molding them out of clay. A CD is playing, declaring the love of God for his people. Candles are burning over the names of friends and family that are no longer walking with God. There has been much prayer over the past couple of days for the prodigals, those who have turned from their faith. Tears have been shed, burdens have been lightened, and people have been laughing and celebrating what God is doing."

From England, the Salvation Army networks around the world began to catch the call to continual prayer. They prayed in Salt Lake City as it hosted the winter Olympics and even in Moscow, during a bitter winter and despite harsh persecution from the police. Increasing numbers of prayer rooms are being opened in countries where Christians are persecuted and forbidden to evangelize. Of course, while it may be possible to legislate against people proselytizing, it is—as Daniel's enemies found out—somewhat harder to stop them from praying for their friends.

## 'WAKING THE GIANT' IN AUSTRALIA

A young guy named Paul Mergard who had worked on the U.K. year of prayer returned home to Bundaberg, a provincial city in Queensland, and enthused about the impact 24-7 was having in England. His home church was fairly conservative, "not the sort of place you would expect to do 24-7, let alone be the first Salvos in Australia to do it. But then again maybe," Paul continued, "it was a prophetic sign of what was to come."

Major Peter Pearson, who leads the Bundaberg center, was clear about the impact their time of prayer has had: "Fifty-five people completed ten weeks of the Alpha Course; fifteen of these were brand new to church. Many people were healed and reconciled, and the church is totally different as a result. Three patients with potentially serious illnesses all came back from their specialists with results totally out of line with the doctors' first expectations.

"Numbers are not everything," he continued, "but since the week of prayer here in Bundaberg, the congregation has risen from an average of eighty-five to 140. We're returning to our roots in incarnational, passionate ministry and prayer. And as we do so, the future has become once more an exciting adventure of 'saving souls, growing saints, and serving suffering humanity.'"

Major Pearson concluded with a remarkable assertion: "In twenty-four years of officership, I have never seen God move in such a mighty way. Over seventy decisions in twelve months with twenty first-time commitments to Christ have been made."

Stories like this prompted the Salvation Army leaders in Eastern Australia to commission an entire year of 24-7 prayer like the one in the U.K. That year was such a massive success that they just didn't want to stop at the end of it and are still going now, praying night and day from corps to corps. Paul Mergard summed up the impact: "God is speaking so clearly and calling us so much closer that this does not have an end date right now. It looks like 24-7 prayer is simply becoming part of our ongoing DNA. We are the most respected organization in Australia, and through 24-7 God is waking the 'Sleeping Giant.' It's an exciting journey to be on."

Commissioner Hughes summed up the initial impact of 24-7 on his denomination: "24-7 Prayer has helped us recapture something of the fire and passion of those early Salvation Army leaders, who didn't make any distinction between prayer and physical care—they simply met people's needs. They knew that people needed to encounter the living God just as urgently as they needed bread and shelter ... so they went for the truly holistic approach and prayed them into the Kingdom while serving them a decent meal." He concluded, "24-7 presents wonderful opportunities of being creative in prayer, but above all, we have begun to relearn what it means to have prayer at the center of our mission and mission at the center of our prayer."

With Zinzendorf's heart for renewal and mission, I'm sure he and The General are applauding heartily from their ringside seats.

## THE NOMAD IN SWEDEN

The screams of people bungee jumping from the nearby crane provided an unusual backdrop to the conversation. We were eating take-out Mexican bought from a van at the Swedish Frizon Festival where 3,000 young Vikings had gathered to rave and praise God. The guy across the table from me picked up a nacho, trailing cheese: "I've lived in ashrams in the East," he said. "I've seen a lot of things, but," he paused smiling and emphasized every syllable of his next sentence, "when I stepped into the 24-7 prayer room in Stockholm, I think it was the most intense spiritual experience of my life."

With that, Lars Johansson, Director of the Forum for Faith and Society based at Orebro Theological Seminary in Sweden, finally popped the nacho in his mouth, wiping a little cheese away as another body hurled itself suicidally from the crane. Nearby I noticed The Nomad, a graffiti-covered 24-7 caravan that serves as a mobile prayer room touring Sweden like a tabernacle, taking the presence of God and the power of prayer to schools all over the country.

More people live in London than in all of Sweden, and yet, in this spacious land on the stroke of midnight as 2001 tipped into 2002, Swedish young people launched themselves into an unprecedented, unbroken year of prayer for their country. Outside it was snowing, but in the large auditorium in Jonkopping, several thousand young people were pledging themselves to prayer as never before. Mia Lind recalled: "Personally, I was too blown away by the mere size and significance of this to have any expectations. I only remember thinking 'this is big!'"

An entire generation in Sweden has grown up with a view of God and church as irrelevant to their lives. The challenges for young Christians are therefore massive, which is perhaps why 24-7 prayer rooms have multiplied around the country so quickly. Before long, "these prayer rooms started talking to each other, sharing their stories and experiences," Mia recalled. "And so we decided to 'join up the dots' with a year of unbroken prayer. We got together a gang of people to launch the Swedish 24-7 office and just four months later found ourselves kicking off 24-7-365 in our nation. Why did we do it? Because Sweden needs God, badly."

From intimate prayer rooms in church buildings to a mud-soaked tent at a rock festival, young and old alike began crying out to God across Sweden. Just one of many stories comes from a church near Stockholm, amazed at the power of prayer when their annual youth camp more than doubled in size, and they baptized fourteen people. At the end of the year, Mia's husband Marcus, who heads up 24-7 in Sweden, said, "It's been more incredible than I ever expected! It's almost like 24-7 has become an excuse for prayer among people who rarely prayed before."

## YOUTH WITH A MISSION, WESTERN EUROPE

Carl Tinnion is one of the most passionate people I know. He is passionate about his wife Mel, food, sculpture, and God too. Built like a brick outhouse with his handsome shaved head, he is one of the gentlest and most creative people I know. As well as being a leader within YWAM, Carl is also part of the Cultural Shift team, which means that he has been around 24-7 right from the start.

But it was Carl's own personal experience in a 24-7 prayer room that was crucial in making him a champion of prayer within YWAM. This is how he described that experience:

"I have always had the sort of mind that struggles in closed, stuffy, quiet environments. Perhaps I will grow up someday and discipline myself to do so—maybe I won't! I have always loved prayer, but mainly when it involved being on top of a mountain or deep in a forest walking and talking with God.

"The old models of sitting in a circle staring at the floor used to drive me insane, and I was always led to believe I wasn't a dedicated Christian if I didn't comply. And then the 24-7 model came along!

"I suppose there's nothing magical about it, but the concept of total freedom alone in a room where I could be me and express myself fully in all my weirdness was THE MOST refreshing, releasing, and exciting experience. The fact that it was okay and that God would still engage with me was like fresh mountain water flowing over my body.

"I was allowed to paint and write poetry all over the walls; I was allowed to sprawl all over the floor listening to godly drum and bass. All of a sudden, an hour or two hours or even three all blended into something that alluded time itself.

"My allotted time slot would be over so fast that I began to feel I was being cheated! How amazing is that? Not to have enough time, even in an hour or two, to pray or connect with God as much as I wanted to! It's something I had only ever read about and never imagined that it could happen to me—certainly not while I was still young! Praying in the middle of the night became exciting, and I would find myself going through the motions of the working day looking at my watch and waiting for my 'time' to come in the prayer room."

Carl's relentless enthusiasm, and that of Mark Markiewicz the inimitable leader of YWAM England, sparked a decision by the mission's Western European leadership team to mobilize prayer rooms right across the continent. They invited Ian Nicholson and me to attend a gathering of leaders in Germany and share about 24-7. For me it was a poignant connection; Loren Cunningham, founder of the mission, had made such an impact upon me through his writings. In fact, it had been the exciting story of YWAM's beginnings that had brought me to my knees so many months before, longing for more of God. I suppose it was the spiritual rocket that had launched Samie and me out on our wild goose chase around Europe.

Standing in front of all those missionaries in the middle of Germany, not so far from Hernnhut once again, it was an awesome thought that perhaps the Moravian anointing for perpetual prayer was coming home to roost in the world's largest missionary movement, with 18,000 staff engaged in the very frontiers of justice, creativity, reconciliation, and evangelism. Once again I could imagine Zinzendorf, Wesley, and Booth cheering us on as we mobilized The Watch of the Lord and married it with mission and ministry to the poor.

*"These I will bring to my holy mountain and give them joy in my house of prayer. Their burnt offerings and sacrifices will be accepted on my altar; for my house will be called a house of prayer for all nations." The Sovereign Lord declares—he who gathers the exiles of Israel: "I will gather still others to them besides those already gathered." —Isaiah 56:7-8*

## DEEPER

### THE SAVIOR-INTERCESSOR

The theologian P.T. Forsyth said, "The real power of prayer in history is not a fusillade of praying units of whom Christ is the chief, but it is the corporate action of a Savior-Intercessor and His community, a volume and energy of prayer organized in (the) Holy Spirit and in the Church the Spirit creates."

## JOURNEY

### SALVATION (ARMY)

"God richly blessed us in ways we cannot begin to imagine—for example, during our worship service on Sunday, about twenty people responded in some way to what God was saying to them. And considering there had only been two responses all year prior to the prayer weekend, we believe that the prayer had a role to play in this!" *Calamvale, Australia*

"Prayers written on the prayer wall and in the prayer journal have had a profound effect on all those who have read them. Many have testified to having been moved to tears on reading the openness of others." *Birmingham, England*

"Through our time of prayer, five people have returned to the Lord—one who had been away for over twenty years. Family relationships have been restored. People have started attending meetings again who haven't been for years. Many are saying things like, 'You can feel God as soon as you walk in to the prayer room,' or 'I came in here really disturbed and am leaving at peace.' We're gonna do 24-7 again and again and again. It's too good to leave at that. I know it's given our people a new desire to pray." *Gosford, Australia*

# WHEN THE SPIRIT
## SAYS, 'COME'
[RUSSIA. GERMANY. MACEDONIA]

*Do you want to look for my fullness?*
*Do you want to make history with me?*
*Do you want to count for my Kingdom?*
*Do you want to see miracles and stand for justice?*
*Do you want to see reconciliation and people set free?*
*Do you want to see nations transformed*
*by the power of prayer?*

*Then come follow me,*
*and I will show you where to go.*
*It's not to the platform and the spot-lit speaker.*
*It's not to the conference, the meeting or the camp.*

*Come with me to the darkest places*
*Come to the hurting, the howling, hollow faces,*
*Come with me to the addicted, convicted and caught*
*Come with your light, run with your salt,*
*Come to the sorrow; the suicide tree*
*Come to the stable*
*Come follow me.*

Ian Nicholson found himself sitting in a prayer room

in St. Petersburg, Russia, at 4 a.m. tapping these thoughts into a computer. "It was as if Jesus was looking me straight in the eyes, inviting me to come and follow Him all over again," he said. And so this challenge came spilling out onto the screen. He smiled, recalling The Arab and the Romanian Christians risking all behind the iron curtain. It had been years since Ian had last felt this stirred.

## BABYLON OF THE SNOWS

St. Petersburg stretches out on the Neva Delta, known as the Venice of the North or Babylon of the Snows. It is the world's most northerly city, on the same latitude as Alaska and Greenland, languishing in near perpetual darkness through the worst weeks of winter. But on summer nights, the sun pauses just nine degrees below the horizon and the glow of dusk meets dawn unhindered. These are the famous "White Nights" (the "Beliye Nochi") when streetlights are never switched on and the city sinks into lilac twilight for just an hour in every twenty-four. The famous skyline, with its shimmering spires and the glimmering gold and blue onion-domes of the Church of the Resurrection of Christ, might seem at such times like the architecture of a fairytale place.

But such romance hides the pain of one of the most tragic cities on earth. The Church of The Resurrection of Christ is also known as The Church of the Bleeding Savior. And in these streets, He bleeds for sure.

The city's very foundations were laid on a hidden holocaust of human endeavor; more than 25,000 people died constructing this fairytale skyline for Tsar Peter the Great 300 years ago. During the Second World War, more than a third of the population died of cold and starvation when the Nazis besieged her for an extraordinary 900 days. St. Petersburg is also a city that has suffered three bloody revolutions; for ten years she was known as Petrograd, and for sixty-seven she was Leningrad before reclaiming her maiden name.

The city today captures such turmoil in the microcosm of many lives.

Life expectancy for men is just fifty-eight (compared to seventy-three in the States), alcoholism is endemic, and more than 5,000 children live on the city's streets.[27] These unwanted kids congregate in "tousovkas," places of shelter and warmth often at the metro or railway stations. It's where they beg for cigarettes and money, sniff solvents, and make the most of the busy rush hours to pick pockets. Both girls and boys get involved in prostitution. But although the tousovkas are dangerous and violent, to the street kids they are "home."

## A SHOWER IN THE STREET

Our Russian friends live in this world, seeking to "preach good news to the poor ... to bind up the brokenhearted, to proclaim freedom for the captives and release from darkness for the prisoners" (Isaiah 61:1). Their church is made up of many people set free from heroin, alcoholism, sexual abuse, and despair. And today they had taken Ian and the 24-7 team down to the shadowy subway where crowds of commuters filter into the Leningrad metro. Outside an old woman in a typical headscarf had been selling an unlikely collection of plastic bags and wild flowers.

Here in the subway, the group simply started to worship, and at first Ian found himself feeling self-conscious. But as he watched his Russian brothers and sisters lifting their hands and offering their praises to God, he began to catch their passion, and a latent longing rose contagiously in his heart too. "The open-air worship times there in Russia," he later recalled, "were more releasing and passionate than I could remember in any Christian meeting for a very long time." The Russians just seemed to abandon themselves to God, amazed no doubt by all that He had saved them from and all that He had saved them for. "They wouldn't just sing, they would jump and shout. One guy who had been a professional dancer in nightclubs worshiped with such freedom, doing these crazy high-speed spins! It was a scene of release and such great joy."

---

27. Médecins du Monde, Sweden estimate between 5-7000 children live on the streets with far more sleeping at home by night but living on the streets during the day.

As they worshiped there in the subway, a small crowd gathered. Ian noticed a young girl wearing a floppy brown cap over short, straight blond hair, and her face was gaunt and boyish. Almost immediately a stream of venomous Russian words and offensive gestures began to erupt out of her slight frame. She began to shout, circling the group aggressively, looking for a fight and becoming alarmingly agitated about their worship time.

Quickly and cautiously, one of the Russians drew alongside her and began to talk to her with gentleness and respect. The girl began to calm down, but still she avoided eye contact, smirking sarcastically at passers by, pretending now to be disinterested in what the Christian was saying. Gradually, even this hostility subsided, until the girl was simply staring down at her feet, half-hiding from the conversation beneath the rim of that floppy brown cap. Eventually, the angry girl seemed to stop being angry altogether. She looked up, inquisitively exploring the kind eyes of the stupid Christian.

The girl who, moments earlier, had been shouting abuse and wanting a fight was now allowing these crazy Christians to pray for her, head bowed while a hand rested on her shoulders, sagging like a half-dismantled tent after a storm. And as the crowds of commuters bustled by, a forgotten street kid in a floppy brown cap stood in that subway and whispered some words to the King of Kings. The worship continued, but now she was standing a little stronger, like a different girl, hesitantly smiling and trying to sing the words for herself. Later she said that it had felt like standing in a shower; somehow the worship was making her clean.

She came back to the prayer room and stayed most of the night talking and asking the team many more questions. Her problems, like those of so many others, were terrible, but the aggressive girl from the street was now beginning a spiritual journey. It had been an extraordinary transformation. She even prayed a prayer of commitment, but for such people such prayers are just the beginnings of a long hard hike. Sadly, that night the girl succumbed to temptation, doubtless her addiction causing her to crave some new fix, and she disappeared into the night having stolen some items from the prayer room. This is the reality of ministry among broken people, but it is nothing short of the ministry of Christ.

And so, sitting in that prayer room at 4 a.m., the eerie brightness of the White Nights streaming in the window, Ian found himself prayerfully reflecting on the day, the girl, the crying needs of this delinquent city. And he reflected on the sense of God's presence he had known as they worshiped in the subway. And then it hit him: Not once had they asked the Holy Spirit to come. It was as though He had been there already. Waiting.

---

Ian's experiences in St. Petersburg were mirrored elsewhere that summer. More and more, we were finding that God's presence was strongest in the streets and clubs and that many of the most powerful prayer rooms were those established like tabernacles in the dark places of the world.

The Spanish island of Ibiza has been described as Sodom and Gomorrah by the media. Having established itself as the undisputed party capital of Europe, it certainly boasts the world's biggest night-clubs and every kind of depravity. And yet it was about this environ-ment that one girl said, "I felt the presence of God with me more on the streets of Ibiza than I ever have before in any church meeting." How could this be? Were such comments just youthful exaggeration, subtle sideswipes at the church? Or were we, in fact, discovering something real about the Father's heart for a broken world?

## FRANKFURT ...

E.merge, the event we had planned in the hot tub at Thun, drew more than 1,500 young leaders to Frankfurt, Germany, from all over the world, people who were pioneering new expressions of church in the emerging culture. A team working with young people in Russian prisons drove in Jeeps from the Ural Mountains. A converted Chinese gangster flew in from Asia. A contingency of German Jesus

Freaks rolled up in their now familiar Mad Max convoys. A girl with a hit music record in Spain came with a large group from Contracorriente. Coach loads had traveled down from Sweden through Denmark. Susanna Rychiger came with her team from Rollorama in Switzerland. Others came to Frankfurt from America, Czech Republic, Poland, and all over Europe.

God was doing as much behind our backs at E.merge as He was doing in the public meetings. Outside the venue in the blistering heat, hundreds of people would sit around talking all day and into the night, catching up with old friends and forging new relationships too. Expecting this, we had made sure there were plenty of facilities for simply relaxing together: Tables, chairs, and food vans serving German sauerkraut and sausage all helped foster this valuable networking time. "Pray, Play, and Obey" has been an important motto for us, and E.merge was a case in point.

I was glad to be in such an environment once again, having spent so much of my year thus far in hospital wards. Catching up with old friends like Markus and Andrea Lägel from Dresden, Jonah and Heather Bailey from Spain, and Marcus Lind from Sweden was wonderful. I had traveled down from England with many of the 24-7 crowd: Ian Nicholson, Kerry Dutton, Phil Baldwin, and Paul Weston. Pete Worthington, our indomitable webmaster, flew in with his wife Kate. It was like a gathering of the tribes, and hearing about the ways in which the movement was continuing to explode was thrilling, a pleasure only tempered by my sadness at Samie's necessary absence as she continued to recover at home.

And of course, as I reconnected with old friends, I made new acquaintances too. One of these was an extraordinary Swedish pioneer named Tommie Naumann who was to have a significant influence on 24-7.

## TOMMIE

*"And now, brothers, we want you to know about the grace that God has given the Macedonian churches." —2 Corinthians 8:1*

Tommie, now in his late forties, has been doing wild and crazy things for God since his conversion as a longhaired hippy in the Jesus Movement of the 1970s. His vision is that "the motherlands of the Gospel might give birth once again." So many of the places where Christianity first took root are now arid and resistant to the Gospel they once cradled.

Tommie began with summer-long missions work in Macedonia, which was at that time a Communist country closed to missionaries. He had been warned that in Skopje (the capital) it was impossible to preach and only realistic to pray. But being a natural rebel, Tommie simply began preaching the Gospel in a park, and they were soon gathering crowds of a thousand people, with many coming to Christ. The following summer Tommie returned to Skopje with a larger team and continued to reap a significant harvest. "We really spoke to the nation those two summers," he recalled. "National media covered what was happening, and we were even granted an audience with the President of Macedonia Mr. Kiro Gligorov. When we finally got to meet him, we laid hands on him and prayed for him!"

But short-term missions are easily compared to planting churches, and things slowed down as soon as they started trying to develop congregations. In 1995 Tommie and his family moved to Macedonia when the church-planting work really started to grow around the country. "Over the years," Tommie told me, "we have seen many people give their lives to Jesus in spite of civil war, crippling poverty, and a refugee catastrophe literally on our doorsteps that almost broke us completely."

At one point, one of Tommie's churches came under fierce attack. A national television station accused them of paying people to join their "sect" and even of killing cats to drink their blood! But God vindicated them when a journalist wrote a newspaper editorial exposing the whole smear campaign that had been operating against them. "The people doing the work of the devil," it concluded, "are those breaking the windows of innocent people's homes, those threatening people with losing their jobs, those spreading lies and not those called a sect and falsely accused of all kinds of strange behavior."

Despite such persecution and limited resources, they have established a medical clinic with Christian doctors, two pre-schools for three- to six-year-olds, and three thrift stores to create jobs for young people in a country where there is 50 percent unemployment and no state security.

And despite being stamped as a sect by the authorities, the church has also seen extraordinary evangelistic growth among young people through coffee bars, heavy metal bands, prayer, and friendship. During the first years, Tommie told me, they saw someone saved every single week, but he added: "We had a big back door," and many fell away as quickly as they had received Christ. But many were being touched by the love of Christ here, just as they were in St. Petersburg.

Talking to Tommie over coffee in Frankfurt, I had no idea that I would one day soon get to visit his church in Macedonia. But when I did, I discovered that the realities of what they were doing were even more remarkable than Tommie was letting on as we talked in Frankfurt. For instance, I prayed one night for a girl who had responded to a talk I had given and watched as the Holy Spirit visibly impacted her and she cried a great deal. Later that night Tommie told me matter-of-factly that she was a girl from the orphanage who had watched her father kill her mother. In that single moment, she had lost both parents: one to prison and the other to the grave. I was humbled when I thought of my usual list of minor prayer requests in the face of such trauma and need.

That significant church has now planted other little congregations around Macedonia and into another country that cannot be named for security reasons. Tommie may thus have sent out the first Macedonian missionaries since New Testament times.

With his burden for the motherlands of the Gospel still burning in his heart and having established a "church-planting-church" in Macedonia against all the odds, Tommie and Gunilla have now moved to Thessalonica to pioneer all over again. He is generally unknown on the Christian conference circuit, but spends himself for the lost and the hurting with quiet perseverance, a passion for life, and lots of laughter.

But sitting in a café one night, Tommie allowed me to glimpse just a little of the price paid by such pioneers: "I'm often discouraged," he confided, with a wry smile. "To be honest with you, Pete, I feel an incredible lack—almost like a failure at times." His clear, blue eyes had fixed unwaveringly on mine. A pause. And then, with extraordinary passion, "But I would rather speak to five people in a house who don't know God than to thousands of Christians at a conference." I felt uncomfortable and challenged. The moment hung in space like a wisp of cigarette smoke, and then we were laughing once more to Tommie's latest lineup of terrible jokes.

Tommie isn't a well-known man, but in God's "underground" movement, he is an apostolic pioneer. We had asked him to preach at the E.merge conference and were deeply moved by what he shared and by his example. There was a spontaneous desire to honor him and thank him for paying the price of pioneering away from the limelight over so many years. We also wanted to recognize that there are many like him, remarkable role models inspiring us as younger people to persevere. Bringing Tommie onto the platform, we asked him to trust us by diving backward into the crowd, and as he did so, we surfed him right from the front to the back of the hall, praying for him as we lifted him high over our heads all the way. Then we took up an offering to help him launch a Bible training school.

## GOD IN A PARKING LOT

Theologian Edwin Orr observed, "There's a greater movement of prayer growing now than ever before in history. Whenever God sets about to do a new thing, He always sets His people praying."

As E.merge drew to a close on Sunday morning, something prophetic was about to take place that would perfectly illustrate this marriage of prayer and God's new thing.

We had rented a club—more of a rock venue than a place for dancing—for our Sunday morning meeting, but it quickly became clear that we couldn't possibly all fit in. I was scheduled to speak, but, standing in front of hundreds of people jammed into that confined space, I somehow knew that I wasn't meant to. Instead I held out the microphone and asked people to share as they felt prompted. Perhaps I was sensing the fact that the real spiritual action was going on elsewhere ...

About 300 people found themselves unable to get into the venue, and being locked out, they decided to conduct their own meeting in the parking lot. Ian Nicholson was one of the people in that meeting, along with many others preparing to be sent from Frankfurt on 24-7 missions to Ibiza, St. Petersburg, and the slums of Delhi. And so, against a background of graffitied walls in the shadow of the nearby railway lines, the crowd began to worship.

There was no sound system, but Ian invited people to come and share "what God had put in them" over the last few days. Many wept as they requested prayer for various nations. Intercession began to sound across the parking lot as passionate shouts of petition and request went up. Ian was stunned by the sheer spiritual passion here in the open without any of the trimmings of a normal meeting. He sensed that God was speaking through this moment, calling His people to get out of the buildings and into the parking lots, out of our meetings and into the streets.

## COME

"For thirty years," Ian reflected later, "The church has been gathering to say 'Come, Holy Spirit,' and in His grace He has come. But perhaps the tables are turning. Perhaps it is now the Holy Spirit's turn and He is saying to us, 'Come, holy people.' Perhaps the Holy Spirit is waiting for us to attend His meetings in surprising places."

As we began to explore Ian's parking lot revelation over the ensuing weeks, we became more and more convinced that this was a word from God. As we went from Frankfurt and began to turn the prayer rooms outward onto the streets in mission, it was a word that would soon be confirmed in signs and wonders as we responded to the Spirit's invitation to come.

Just as Jesus 2,000 years ago spent His time at parties, engaging with the disreputable and apparently non-religious, so today He seems surprisingly comfortable among the crowds of partygoers, the non-religious pilgrims of our time. Perhaps He longs that we would vacate our buildings from time to time, that we would turn our temples into tabernacles, that we would become like Him, the friend of sinners. We are the light of the world, but no one wants to stare at the bulb. We are the salt of the earth, but a whole plate of the stuff will make you sick. The people of God are called to scatter and mix, to mingle and move, to influence from a position of weakness, like a small child in a large family, like yeast in a loaf, like a mustard seed beneath a pavement.

Could it be that the Holy Spirit is weary of attending our meetings and hungers for our presence at His? Perhaps He's dreaming up a thousand new meeting places, where new sounds and sights burn the eyes and break the heart! Maybe the time has finally come when it will no longer be possible to encounter the fullness of God in Christian conferences and classic meetings. Maybe this is a new day in which the fullness of God awaits us in the streets and clubs and pubs. But will we hear the Holy Spirit saying, "Come, holy people?"

He waits with Jesus in the darkness until we come, and yet we wonder why maybe He didn't show up the way we hoped at some of our grand events.

Of course, God will still attend our meetings—Jesus has promised to come whenever we gather in His name. And He is, let's remember, omnipresent! But perhaps there is a weariness, even a reluctance in His heart, as He gazes back over his shoulder, out the church door, and into the street.

> *"When he saw the crowds, he had compassion on them, because they were harassed and helpless, like sheep without a shepherd." —Matthew 9:36*

Maybe our 24-7 war cry "Come On!" is flipping around. Maybe we're in store for some backdraft as the angels yell "C'mon!" at us while we hide in holy huddles and Christian cuddles—even in prayer rooms—so safe and sound in every way. We've spent thirty years saying, "Come, Holy Spirit ..." and He came. Now, if the Spirit says, "Come," the question is this: Will we obey?

## DEEPER

### SACRAMENTAL LIVING

> *"Whether we think of, or speak to, God, whether we act or suffer for Him, all is prayer, when we have no other object than His love, and the desire of pleasing Him. All that a Christian does, even in eating and sleeping, is prayer, when it is done in simplicity, according to the order of God ... In souls filled with love, the desire to please God is a continual prayer."*
> —John Wesley, *A Plain Account of Christian Perfection*

What does it mean to pray 24-7? It means living our whole lives, twenty-four hours a day and seven days a week, in the grateful awareness of God's presence and with a desire to please Him always. Prayer is not just about the contemplative moments or the moments when I'm consciously firing words at God. The call to "pray without ceasing" (1 Thessalonians 5:17) is a call to remember Christ's presence continually in the subconscious as well as the conscious realms of my life. But how am I to do this? How am I to keep Christ in my subconscious, in my reflex-reactions even when I'm sleeping or working or watching a movie? How am I to be Christian by default as well as determination?

The key is to maintain a rhythm, a heartbeat of disciplined prayer, in which I encounter Christ regularly, deliberately, and consciously. The spinoff of these times, as you will see in the character of any older person who has spent a great deal of their lives contemplating Jesus, is that His presence thereby moves by a process of osmosis from the conscious into the subconscious mind. As we open the door, again and again, to Christ, He comes in day by day and eats with us, laughs with us, shares with us, until we acquire His mannerisms and know His very thoughts. A season of 24-7 prayer can be a useful tool for bringing Christ consciously back into the midst of our ongoing lives as individuals and as communities. And prayer rooms are an interesting expression of God's intention, which has always been to walk in continual communion with His people.

But just as no person could or should spend every waking moment in a 24-7 prayer room, so we must understand that the prayer room is an expression of the continual communion between God and His people, but it is not the same thing. The ultimate 24-7 prayer room is the human heart fully surrendered to God and not a room full of coffee mugs and hand-drawn pictures!

What we want to do, in Wesley's words, is live lives of prayer as "souls filled with love and the desire to please God." So the place of prayer creates the moment of conscious disciplined prayer that then enables me to live prayerfully in front of my VDU screen, or while teaching a sixteen-year-old to drive, or working at a check-out or whatever job I do. We don't want to withdraw people from society to live in spiritual bubbles of perpetual prayer; rather we want to immerse ourselves in society, having immersed ourselves in the Spirit—in the world, and yet full of God and overflowing.

## JOURNEY

## SICK OF CHURCH?

I brought a few of the Goth kids who hang out in the park into the Boiler Room (24-7 House of Prayer) yesterday, and we had an amazing time talking about God and witchcraft. After a while one girl was sick all over the place, and she had to call her dad and arranged for him to collect her from the station. I then spoke to him because I felt she was too ill to walk far, and he was totally freaked out: "So, run that past me again—she's in a prayer room?" he said. "But she won't come near a church!" It turned out that the girl's parents are Christians, live about an hour's drive away, and when her mum came in, her comment was, "Maybe you are the lifeline we need!" It's hard work running an always-open prayer room, but then if stuff like this is happening—why are we surprised!

*Penny, Reading Boiler Room, U.K.*

# CHAPTER SEVENTEEN

# LADIES AND GENTLEMEN, CHURCH HAS LEFT THE BUILDING

[MEXICO. MACEDONIA. CYPRUS.]

AND SO, SHOT OUT FROM A PARKING LOT in Frankfurt, we began to attend the Holy Spirit's meetings whenever and wherever we could find them. And they really were held in some very surprising locations and at some very inconvenient times indeed. Just as Jesus paid a price to dwell among us, risking His reputation among prostitutes, lepers, and crooked accountants long before He paid the ultimate price on the cross, so too we found ourselves praying and preaching in places that some Christians would probably boycott.

## AYIA NAPA

One of the people in the crowd at Frankfurt was Bex Walker, a twenty-one-year-old petite English girl whose blond hair fell in stunning ringlets halfway down her back. As Bex received prayer that day, she had no idea that she would soon find herself walking in the footsteps of Paul and Barnabas: "After they had fasted and prayed, they placed their hands on them and sent them off ... to Cyprus" (Acts 13:3-4).

It was only meant to be a vacation in Cyprus straight after E.merge, but even on the lazy, hazy beaches of that sun-soaked island, Bex found herself haunted by her experiences in that German parking lot. God was stirring her spirit. Driving around the island one day, Bex sensed that the Holy Spirit was calling her to return to Cyprus. In her hotel room later that night, Bex just broke down, weeping uncontrollably as she began to catch God's heart for the people who flock to this sparkling island in the Mediterranean Sea.

And so she returned the following year to target the party town of Ayia Napa in the southeast of Cyprus where a third of all visitors to the island end up. This was to be the start of a series of spiritual adventures, at the invitation of the Church, which would become an incredible roller coaster of mission in the summer of 2003. Napa is a club capital, a party place, but unlike the chilled Balearic Beats of Ibiza, it is permeated with a more aggressive mix of garage and rap music. Prior to our arrival, there had been escalating gang tension and violence even reported by the international media.

Arriving in such an intense environment, the priority for the team was to establish a 24-7 prayer room in a convenient shop they had arranged to rent. But when they started to pray, the owner accused them of witchcraft and threw them out onto the street. Finding themselves charged with devil worship and now homeless, the team relocated to the ancient monastery that sits incongruously by the neon-lit central square at the heart of the town's nightlife, and in the cloistered hush of the tiny chapel, they began to pray as people have done in that peaceful place since the sixteenth century.

On the street outside, a man selling freshly roasted corn on the cob from a makeshift stall soon gave his life to Jesus. Suffering serious problems from a past riddled with drug abuse, he slowly began to grow in his faith, coming into the prayer room at 5 a.m. every morning, when, he said, the presence of God seemed strongest!

Without a permanent base, the team began to prayer walk, make friends, pray in clubs, and break-dance on beaches. One of the team members, a gospel singer named Heather, was invited to sing to the crowds in the Planet Dance Bar over the DJ's dance beats. She used the opportunity to worship, and yet no one seemed to mind.

*The Times* newspaper sent a journalist to shadow Bex and the team, and the ensuing article by Michael Thodoulou painted a vivid picture of the debauchery confronting the clean-living young missionaries in Ayia Napa:

> "The resort would seem to be a big challenge, given its reputation for raunchy behavior and hedonistic excess. A sign over one open-fronted bar exhorts patrons to 'Fuel Up, Party On, Shag On.' Brandishing a bottle of lager, a British tour rep leading a pub crawl through the square intones an irreverent rendition of the Lord's Prayer: 'Hallowed be thy drink, thy will be drunk, I will be drunk, on holiday as it is at home in the local.' Nearby, a bar has free entrance to a male strip show post-midnight on Fridays with a sign screaming: 'Get 'em off!!!' Another offers shots of garish alcoholic concoctions with sexually suggestive names. But because of the Cypriot resort's good-natured, 'anything goes' atmosphere and the impressive clubbing skills of the 24-7 mission, the confident young Christian evangelicals do not seem out of place … 'Sometimes you just go up to random people and say: 'Man, can I pray for you?' Justin Hirschorn, a 22-year-old student, said. 'There's generally a good response. It's really cool.'"[28]

Drawing to a close, the article reports an apparent miracle that occurred in answer to prayer: "Elle, a micro-skirted 24-year-old from Birmingham who works as a 'PR' for a dance bar, is grateful to them for resolving an earthly problem. 'They chatted me up, they prayed for my wisdom tooth and it worked,' she grins. 'My teeth are fine now.'"

---

28. *The Times Newspaper*, Michael Theodoulou, "24-hour Party People On Mission to Convert Europe's Hedonists," August 7, 2003.

## SEX AND SALVATION

The team's break-dancing obviously impressed the right people because they soon found themselves invited to attend a highly exclusive party on a boat with famous musicians they had only ever seen on TV before.

On the boat, a video reporter filmed a short interview with the team, fascinated that they were Christians and asking them questions about their views on sex and why they were in a place like this anyway. The video was later shown at one of the big bars in town, allowing the team, indirectly, to share their message with a crowded and attentive pub.

Meeting up again later in the week to talk about faith, the video man closed the conversation with an amazing offer. He was the host of a regular Friday night beach party, which included a rap battle. Would the 24-7 guys, he asked, come to break-dance and then talk to the whole crowd for two minutes about Jesus? "They'll all be off their heads with drink," he admitted, "but they still need to hear about Jesus!"

It was to be another of the Holy Spirit's unusual meetings in a very dark place. The team felt embarrassed surrounded by the usual rounds of drinking and sex games, but reminded themselves of the apostle John's encouragement: "You, dear children, are from God and have overcome them, because the one who is in you is greater than the one who is in the world" (1 John 4:4). If this was to be a clash of two kingdoms; they knew that it wasn't them that needed to be afraid. They had the Holy Spirit, and He was about to hijack this meeting!

And so it came to pass that a diminutive blond prayer warrior got to preach to the hardcore rap elite of Europe on Nissi beach that Friday night. The break dancing display had been popular enough, but as Bex spoke about Jesus, chaos broke out. Some girls began to yell obscenities from one corner of the crowd, while a group of men shouted, "Go for it!" Many sat in semi-drunken stunned silence, and one man turned to a team member and said, "I haven't got a clue what this is about, but I want to find out about God."

"We spent the rest of the night having loads of conversations," Bex recalled. "People wanted to know about Jesus, wanted to be prayed for, wanted to tell us their problems, and a number of real friendships were formed." The video man was delighted and asked Bex to come back and preach the following week too! Yet again a team had stepped out in obedience into a most unlikely setting and found the power and presence of God powerfully at work.

## MACEDONIA

Meanwhile in Macedonia, Markus Lägel had gone with a team from Tommie Naumann's church to the beautiful resort of Ohrid where young people fill the streets like sheep without a shepherd. A Macedonian team member named Sonia visited the apartment next door for half an hour and was quizzed by two guys about her prayer life. Most people in Macedonia are either nominally Orthodox, Muslim, or atheist, so the idea of praying to God any time, any place was fascinating to them. To prove that it really was possible, Sonia simply put her hand on a couple of them, asked God to meet with them, and then left. But a couple of minutes later, one of the men came anxiously banging on her door saying that his friend was shaking all over and asking what was going on. Sonia explained that it was just the power of the Holy Spirit at work in his life, and that it would probably stop eventually!

## PRAYER PALAPPA IN MEXICO

As Bex rapped in Ayia Napa and Sonia's neighbor shook in Ohrid, 24-7 guys in Mexico were having a more mundane encounter. They had been trying for days to get a place they could use as a prayer room at an international surf festival in Puerto Escondido. Nothing was coming together, and after a week of prayer, they felt like giving up. But then, unexpectedly, they were offered a big, open hut called a Palappa on the beach right in the middle of the festival, just a stone's throw away from where the adjudicators sit to judge the surfing. "We can see it all from the prayer room—its on the beach and has the most incredible view imaginable!" wrote Carlos Sanchez excitedly. "We've even had non-Christians coming in, crying and praying. This Palappa used to be the number one drug dealing spot here in Puerto, and now it's a prayer room that we got given free of charge right in the heart of this International event … it's totally mind blowing!"

Another team member drew out an important lesson: "God has been so faithful, but has taught us a huge lesson to do with patience and perseverance. I really want people with a heart to do prayer rooms in specific locations to be encouraged and challenged that when God clearly speaks about His heart for prayer in that location, He means it. We need to take God at His word and persevere in prayer until it happens."

## P.U.S.H.

Perseverance has been a key theme for 24-7. In many ways continual prayer is exactly that—a refusal to quit! With all the encouragements and even miracles of the first few years of this crazy movement, it would be easy to make it sound like everything is easy or automatic. The reality is that we all live with far more frustrations in prayer than breakthroughs. And we are all called to persevere as we seek to love God, love one another, and love the lost.

Sometimes as we attend the Holy Spirit's meetings, people become Christians, are healed, or journey farther down the road to faith, but sometimes it's just hard work with few obvious results. Perhaps that's why Jesus "told his disciples a parable to show them that they should always pray and not give up" (Luke 18:1). Mission pioneers such as Jackie Pullinger, working in Hong Kong, waited seven years for her first convert. William Carey, who was inspired powerfully by Zinzendorf as he pioneered in India, waited eight years. He spent the time serving the community and earning their trust. We too must be prepared to dig in for the long haul.

If we are to persevere in faith, it is vital that we know clearly what God has said to us. His Word is our strength, enabling us to keep going when others would quit. I have often been forced to cling to the promises of God when I've felt like giving up or giving in. Through my own personal struggle with Samie's illness, not to mention many sleepless nights with the stresses and strains of spiritual warfare and the daunting challenges of a movement growing at such a pace, through many trials, I have often needed to remember the things God has said to me. These have helped me persevere in prayer and in practice. So, I guess I had better introduce you to Justin …

## JUSTIN

Justin Blake, the prophetic guy who predicted 24-7 six months before it happened, has often had remarkable insights into my life. He's an old friend who loves practical jokes, laughs like a hyena, and carries his beaten-up pocket Bible with him almost everywhere he goes. He's someone who has learned to listen for the whisper of God at all times. He even took pen and paper into the movie *Braveheart* because he wanted to take notes!

Several months before the accidental advent of 24-7, as Justin and I were having lunch in a diner one day, God began to show him some important things for my life. You can always tell when Justin is about to prophesy because he suddenly looks serious and clears his throat. On this particular occasion, I noticed Justin studying a man shooting pool at the nearby table. "You see that guy's T-shirt, Pete?" he said, clearing his throat ominously. I glanced across as the man stood up from his shot and saw the phrase "Global Connections" emblazoned across his chest.

"Pete, God is going to give you global connections," he said, looking earnestly at me. "I see a world wide web of relationships, or maybe it's more like a word wild web. There's going to be a wildness, and yet there will be a web, a matrix, a strong sense of connection. And it's going to be to do with the Word of God and the wildness of His Spirit. Word and Spirit working together."

I had learned by now not to interrupt Justin when he was in the flow. I had no idea what he was talking about, but it sounded exciting, and I knew I needed to concentrate.

Next Justin picked up the bottle of mineral water in front of him. "This caught my eye the moment we sat down," he said pointing at the small print on the label. Squinting at the bottle, I read something about the softness of the water that flows from the particular spring at which this bottle had been filled.

"Pete, as well as a world wide web of relationships, God is going to bring you people who will be like soft water to you. They will be older people, advisers, but they will not try to control; instead they will be gentle, wise, and their wisdom will flow from some place long ago, a deep place like the spring from which this water came."

## SOFT WATER

With glorious common sense, the book of Deuteronomy says that the way to work out if someone is or is not a prophet is to wait and see if their prophecies come true.[29] Justin's track record in this respect is exceptional, and looking back on this occasion, I am forced to accept once again that he was indeed speaking prophetically into my life. Looking at the World Wide Web—literally and metaphorically—that God has given us, it's quite clear that the man playing pool had unwittingly picked the right T-shirt that morning.

And as for the soft water: One of the main fulfillments of that had come in the form of Ian Nicholson. The Bible-smuggling adventurer was now living a more ordered existence in Guildford where 24-7 would one day be launched, and he had called me out of the blue one day to ask if he could come down and simply hang out from time to time. I was surprised because I vaguely knew him to be quite a bit older than me, but there seemed to be no agenda other than a sincere desire for friendship.

---

29. Deuteronomy 18:21-22

For several years Ian and I shared occasional coffees, walked my big black dog, Wellie, and talked about the things on our hearts. This growing friendship with Ian was to be crucial in all that God was preparing us both for. He was one of the people who would often offer me humble advice, encouragement, and exhortation without ever trying to control. To use Justin's metaphor, Ian was like a source of soft water.

God often blesses relationships. I sometimes think He likes to use relationships more than individuals. There was Moses and Aaron, David and Jonathan, Naomi and Ruth, Elijah and Elisha, Mary and Elizabeth, Jesus and his cousin John, and Paul and Timothy, to name but a few.

As Ian and I walked and talked, he would often refer to his days in Vienna and his longing to see a fresh mission movement capturing the hearts of young people the way his had been captivated as a new Christian. I in turn shared with him my journey: the vision of an army, the visit to Hernnhut, the encounter in Dubi, the struggles and concerns. And when the prayer rooms began to multiply, I turned increasingly to Ian, with his experience of training teams and pioneering in difficult places, to help us shape our vision for mission. He has pioneered this core dimension of 24-7 brilliantly (as the stories in this chapter show), ensuring that we don't become insular and inward looking in prayer, but continue to seek out the Holy Spirit's meetings whenever and wherever they might be.[30]

## DEEPER

## AZUSA STREET

The Azusa Street prayer room of 1906 ushered in an era of church growth and mission unprecedented in world history. Church groupings, believed to number 400 million, trace some of their spiritual roots back to the momentous meetings that took place in

---

30. 24-7 Mission is committed to following codes of good practice developed by U.K. mission agency Global Connections. We also draw heavily from Youth With A Mission for training support. A key value is a commitment to work alongside local Christians in building and planting church.

Azusa Street, Los Angeles, where they gathered continuously for more than three years. One newspaper writer was scandalized because "they never dismissed church." The impact of this prayer room quickly touched the poor and destitute. For instance, a church in Los Angeles associated with the revival, Christ Faith Mission, established a center called Pisgah. By 1911, the Pisgah Home provided regular housing for 175 people, plus an average of 9,000 beds and 18,000 meals a month to the urban homeless, the poor, and the social outcasts, including alcoholics, drug addicts, and prostitutes.

At the heart of this extraordinary movement was a passion for mission and a commitment to prayer. William Seymour, the pastor who helped shepherd this move of the Spirit, was known to pray for up to five hours a day. His own spiritual mentor was Charles Fox Parham. Parham had for some years run a Bible school in Topeka, Kansas, where the students took turns to pray in groups for three hours maintaining 24-7 prayer in the college prayer tower. For more on this, visit *www.redmoonrisingbook.com.*

## JOURNEY

### PEACE AND HARMONY

The Notting Hill Carnival attracts more than 250,000 people, but the Lord heard our prayers, and this year there were fewer arrests and, incredibly, no violent crime. A DJ played trance music, some of which had Christian lyrics, out onto Portobello Road, and a crowd of more than 400 started partying. We were planning to close at 6 p.m., but the police asked if we could keep the music going till 7 p.m., as the crowd was so calm and the atmosphere so good. As people were partying, the YWAM team went around the crowd praying for people and dancing with them! The policeman radioed his colleagues saying, "Don't worry about Portobello Road. The Salvation Army has it under control." We didn't of course; it was God answering our prayers for peace.

*YWAM, England & Notting Hill Salvation Army, London*

# THE **RAINMAKER**
[IBIZA. NORTHERN IRELAND.
PORTUGAL]

"COCAINE?"
"I'm alright, thanks."

It was breakfast in Ibiza: a traditional British "fry-up" of sausages, eggs, and bacon, and James Bullock was sitting in the sunlight trying to explain Jesus to a guy doing a line of coke. They had become friends in one of the island's coolest clubs, DC10, where the DJs themselves go to party when it opens at 6 a.m. at the end of a hard day's night. James and the other 24-7 guys had somehow managed to blag their way in a few weeks earlier, and now, incredibly, you only had to turn up and say you were one of the Christians, and the large iron doors would swing open wide. DC10 lies at the end of an airport runway, and every Monday morning of the party season, you will find it full of wild and wonderfully exotic personalities, short on sleep, drugged up, and ready to party. James, who loves DC10 probably more than any place else on the island, often found himself looking around the dimly lit club wondering, "What sort of church would these guys fit into?

What sort of church could these guys become?"

Ibiza (pronounced 'Eye-bee-tha' by U.S. tourists) basks in
Mediterranean sunshine for 300 days of the year, one of five Spanish
Islands that together make up the Balearic enclave. Secluded beaches
with crystal clear waters ring the coastline, interrupted occasionally
by fishing villages or brash and bustling tourist towns, while elsewhere on the cliffs, traditional whitewashed churches cut their shapes
in the deep blue ocean beyond. Moving inland, palm trees soon give
way to almond, fig, and olive trees before the terrain swoops up to
the great, pine-forested hills that dominate the center of the island.
The Ancient Greeks called the island "Pitiusa" which simply means
"the Pinery."

This beautiful place was ruled by almost every ancient superpower,
from the Greeks and Romans to the Muslim Moors, but none of
these invaders ever treated Ibiza with the disdain shown by the
forces of hedonism over the past fifty years.

## ISLAND LIFE

It all began quietly enough in the 1950s, as General Franco's fascist
regime oppressed the Spanish mainland, turning Ibiza into a laid-back
hideaway for liberal and left-wing dissidents and artists. Next came an
influx of beatniks and hippies in the '60s, American draft-dodgers and
North Europeans on the hippy trail to Marrakech. This was when the
island began to acquire its reputation for drug-fuelled excess, free
love, and wild parties. In the '70s, Ibiza's legendary, high-class clubs
were born: Pacha, Amnesia, and Ku (now Privilege) attracting the
likes of James Brown, Freddie Mercury, and Mick Jagger.

The scene was set for this little island in the middle of the
Mediterranean to become a major influence upon youth culture
around the world. And sure enough, as the 1980s danced to Duran
Duran and the Beastie Boys, Ibiza was developing its own, unique
sound; Balearic beat: an eclectic mix of electronica, Latin, Afro, and
funk music that would give rise to the massive sounds of Acid House

and Chill Out music today. By now a dance floor hit in Ibiza was a guaranteed chart-topper in many parts of Europe.

And then in the '90s, the super clubs landed their vast enterprises on the little island; Cream, Ministry of Sound, and Manumission began to compete for market share with ever more outrageous stunts. Before long there were live sex shows, circus acts, and the streets of San Antonia were sprawling with pre-club bars and staggering, sunburned revelers.

---

I was standing in the kitchen at my folks' house drinking coffee when the newspaper headline jumped up at me. In the wake of titillating MTV documentaries "uncovering" Ibiza's immorality, the island was being branded as a modern-day Sodom and Gomorrah. These biblical cities, infamous for their sinfulness, once provoked an interesting exchange between Abraham and God. The Lord promised the patriarch that, if just ten righteous citizens could be found, He would spare the entire region. "God, please don't give up on Ibiza," I whispered, taking a sip of coffee and reading on. The article described depravity, violence, rape, sexual perversity, and every kind of sin, and yet, instead of outrage, I found a longing welling up inside: "What a great opportunity for Jesus!" I thought. "Wasn't He the friend of sinners? Didn't He say that He had come for the sick and not the healthy? What a perfect place to take the Gospel!"

The question, of course, was: "How?" But God, who never forgets a single prayer His people utter, would remember this little exchange too. I guess that's why, a few years later, an invitation would come out of the blue: "Could 24-7 open a prayer room in Ibiza during the party season?" It was an opening that would have an impact beyond anything I could possibly have imagined that day.

## INVITATION TO COME

The three mind-blowing days at at Contracorriente in Valladolid had one more surprise in store for a guy who felt like he just couldn't take any more. Already there had been the people crying over my interview in the magazine, the Spanish-American dance of The Vision, the discovery that these words were even impacting the relatives of Columbine victims, the revelation that God never forgets a single prayer, the moment I realized that I had been in Valladolid before, the cries of "Venga!," the fifty kids who prayed right through the night, and then, just when I thought I couldn't cope if God tried to download anything else onto my hard-drive, Sara Torres approached me in the prayer room: Would we come to Ibiza? Would we come and help the churches on the island pray? It was not just an invitation to Ibiza. It was an invitation that would trigger many other frontiers for 24-7 shaping our very model of mission at a critical time.

## THE CHRIST-HAUNTED LANDSCAPE [31]

A team of four landed in Ibiza the following autumn to spy out the land. We knew that if we were going to do anything in such an extreme location, we would need to prepare ourselves spiritually as well as logistically and that it would be vital to work closely with the local churches on the island. Kerry Dutton, James Bullock, Vicky Ward, and Carl Barkey flew out and met with the Ibizan church leaders. As they simply shared the vision for Ibiza, tears were shed on both sides. "See," God was saying, "I have placed before you an open door that no one can shut" (Revelation 3:8). The Holy Spirit said "Come," and although we had no idea what would happen, we were determined to obey.

Straight after E.merge, a team flew out to Ibiza. They quickly adjusted their sleeping patterns to be awake all night and to sleep all morning. They learned to only drink bottled drinks and never to put these down to avoid any kind of drug being slipped in. They set up a prayer room near the center of San Antonia and began to pray 24-7. They also took turns visiting the better clubs where they would worship and intercede all night. Every night they would go out in

---

31. Susan Ketchin coined this phrase to title her book *The Christ-Haunted Landscape, Faith and Doubt in Southern Fiction* (University Press of Mississippi, 1994).

teams onto the streets and among the pre-club bars, making friends, talking to people, and gathering prayer requests. They would often end up helping people too hammered on drink or drugs to find their way home, or listening to people pouring out their troubled hearts. A year later, we returned for the whole of the party season. Those who could DJ got residencies in local bars, and whenever they could, the team would throw parties giving away fruit.

They also helped clear the beach of rubbish, filling hundreds of garbage bags with cans, used condoms, cigarette packets, and worse. The island's Minister of the Environment said that certain species of endangered wildlife might return to the area if it was clean and that this in turn would give them the grounds to reject the building of another resort on the site.

It quickly became clear that Ibiza was not a godless place at all. In fact, His fingerprints were everywhere: in the extraordinary creativity and innovation. In the lives of some of the people they met. In the fun and the joy of many of the parties. In people's openness to talk and share their spiritual quest. This was, in many ways, a "Christ-Haunted Landscape" where clubs carry names like Eden, El Divino, and Es Paradis, and club nights are called Soul Heaven, Salvación, God's Kitchen, and even Judgment Sunday. It seemed ironic that, while we were walking purposefully away from religious jargon in case it didn't communicate, we were passing pagan dance culture speeding in the other direction with the windows down and the music loud.

But in spite of the spiritual overtones and the awesome creativity of the scene, Ibiza is also a mess. Human waste spoils many of the beaches; people stagger back to lonely apartments paralytic with alcohol-poisoning night after night, week after week. The faces change, but the problems don't. Date rape drugs are widespread, along with every kind of sexual and spiritual perversion. This is a place riddled with sin and sickness in need of prayer and practical Christian love like few others.

## PRAY, PLAY, AND OBEY

Whether it's St. Petersburg, Ibiza, Mexico, Delhi, or any of the other places we have sent teams, our approach is essentially the same: We go to Pray, Play, and Obey.

*Pray:* First we go to pray in the place. We believe that this is the very essence of all effective outreach, and so we generally try to set up a 24-7 prayer room and maintain shifts of prayer throughout the time we are there.

*Play:* Secondly we aim to find the traces of God's goodness in every culture and fully enjoy these graces. We're not there to condemn the place, but to celebrate the life and the love of God in it. One aspect of bringing redemption, we believe, is to magnify all that is wonderful about the world. This might mean visiting The Hermitage museum in St. Petersburg, the Taj Mahal in India, or the beach in Ibiza.

*Obey:* We believe that it's not enough just to pray a lot and have some fun. It's important to actually share Jesus in word and deed. Whenever there are local Christians, we take their advice about appropriate and effective ways of doing this, but we have a natural tendency toward "servant" style evangelism.

## SPECTATOR

Maybe the best way of depicting our work in Ibiza—and thus our ethos wherever we go—is through the eyes of an objective observer. *The Spectator* (est. 1828) is one of England's oldest satirical magazines, and yet they flew a reporter out to visit our team in Ibiza one summer. The resulting article (entitled "Jesus goes to the disco"[32]) was surprisingly fair. The journalist who is known for her sarcastic treatment of crystal balls, haunted houses, and psychics exploiting 9/11, admitted in the resulting article: "I had hoped for solemn, pasty faces,

---

32. *The Spectator,* "Jesus goes to the disco: Mary Wakefield finds a gang of missionaries in the sex-and-drug-fuelled raves of Ibiza," October 12, 2002.

biblical samplers and sensible shoes. Instead there were eyebrow rings, gelled hair and tanned skin." In crisp, straightforward English, Mary Wakefield wrote:

"At 4.00 a.m. when the bars begin to close and street cleaners start to hose the puke and urine off the pavement with neat bleach, an incongruously sober and cheery group appears. They stop and talk to the stragglers, ask lost girls if they are all right, unstick passed-out teenagers from the street and heave them over to the taxi rank. Sometimes they ride home with them; occasionally they take a comatose boy to hospital."

Earlier the journalist had accompanied team members on an evening stroll through San Antonia's bustling "West End":

"Throughout the evening waitresses, seasonal workers, girls hand-ing out flyers stopped group members in the street and poured out their problems. On the way to Café del Mar, a woman with bleached dreadlocks and bondage trousers, who looked as if she'd rather boil to death than be seen talking to a Christian, approached a girl called Claire. 'I've finally been fired,' she said, and offloaded fifteen minutes' worth of anxieties and frustrations. Outside a restaurant, a waitress stopped Becs Lindford and started worrying about her debt. 'I want to go home, but I can't because the tax men will be on to me,' she began, apropos of nothing, and continued for a further twenty minutes. Becs offered cheerful advice. Inside the restaurant, Jez, the director of a documentary about the group said, 'People all over town are starting to talk about 24-7. I keep overhearing discussions about the work they're doing and their lives. They've had a huge impact."

As you may have deduced from her article, Mary Wakefield wasn't exactly a natural "clubber," and she concluded her piece like this:

"The next day, I recovered while taking tea with the Anglican priest on the island, the Rev. Edrick Corban-Banks, a Lebanese man from New Zealand … 'The most important aspect of the project is, of course, the missionary work,' he said. 'A lot of the holidaymakers who come here to do vast quantities of drink and drugs are in a very bad way. They have a grief inside them and a need to open up to people their age who understand them.' 'But isn't it terrifying for ... everyone to go into town and confront drunken thugs?' I asked. Edrick sighed from under his fine black moustache. 'Your readers won't like my answer—I don't imagine this sort of thing goes down very well in print— but they go out with confidence and purpose because they know in their hearts that they've been called here by God. He is with them; how can they be scared?'"

Edrick was right; we did have a sense of calling. And as we sought to attend the Holy Spirit's meetings in the pubs, clubs, and streets of Ibiza, we would soon experience the reality of the fact that "the kingdom of God is not a matter of talk but of power" (1 Corinthians 4:20).

## THE HEAVENS OPENED

*"I will send rain on the land."* —1 Kings 18:1

The people of Ibiza were suffering their worst drought in years, and the Christians had asked us to join with them in praying earnestly for rain. The island is renowned for its low rainfall, but this particular year was proving especially severe. In fact, the priest said that the biggest blessing the team could bring to Ibiza would be rain! And so we prayed for rain.

One Sunday we gathered in the hills with a number of the local churches at an open-air restaurant where we worshiped together in unity, and I was asked to speak. At about 10 p.m. we jumped into our various cars, waving to our new friends and thanking them for a memorable evening. As we drove away, the first fat drops of rain in three months started to splat on our windshields. By the time we arrived back at our villa, it had become a downpour.

Just then, as if to confirm the significance of the moment, Kerry received a text message from Ian in Russia: "1 KINGS 18." It was midnight in St. Petersburg, and with the "White Night" shining its eerie brightness outside, Ian had been praying for the Ibiza team with two of the Russians: Vanya and Dema, when an intense sense of the presence of God entered the room. Vanya received what he felt was a word from God for Ibiza about Elijah's battle with the prophets of Baal. This comes in 1 Kings 18, a chapter which starts with God's promise to send rain and culminates with a mighty downpour ending years of drought. Without any knowledge of our situation and thinking it was something to do with the prophets of Baal, Ian texted the passage to us from the other side of the world. "Meanwhile," as we drove home from the prayer time in Ibiza, "the sky grew black with clouds, the wind rose, a heavy rain came on" (1 Kings 18:45).

Back at the villa, some of the team climbed the ladder onto the flat roof to splash and yelp their childish praises to God as a torrential storm swept the island all night and into Monday morning. The heavens, it seemed, had opened.

This was a significant rainstorm, but the timing was even more amazing. We were later informed that it hadn't rained like this in Ibiza during July since 1976.[33] We had, it seemed, just witnessed a miracle in answer to concerted prayer. By Monday afternoon the rain was so heavy that one of our team cars broke down in the center of San Antonia.

## TOKENS OF FORGIVENESS

Lucy Cooke had received a vision two days earlier in which the dirty streets were gushing with water washing them clean. The symbolism was obvious, and she had shared it with the team as a simple encouragement for prayer. But, climbing out of her broken down

---

33. The Hong Kong Observatory in its Climatological Information based upon data between 1961–1990 says that Ibiza may expect just 0.6 days with rain in July and that the average rainfall in this month for the island is just 0.2 inch.

vehicle in the pouring rain that Monday, Lucy looked up and gasped with instant recognition. She was standing in her vision, watching a great river of water gushing down the road: "I just couldn't believe it," she recalled. "I was looking at the exact waterfall I had seen. At the top of the street it was gushing pure and clean, but by the bottom the water was filthy washing away so much dirt."

As Lucy shared this experience with the team later, a girl named Lora looked crest-fallen: "God gave me a Bible verse to read earlier in the week," she said with a sheepish grin, "and I was too embarrassed to do it. Now you probably won't believe that I've had it in my head all week." She looked around the room, shrugged, and opened her Living Translation of the Bible. "Okay, here goes: 'Rejoice, O people, in the Lord your God, for the rains he sends are tokens of forgiveness'" (Joel 2:23, Living Bible).

The room fell silent. It was another "fear of the Lord" moment. As the rain continued to drum on our windows, we knew for sure once more that God was with us, hearing our prayers. He had sent rain in July (the first in thirty-five years). He had spoken to an unknown Russian on the other side of the world. He had flooded Lucy's car to show her the cleansing of the streets. He had spoken to us now through Lora about salvation, these "tokens of forgiveness."

Sitting staring out of the window at the rain falling on the pine covered mountains, a girl with a deep tan and dark brown curls made a solemn deal with God. It was obvious that the Holy Spirit was on the move, but Carla Trundle found herself nervous of missing the moment, terrified of averting these "tokens of forgiveness" just because she was shy. She determined that tonight would be different; tonight she was going to be bold. "Tonight," she promised God, "I'm going to pray for at least one sick person in the streets of San Antonia to be healed, then and there."

## CARLA

Eight years earlier and more than a thousand miles from Ibiza, growing up as a nominal Catholic in Northern Ireland was a bewildering experience. The playground was full of subconscious sectarian prejudice, and Carla found herself ostracized by hard-line Protestants for being Catholic and spat at by hard-line Catholics because her dad was doing building work for the RUC (seen as a Protestant police force). Without any understanding of real Christianity, Carla just found it all confusing. "I used to wonder why people who believe in the same God hated each other so much," she recalled.

When she was eight, the family was forced to flee to England with a death threat hanging over their heads, and, under such intense pressure, her parents became followers of Christ, ambassadors for the Prince of Peace. Such experiences were preparing Carla Trundle for the role she would play in 24-7 prayer in years to come. Like Markus Lägel in Leipzig, Ian Nicholson in Vienna, and many others, Carla was being shaped and prepared for the call of Christ to mobilize prayer and mission. In particular, He was preparing her to be a passionate advocate of Christian unity: "After my experiences in Northern Ireland," she said, "I just love the fact that 24-7 unites Christians in prayer, bringing so many different denominations together in one place with one heart."

At the age of eighteen, Carla left home and ended up at University College, Chichester, studying dance. Little did she know that she was arriving in town just a few weeks into the first 24-7 prayer room. "I didn't really have a relationship with God," she recalled, "although I did have lots of religious head-knowledge after years of attending my parents' church." Carla was also having serious doubts as to whether she really wanted to live the Christian life, having met a guy at college. "A life without God seemed uncomplicated and appealing, especially compared to the things I had seen religion do in Northern Ireland."

Carla came along to church to placate her parents, but behind the dazzling smile and sunny personality, real spiritual struggles were raging. Unaware of any of this, a friend invited Carla to come to the prayer room for an hour one day. "I figured I would go for ten minutes," Carla laughed, "but I ended up on my knees talking to God for two hours. When I stood up, I knew that something was changing in me; I couldn't ignore what I had just experienced."

From that point on, Carla barely looked back, and as she grew in her faith, 24-7 continued to be a key discipling factor in her growth. "For me, prayer rooms have always been the space and time when God has challenged me the most and moved me on in my faith," she said. It was in another prayer room, this time in Manchester, that God spoke to Carla about working for 24-7 after graduation. But first He was calling her to join the team heading off to Ibiza …

---

The unseasonal rain was finally dying down as we got ready for our night on the town. Some were heading off to the prayer room first, others were going clubbing to intercede, but Carla, mindful of her earlier pledge to God, was going to hit the pre-club bars with a determination to pray for someone.

The narrow, sloping streets between the bars were buzzing with raucous, laughing people as usual. Many sat at tables outside on the sidewalks while tribal groupings of happy tourists streamed past in their smart-casual designer clothes. As usual there was a TV camera following members of the 24-7 team for a British TV documentary, and tonight, of all nights, it had chosen to follow Carla and her partner for the evening, a girl named Jo.

## SMOOTH GAV

A gang of guys came swaggering and laughing toward Carla and Jo, hoping to snatch fifteen seconds of fame from the camera and perhaps a little recognition from these two pretty girls as well.

"What are you filming there, darling?" enquired the ringleader, who introduced himself as "Smooth Gav" with a surprisingly cute smile. He was tall with dark hair, wearing a red polo shirt and jeans. Remembering her promise to God, Carla glanced nervously across at

Jo. Then, with a big grin that belied her nerves, she looked straight at Gav and began to tell him all about God.

Some of the group were immediately uninterested. "Come on, Gav—it's the God Squad!" they groaned, trying to pull him away. Carla drew a deep breath: "Have you got something wrong with you?" she enquired a little too loudly, and then, seeing their quizzical expressions and realizing that she had pretty much just insulted them, she blurted, "I mean, um, have you got any problems?" This was getting worse. "Any medical conditions. You know, stuff you would like God to, um, maybe heal."

This was too good to miss, and Smooth Gav was there again immediately with his cheeky grin: "My knee," he said. "I can't bend it more than about five degrees," and he demonstrated. Sure enough, the knee was almost completely locked straight. Jo asked what had caused it and Gav described a Rugby injury six months previously. "Haven't been able to move it more than a few degrees for half a year," he repeated.

They sat him down on a chair outside the bar and began to pray, the two girls with their eyes closed and their hands self-consciously hovering above his knee, while Gav looked around trying not to giggle, and his friends just laughed at him. But then, suddenly, he went silent; Carla said a hurried "amen" and opened her eyes to see that Smooth Gav was no longer looking quite so smooth. In fact, he appeared distinctly troubled.

"We've totally freaked him out," she thought, but before they could make their excuses and run, one of the other boys in the group stepped forward. He was shorter than Gav with a shaved head, wearing a plain white T-shirt and obviously shy.

"Do you pray like that for anything?" he asked quietly, no smile on his face. "I feel really stupid telling you this, but I've got ingrown toenails on this foot," he waved his left one, "and they hurt like crazy all the time. Doctor says I've got to have an operation." There was no sign of a punch line—this guy was serious. He wanted them to pray for his toes, then and there, in the streets of San Antonia.

"By the way, my name's Nigel."

Carla watched as Jo knelt down on the sidewalk and gently touched Nigel's white trainer, speaking out a prayer which was impossible to hear above the cheers and jeers of passers by.

Suddenly Nigel started shaking his head: "No way. No way," he exclaimed in disbelief. "The pain has gone. The pain has totally gone!" Suddenly the other boys in the group who had been joking and laughing throughout fell very silent.

"Why don't you take off your shoe?" said Jo with a confidence that left Carla terrified.

"You don't wanna do that, Nige," laughed one of the group, regaining his confidence, and then, addressing himself to Carla, "his foot is disgusting. You really don't want to see that."

But Nigel already had his shoe off, and he was now carefully peeling away his sock too. And then he started screaming. Everyone scrambled to stare at Nigel's perfectly ordinary pink foot as if it was the Eighth Wonder of the World, while its owner yelled, "I don't believe it! I don't believe it!"

"It's not manky any more!" exclaimed one, before swearing repeatedly very loudly.

A familiar voice suddenly rose above the others, "Look at my knee, boys. Look at this!" Smooth Gav was dancing round the street swinging and kicking his leg around like a chorus girl in Riverdance. He had clearly regained complete mobility in the joint. It was an extraordinary sight as Smooth Gav hopped around, swinging his leg at an invisible football while Nigel stood in one shoe, pointing at his naked foot in speechless admiration as if he'd never seen anything quite so beautiful in his life.

The rest of the group was now surprisingly sober and silent. Suddenly, they all had their own prayer requests to bring as faith surged in their unbelieving hearts.

"Can you pray for my dad? He's sick."

"Could you pray for my younger brother? He's just gone into prison, and he needs God to look after him because no one else is going to in there."

Nigel wanted to know how to pray and if he could do it too. They all wanted to know: "How did you do that?" For fifteen minutes Carla Trundle, the girl from Northern Ireland, the girl who'd almost given up on God before she ever even started, stood in the streets of San Antonia, crowds of party-people drifting by, and explained to a bunch of rough, tough men about the God who made them, loves them, and wants to wash away their sins the way the rain had washed away the dirt from the streets of Ibiza the previous night.

The following night Carla saw the group again. "We've never even mentioned God to each other before we met your lot," Gav said. "But since last night, that's all we talk about! Look at this," and he began swinging his leg back and forth, bending his knee as far as it would go. Still healed.

It was an amazing night as we talked and prayed and partied; somehow evangelism and prayer had become a whole lot easier since the rain. Maybe it's what people mean when they talk about "operating under an open heaven." The miraculous storms really had, it seemed, been portents of something spiritual, "tokens of forgiveness."

---

A year later, Carla was back in San Antonia feeling down and discouraged after a fruitless few weeks. The team had just been burgled. Everything had gone: passports, money, record decks, the lot. "Lord, I really need an encouragement tonight," she said without exaggeration.

A while later she caught sight of a familiar figure with a cute smile.

"Smooth Gav?"

"Hey!" he cried, "It's the Fit Christian Chick!"

"How's your knee?" blushed Carla. And with a grin of recollection, Gavin arced his foot at an invisible ball: "Never been better, thanks!"

---

We returned from that first great 24-7 missionary push rejoicing. The stories from all the different teams were simply amazing, and we had much to praise God for, especially the ways in which He had worked in our own hearts, changing each one of us through times of hardship as well as encouragement.

When the seventy-two disciples Jesus sent out "like lambs among wolves" returned full of the stories of how God had used them, Jesus was filled with joy exclaiming: "I praise you, Father, Lord of heaven and earth, because you have hidden these things from the wise and learned, and revealed them to little children ..." Then He turned to His disciples and said privately, "Blessed are the eyes that see what you see."

We certainly knew that we were blessed children. We had taken the prayer onto the streets, seeking to attend the Holy Spirit's meetings instead of our own, and the results had been truly remarkable. The prayer rooms continued to multiply, each one a place of intimacy with the Father and a mini mission station closer to home. To cap it all, we had now been praying together continually for two years.

For Samie and me, it was to be a time of rejoicing and relaxing. She was recovering well from her operation, and her seizures seemed to be subsiding. Looking back on a crazy two years since that first prayer room, we felt as if we had aged about three decades! It was time for the vacation to end all vacations: a celebration of all that had happened with 24-7, a celebration of our family, and a celebration of the fact that Samie was even alive. Remembering my blissful days hitching along the Algarve in Portugal, I wanted to show Samie and the kids these beautiful beaches. Maybe we would even light a fire and cook fish one night. Of course we would also have to visit the rugged cliffs of Cape St. Vincent for a day. For me it would be a profound pilgrimage, and I knew I had much to thank God for.

---

I guess we all remember where we were and what we were doing when the first plane hit the first tower of the World Trade Center. By some surreal twist of faith, the meaning of which I cannot fathom, we heard the news on a Portuguese radio broadcast, driving home to our rented villa from a day on Cape St. Vincent. It had been my first visit in almost exactly a decade to the place of my commission.

By the time we got back to the villa and switched on CNN, the world had changed forever. The stakes were raised. Within days, hundreds of prayer rooms and thousands of people all over the world would want to know how to pray in a time of terror such as this. We were walking blind into an era of "wars and rumors of wars" and it was slowly dawning upon us that 24-7 had perhaps been raised up by God "for such a time as this" (Esther 4:14).

It was still great to hear the stories from the mission teams of individual salvations, isolated healings, and opportunities to show the love of God. But what might the Gospel mean to nations at a time like this? How should we pray for the tribes and cultures of the earth? What did it mean to stand in the gap now, interceding for the peace of entire communities? The Lord had called us to pray, and we were praying. He had called us to attend His meetings, and we were there having a ball. But there was another important foundation that He wanted to lay into 24-7 alongside prayer and mission.

God began to make it clear that He was calling us to establish long-term "houses of prayer for the nations" with the dream that these might somehow become redemptive communities at the heart of people-groups.

We had started off praying for situations from a distance, and God had called us to plant our incongruous little tabernacles in the heart of messed up communities. That's what we'd been doing in Ibiza, Ayia Napa, Mexico, Macedonia, and many other places. All over the world, people were launching Moravian prayer rooms in all sorts of crazy places. But even this was not enough. God didn't just want us to pray that people might somehow leave their world and climb aboard our spaceship, which occasionally touched down in the neighborhood. In theological terms, the call was to long-term, incarnational transformation. It was to live and pray among the lost in such a way as to journey with them into the likeness of Christ together. And so, sensing such things at such a time, we began to dream again. How could we bring transformation through the power of persevering prayer and long-term presence to the very subcultures of the generation? And what might such lofty concepts look like in practice?

## JOURNEY

## BACK TO BASICS

The youth have been praying for a woman in our church who has severe nerve damage in her back. This nerve condition has caused her great disability and pain for a number of years. She requires special chairs to sit in and so forth. We just learned that today her back was completely healed when she woke up this morning. She's at the church right now cleaning for God. She has always wanted to clean at the church as a ministry, and she is dancing around shouting "hallelujah!" with a broom in her hand.

*Matthew, New Brunswick, Canada*

# CHAPTER NINETEEN

# THIRD MILLENNIUM
# MONASTERIES
[U.K.]

*"Rescue those being led away to death;*
*hold back those staggering toward slaughter."*
—*Proverbs 24:10-12*

THE TEENAGE GIRL ARRIVED VERY
drunk, her thick black make-up now smeared and
her skin even whiter than usual. She walked
unsteadily into the House of Prayer where many of
her friends were hanging out these days. Sure
enough, some were clustered around the computers
using the Internet, a couple of girls were sitting in
the corner drinking coffee, up at the other end of
the building the guy with the beard was trying to
pray as usual, and a small group of her friends was
standing by the bar, no doubt talking to Penny
about God and stuff. A Bible verse on the wall
caught Sarah's eye, but by now the room was spinning and swirling like a slow-motion merry-go-
round, and the music sounded far, far away.

Clearing up Sarah's vomit a few minutes later,
Penny reflected that this was not quite what any of

them had anticipated when they first imagined a 24-7 house of prayer. Andy, the leader of the project, was now on his usual Saturday visit to the ER; this week it was with Sarah, next week, who knows? And kneeling now on this holy ground, Penny chuckled. Wasn't prayer meant to be a serene activity in pretty places with pictures of waterfalls on immaculate walls? Yet here she was on her hands and knees, not praying but gagging at the smell of Sarah's leftovers.

It was undeniably tough, often frustrating, but deep down Penny loved it; she loved the kids who had never been to church and were now regularly praying, she loved the fact that some were changing their minds about God, and she loved the way that the heartbeat of it all was a rhythm of prayer and intercession. It wasn't easy for Penny, Andy, Malc, Pete, and all the other faithful prayer warriors, but on a day like today, it somehow seemed like it was worth all the effort. What was it that old missionary to China had said?

*"Some want to live*
*within the sound*
*of church or chapel bell;*
*I want to run*
*a rescue shop*
*within a yard of hell." —C. T. Studd*

Penny pondered this as she carried the bucket to the kitchen. Strictly speaking, this might not be within a yard of hell, but it was definitely in the neighborhood.

## PRAYER AND THE POOR

Maybe this is what prayer is all about; one minute you're kneeling in quiet contemplation, and the next you're kneeling by an unconscious girl; one day you talk to God about people, and the next you talk to people about God. This marriage of intimacy with active involvement in a hurting world is the very meaning of the word intercession. There have been times throughout history when God could no longer bear to hear the cries of the poor and the oppressed while the religious leaders turned the temple into a social irrelevance and did nothing at all to care for those who were hurting. At such times, as the flood of God's anger threatened to burst the very dams of His grace, He would search for someone, anyone, who might "stand before me in the gap on behalf of the land so I would not have to destroy it." Tragically, He told Ezekiel, "I found none" (Ezekiel 22:30). If this is what it means to intercede, "standing in the gap" between God and hurting humanity, I guess it isn't a task that can be cloistered away all the time in sanitized environments. Standing in the gap for the poor and marginalized may well mean that it matters where we pray and how we pray, and that our prayers for the poor are worked out in practice.

When churches in Reading near London clubbed together to turn a derelict drinking house into a 24-7 prayer house, intercession became very practical very quickly indeed. In the neighboring park, gangs of young people hang out getting drunk, getting high, and getting into trouble; many of them are Goths with dark clothes, dark music, and a dark worldview to match. At a very young age, some are well down the road to addiction, but whether the danger is drugs, drink, or promiscuity, such symptoms belie an underlying need for healing, hope, and ultimately, we believe, for the love of God.

In the city of Manchester, our Prayer House was based, for a while, in an old downtown warehouse, close to the gay district and the famous "curry mile" where more than fifty neon-lit restaurants offer every Punjabi dish known to man. Stepping into this venue on one occasion, I was surprised to see a large sign on the wall: "No drugs allowed." I don't suppose many prayer houses have ever needed a sign like that. 24-7 houses of prayer are proving wilder, much harder, and yet way more exciting than anything we could possibly have imagined back when we first started exploring the idea.

---

24-7 prayer rooms had begun to multiply, and many churches were beginning to build regular rhythms of Moravian prayer into their community life. But some locations began to talk about "joining up the dots" and establishing houses of continual prayer: 24-7-365! Of course, most towns and cities in the western world have someone somewhere with a vision for such a "house of prayer for the nations" (Mark 11:17), and they usually have an accompanying filing cabinet full of confirming words from the Lord. However, relatively few such houses actually exist for three important reasons:

- People
- Money
- Motivation

## People

To pray without ceasing through every minute of every day and every night requires a lot of people! It is attainable if you have a whole bunch of full-timers dedicated to the task of prayer, as did many of the old monasteries. It's also easier for mega-churches with lots of resources at their disposal. But for the vast majority of Christian communities, continual prayer is a completely unrealistic ambition.

## Money

If you are going to run a permanent facility with a constant stream of people coming through the doors, there are major logistical challenges, not least the financial ones.

## Motivation

Both of the previous obstacles are surmountable. Funds can be raised. Smaller churches can work together regionally to establish a house of prayer for the city, staffed from a much greater pool of believers. But the real problem has always been this third one: motivation. You just can't get people to do it. A few hardy intercessors might turn out faithfully, night after night, but most people will nod enthusiastically but never show.

But as 24-7 grew, it became clear that the impossible one was now possible. Night after night, around the world, God's people were now rising to pray. And this means that wherever a few churches are prepared to cooperate, they can fill an entire year with prayer quite easily. We had already seen the potential of this at a national level with groups like the Salvation Army linking all their churches to pray, but what would happen, we wondered, if we focused the idea of 24/7/365 down onto specific locations in specific cities?

Suddenly, with a bit of church unity, a venue, and some funding, towns and cities all over the world could become like Hernnhut: hosting continual intercession at the very heart of their communities. The possibility seemed extremely exciting, and a number of places were starting to seriously discuss it.

## ON THE BOIL

As we began to explore the idea of such prayer houses, we nicknamed them Boiler Rooms without much thought, and it just sort of stuck! However, as is often the way, we've since discovered quite a bit of significance to the name:

In the great days of steam, boiler rooms were a familiar concept all around the world. They powered everything from vast machines in factories to household heating systems. A boiler room was a well-known powerhouse, a driving force, a place of pressure and creative energy. From the furnace came power.

Of course, a boiler room was also functional, dirty, and hot, often tucked away in the basement. It wasn't a comfortable setting for entertaining or relaxing. It was a place of essential work.

We realized that these were great metaphors for the role of a prayer house in a community. As we stoke the fires of intercession, prayer-power is released to energize God's purposes in the surrounding area. In most towns and cities, there are already many wonderful, God-inspired projects to which faithful people are giving their all. We sensed that a 24-7 Boiler Room should not be just another project to add to the menu, but rather a source of prayer-cover for these projects, empowering and protecting the work of God and the people of God in the host community.

## AND THEN ...

In our usual bumbling way, it was several weeks after the launch of the first Boiler Room that we discovered another significance to the name. Lou Engle, the prophetic figure behind The Call prayer gatherings around the world, walked into our converted pub in Reading and said in his grave voice, "I love the name, guys ... You do know the significance of the name?"

Seeing our blank expressions, he explained that C.H. Spurgeon, perhaps the greatest preacher of the late nineteenth century alongside Charles Finney, attributed the fruitfulness of his entire ministry to what he called his "Boiler Rooms." These were prayer rooms—often in the basement of whatever building he was speaking in—where people would intercede as Spurgeon preached above. They were the very power-source of his remarkable ministry.

## ANCIENT CELTS

I began to wonder what a Boiler Room might look like in practice. If there was to be nonstop intercession in certain locations for years at a time, it would be absolutely vital to get the "genetic code" right. Everything we knew of the Moravians taught us that prayer had to be outward looking as well as contemplative, otherwise there would be a danger of creating very labor-intensive Christian ghettos.

> *"Stand at the cross-roads and look;*
> *ask for the ancient paths,*
> *ask where the good way is,*
> *and walk in it."*
> *—Jeremiah 6:16*

I found my mind wandering back to the earliest settlements of Christianity in the British Isles, those of the Ancient Celts who evangelized Britain more effectively than anyone before or since. Ian

Bradley, one of the most widely respected experts on Celtic Christianity, described the prayer houses at the very heart of the Celtic witness:

> *"The dominant institution of Celtic Christianity was neither the parish church nor the cathedral, but the monastery ... a combination of commune, retreat house, mission station, hotel, hospital, school, university, arts centre and power-house for the local community—a source not only of spiritual energy but also of hospitality, learning and cultural enlightenment."*[34]

These ancient communities of prayer, mission, pilgrimage, care, creativity, and education had a profound impact on the British Isles for a thousand years or more. The Celts didn't just plant churches in the sense that we know them today; rather they developed these extraordinary, redemptive communities like little "colonies of heaven" called *muintir*.[35] As we began to dream about Boiler Rooms, we became increasingly excited by the idea of tapping into these ancient Celtic roots and exploring their model of holistic prayer and mission in a contemporary context.

## SIX PILLARS

And so we distilled the ideas of the muintirs down into six essential components of a 24-7 Boiler Room:

- Prayer
- Creativity
- Pilgrimage
- Mission
- Justice
- Community

We believe that it is precisely because Boiler Rooms are prayer hous-

---

34. Ian Bradley, *The Celtic Way* (Darton, Longman and Todd, 1998).
35. To the best of my knowledge Dietrich Bonhoeffer first coined this much-used phrase.

es that they must also, with a certain inevitability, be mission stations, pilgrim hostels, art studios, and centers for community and outreach to the poor.

## Prayer

The Moravian model of continuous prayer would, of course, be right at the heart of every Boiler Room. The atmosphere of continuous prayer is the driving force for everything else we do and a power-house for transformation in the community at large. Through the watches of the night, as people come and go, their prayers lift every-thing else to another dimension. Boiler Rooms aren't just hostels, art centers, and mission stations. They are, in some mystical way, a place where God can be found. It's all about intimacy with Him, infection with the Gospel, and increased effectiveness in our Christian lives.

*Intimacy* ... 24-7 prayer is not simply about functionality: adding effectiveness to the things we do. First and foremost, a Boiler Room is about friendship with God. Like all relationships, intimacy grows from hanging out with the one we love.

*Infection* ... And the thing about hanging out in God's presence is that it's contagious. When an individual develops intimacy with God, they inevitably become infected with His life and love. Just as infec-tions spread when one person breathes on another, so God's breath conveys the same life-giving power today that it did on the day He created Adam from dust. It is through intimacy with God that we become infectious carriers of His life-breath. And a contagious Christian is an effective one.

*Effectiveness* ... A Boiler Room is a center for transformation, but before we see the changes reported in the newspapers, we will expe-rience them in our own lives. You don't need 24-7 or a Boiler Room to discover intimacy with God, but maybe it can help!

## Creativity

"The earliest Christian assemblies, gathering in homes and cata-combs, adorned the walls of their meeting places with scenes from the Scriptures. The whole of the Scriptures is depicted in the windows of the great medieval cathedrals, such as Chartres."[36]

24-7 Prayer is all about creativity in communication with God. How can prayer be limited to words? And because God is the Creator, His presence catalyzes artistry and often lends an "anointing" to artwork created in His presence. Boiler Rooms seek to nurture the relationship between creative people and the Creator God by offering studio space for artists. This means that they can work in a unique environment of prayer.

**Pilgrimage**
Now is surely the time to become open again to the Spirit of God, who desires to come to the most intimate places of our lives, praying, healing, and transforming us that we may be released to a new sense of pilgrimage and divine restlessness (Michael Mitton, *Restoring the Woven Cord*).

We've always known that God's Spirit can fill people. But sometimes we forget that He can fill places too! When a place hosts hours of continuous prayer, it can sometimes become so full of God's presence that even non-Christians sense His proximity.

The ancient Celts called such environments "thin places" because God is close and prayer becomes easier. The journey to such places may be called a pilgrimage—whether it's undertaken by a teenager cycling across town to a prayer room or someone crossing oceans to seek God. "As I walked through the wilderness of this world," wrote John Bunyan, "I saw a man clothed with rags, standing in a certain place, with his face from his own house, a book in his hand, and a great burden upon his back" (*The Pilgrim's Progress*).

Some traditions have almost forgotten the importance of pilgrimage, but the Bible is full of "spirit-journeys," such as Abraham's nomadic call and that of the people of Israel journeying to the Promised

---

36. M. Basil Pennington, *Seeking His Mind: 40 Meetings with Christ* (Paraclete Press, 2003).

Land. God, it seems, loves mobility. His Spirit is described as a fire, a wind, a river, a bird in flight, and His commission is invariably to "Go!" Jesus Himself became a traveler of no fixed abode (Matthew 8:20). The Christian life can be described as a journey, a pilgrimage home to heaven (check out John Bunyan's classic parable, *Pilgrim's Progress*).

Boiler Rooms seek to offer limited accommodation for pilgrims to stay and pray a while.

## Mission

*"These (Celtic) monastic communities were not only places where interested people could come and learn about the faith … these communities acted as mission stations which trained men and women in preaching and healing, and sent them out on missions."*[37]

The Enemy will do anything to divorce prayer and proclamation—to stop the evangelist from praying and the intercessor from evangelizing. Why? Because the two combined are explosive! Boiler Rooms are not just Houses of Prayer. They are also Mission Stations where people gather to train, become infectious in prayer, and get catapulted out, contagious with the Gospel. Jesus promises that if we "remain in Him," we will be fruitful (John 15:5). He also commands us in no uncertain terms to "go and make disciples" (Matthew 28). At the beginning of time, God commissioned Adam and Eve to go forth and multiply (Genesis 1:28).

In prayer we become more effective evangelistically because we are walking closer to God, but we are also sensitized to the needs of those who don't know Jesus as we pray persistently for their salvation.

## Justice

*"And will not God bring about justice for his chosen ones who cry out to him day and night?"* —Luke 18:7

---

37. Michael Mitton, *Restoring the Woven Cord*

Prayer without action is just religion in hiding. So, as we cry out to God night and day, He calls us to acts of compassion and social justice. Jesus' own mission statement was to "preach good news to the poor," and He didn't just long for it, He left heaven and did it! Boiler Rooms are all about bringing transformation to our communities, starting with you and me, alone in the place of prayer and radiating out to touch every stratum of society, especially the poor. Having met with Jesus, we become a tremendous blessing to the world in which we live.

Boiler Rooms partner with local projects to minister to the poor. In fact, we ask people to give one hour for every seven they pray to the poor. They spend this time actively outworking their prayers among those who are suffering in some way. It might mean feeding the homeless or volunteering at a pregnancy advice center.

Of course, the projects not only benefit from an influx of volunteers, but also from the prayer support they receive from so many concerned Christians! Wherever possible, Boiler Rooms connect with social services, local schools, and even the police to receive prayer requests for the local community.

In one of the more important books of the twentieth century, *The Cost of Discipleship*, the martyr Dietrich Bonhoeffer wrote, "The renewal of the Church will come from a new type of monasticism which only has in common with the old an uncompromising allegiance to the Sermon on the Mount."[38] Boiler Rooms are a context in which we are trying to work out what it means to build a spirituality that is all about the meek, the poor in spirit, those who mourn. After almost a year of night-and-day prayer in our first Boiler Room, a book of prayer-poetry was produced. Beautifully bound and stunningly illustrated, it is a unique chronicle, exposing the underlying spirituality of this house of prayer. The remarkable thing about this modern-day book of Psalms is that almost every poem reveals a sense of meekness and even of brokenness.

---

38. Dietrich Bonhoeffer, *The Cost of Discipleship* (MacMillan Co., 1959).

If this is the army God is raising up, it is a broken army of the "frightened and forgotten," an army marching on its knees.

## Community

> *"How good and pleasant it is when brothers live together in unity! ... For there the Lord bestows his blessing." —Psalm 133*

By definition, a Boiler Room is a community on the go every day of the year—not just once a week. People pop in on the way to school. Mothers bring their kids in to draw and paint while they pray. Students sign up for the night watch. Boiler Rooms unite all sorts of people from different churches and different backgrounds in one prayerful community. A Presbyterian might pray for an hour and then pass the baton on to a Catholic for the next! Older Christian leaders have taken over prayer shifts from young, new believers whose simple "handover" prayers have blown them away—so many different believers with differing styles of prayer, yet part of the same prayer meeting together.

In ancient times people sought sanctuary from persecution in church buildings. Today many church buildings are locked shut six days a week, and even if they're open, they are deserted. Boiler Rooms can be magnetic for non-Christians because they are full of God, full of His people, and always open. As a result, they can act as places of sanctuary for people who are scared or looking for God.

> *A guy leaves a nightclub on a bad trip, but he knows where the Christians will be ...*
> *A girl wakes in the night terrified by a demonic dream, but she knows there's a place she can go for safety ...*
> *A businessman lands in a foreign city and knows there's a place he can go to sleep off his jet lag and reconnect with God before a day of high-powered meetings ...*

We had little idea when dreaming these six pillars into being of the impact they would one day have ...

It was 5:30 p.m. on a winter Saturday night, and the soccer hooligans wanted a fight. Advancing across the park near the Reading Boiler Room, they shouted aggressively at the usual crowds of kids just hanging out. One of the thugs grabbed a brick and threw it at the group, and suddenly the park erupted into a violent chaos of breaking glass and broken bones. By the time the riot police arrived, it was mayhem. Screaming and terrified, many of the young people had run down the road, seeking sanctuary at the Boiler Room, pounding on the doors to be let in.

Andy Freeman, "Abbot" of the Reading Boiler Room, takes up the story: "We opened our doors and just tried to help, getting people off the streets and somewhere safe, taking people home or to the hospital. About forty teenagers stayed till around 10 p.m. Goths in black coats stood outside the building guarding the doors with mounted police. Others were getting people organized, telling them to quiet down and respect the place. Still more were making coffee, cleaning up, and just making the place their own.

"There were lots of tears and worry, but in God's house, many people were finding a place of safety. Many wanted to pray that day, others simply wanted to talk. One guy remarked the following day that he hadn't ever thought about God until the Boiler Room opened; now he did."

## THE ABBOT

Andy "The Abbot" Freeman is ideally suited to the job of leading a third millennium monastery. He is kind, gentle, thoughtful, and passionate about young people—especially those who are marginalized by society. He also, it so happens, looks just like a monk. Perhaps it is God's sense of humor, but the one who counts the hairs on every head has chosen to remove most of Andy's, leaving just a strip of brown hair around the back and sides. As a result, Andy, with his bony frame, small, round glasses, hooded tops, and apparent tonsure, looks very much the man for the part!

At thirty-four, Andy Freeman had been involved in Christian youth ministry for seventeen years when he heard about 24-7 and casually suggested the idea of praying nonstop for a weekend to his youth group at Greyfriars Church in Reading. Little did he know that it would change his life and impact tens of thousands of others.

Despite their initial uncertainty, every slot was filled, and before long, a whole week of 24-7 prayer was planned. The response during that week was extraordinary. Christian kids from one school brought fifteen specific prayer requests to the room. By the end of the week, every single one had been answered, including the salvation of specific people. One person even came to the prayer room and actually asked to become a Christian!

The momentum of prayer was growing, and next they prayed 24-7 for a whole month. "People were just encountering God in amazing ways in the prayer room," Andy recalled, to the extent that the idea of a year of continual prayer was already beginning to germinate in certain minds. But Andy was terrified by the idea!

Of course, the Boiler Room concept had also been germinating in my mind, and in January 2001 I shared it briefly at a 24-7 gathering. Andy began to cave in to the wild voice of God; he came to see me, and the roller coaster ride began.

## HISTORY

As we began to draw up plans for our first Boiler Room, we had the unsettling sense, once again, that God had been here before us. Just as He had predicted our first prayer room in Chichester and the reading of Joel chapter two and had awaited our launch in Hernnhut, so now we found the footprints of God, one step ahead of us, as we walked hesitantly down this ancient path.

Reading was no stranger to prayer, having grown up around a massive Abbey, which dominated the town from 1121 until the fifteenth century when King Henry VIII had the abbot hung, drawn, and quartered. As Andy studied the history with his friend Pete Ward, it became clear that all the pieces of the Boiler Room jigsaw were in the spiritual heritage of this place already. The old abbey had practiced all six of the proposed Boiler Room pillars more than 300 years ago, and it seemed that we were unwittingly just picking up where they had left off.

First the abbey had been a place of prayer influenced by the seventimes-a-day Benedictine prayer cycle. It sent shivers down my spine to learn that the church of Reading Abbey had been consecrated "to the worship of God forever and ever"[39] in 1164 by no lesser a figure than Thomas à Becket, the famed Archbishop of Canterbury. The prophetic nature of these words from this martyred apostle amazed us as we witnessed continual worship bubbling up once again beside the ruins of the old abbey. It was as though a dormant promise was coming to life again.

As well as being a place of prayer for centuries, the old abbey had been a place of pilgrimage, a place of ministry to the poor, and an exceptionally creative community too. A monk there had written down a song that is the earliest recorded piece of music in England. "The Abbey," Pete Ward said, "contributed to the progress of education, literature, art, commerce, and brought the life of the borough into touch with the life of the nation. The Abbey was also concerned for the welfare of the poor and sick and with hospitality for pilgrims."[40]

Most of the local churches had come behind the Boiler Room vision; everything was coming together well except for one vital piece—they still had no venue. The team scoured the town without success. And then an elderly lady named Dot received a word from the Lord: "The answer is in the abbey." It seemed pointless to go tramping around the old ruins once again, but in desperation one night, Andy and the team returned to the site of the old abbey in obedience to Dot's word.

---

39. Ed. Reading from *God's Perspective*, Tilehurst Free Church 1997
*http://www.curve.org.uk/RFGP/RFGP_Middle_Ages.htm*
40. Ibid.

## ROOM AT THE INN

This time, in a back street just yards from the old ruins, they came upon a massive old bar called The Forbury Vaults all boarded up and awaiting destruction. Andy wandered around it with mounting excitement as he realized that it had everything they could possibly need for a Boiler Room—and more. There were apartments for pilgrims, a cellar for skaters, commercial kitchens, a conservatory area with natural light for artwork, and a massive old bar area for 24-7 prayer. It even backed onto a river called Holy Brook with an arch of the old Abbey still standing in its backyard.

They found an address for the owners on a legal notice pinned to a nearby pole and called them the next day, offering a twenty-four hour, round the clock security service! Within weeks they were in, and on October 20, 2001, the third millennium monastery was launched with the blessing of the bishop and many local churches.

Despite such amazing historical symmetry, an awesome building given us for free, and other amazing answers to prayer, the Boiler Room has had a bumpy ride. By Christmas of the first year, Andy was ready to burn out, which is neither godly nor clever. We insisted that he take a well-earned Christmas vacation. When we re-launched in the New Year, it was with a much expanded team and a much happier Abbot. We were learning many lessons on this first Boiler Room that would be invaluable for the future. It was like the "best of times and the worst of times."

A wave of encouragement would roll in. The answered prayer book would get very busy. An evangelism course in a local school attracted more than sixty kids. Local youth events were suddenly booming. People reported many more conversations about Jesus than normal.

But then it would get difficult. Each day, lots of unchurched young people were coming to the Boiler Room. Prostitutes were coming for a look and to pray. Drug addicts, alcoholics, and people from very needy backgrounds were wandering through the building. The team were disconcerted—why were all these people coming into a "prayer" room? Was this right—had they lost their focus?

## INVADING MY (PRAYER) SPACE

As Andy and his team prayed, they realized that they had to keep going. They had to keep working with people who were searching. The Boiler Room was as much about mission and serving others as nonstop prayer. One couldn't be separated from the other.

Prayers were continuing night and day with artwork covering the walls. Pilgrims were arriving from all over the world to stay and pray a while. A Nigerian named Matthias would often take an entire night to keep his own personal prayer vigil in the building. Unassuming older prayer warriors would meet every Wednesday morning to pray for the town and for all these young people. But Saturday was becoming mission day. Up to sixty young people were coming in just to hang out, to skate, and to chat. The team decided to go with the flow. But the flow soon threatened to drown them.

Imagine this: It's lunchtime, and things are quietly chugging along with a few people praying, a few people chatting. And then, within thirty minutes, 150 young people arrive. Thirty are outside drinking beer and spirits out of soda bottles. Some are aggressive, and a boom box on the street is blasting out Marilyn Manson to the entire neighborhood. Thirty skaters have made themselves at home in the parking lot. Only two staff are on duty. It's not good.

Andy recounted what happened on this particular occasion: "The alcohol and the music we dealt with. One guy came inside and blasphemed very loudly only to be reprimanded by his friend: 'Jason, don't swear! God lives here.' Although these guys are not from church, they have a respect and some understanding of what we're about. For all their black clothes, many seem to have had experiences of church. For the next few hours, things calmed down, and we had lots of amazing chats, some about God and faith, others about difficult issues they are facing. The really staggering thing about Saturday was that all the momentum was coming from this group of kids who don't know Jesus. They were asking us why we believe in a God we can't see. They were starting the conversations. They were even starting to join in the prayer as if it was the most natural thing in the world. A small group asked if we would organize a 'kinda church type thing' on Saturday evenings. We found ourselves surrounded by people just begging us to witness to them."

As the months have passed, there has been less drunkenness among the youth, less violence, and a change in the conversation. There is less talk of the occult and more of Jesus.

A redemptive community is going about its task, and slowly the goodness of God has begun to permeate the district. At the time of writing, a number of cities in various countries are making plans to establish Boiler Rooms. We find ourselves dreaming about some kind of crazy network of these Millennium Three monasteries around the world, praying like mad, ministering to the poor, sending out missionaries, and producing amazing works of art inspired in places of prayer. We see many plans, many dreams, masses of potential. But ...

**For Further Reading:**
Historical detail in this chapter draws from insights in the following books:
Michael Mitton, *Restoring The Woven Cord* (Darton, Longman and Todd)
John Finney, *Recovering the Past* (Darton, Longman and Todd)
Roger Ellis & Chris Seaton, *New Celts* (Kingsway)
Ian Bradley, *The Celtic Way* (Darton, Longman and Todd)
George C Hunter III, *The Celtic Way of Evangelism* (Abingdon Press)
*The Golden Legend or Lives of the Saints,* Compiled by Jacobus de Voragine, Archbishop of Genoa, 1275.

**DEEPER**

# A WEEK IN THE LIFE OF A BOILER ROOM

· Between 120 and 168 hours of prayer and intercession.
· Five afternoons a week of drop-in working with young people who hang out in the local area.
· A youth alpha for forty unchurched eleven to fourteen-year-olds.
· One night of prayer covered by local college students.
· One alternative worship evening.
· One weekly "Compline" Service and Evening Prayer.
· Daily food collection for the homeless from two local cafés.
· Four prayer meetings for local offices and businesses every month.
· Two local school Christian Unions come in weekly to pray.
· More than thirty people come in faithfully for the same prayer slot each week.

## JOURNEY

## ADAM PAUL COOLEY R.I.P.

This afternoon I went to the funeral of one of the kids who came regularly to the Boiler Room. His name was Adam and he died of an overdose about two weeks ago. Sitting in a squat in the center of town, he either took too much or took something that was too dodgy. I don't know.

The funeral hit me hard ... I wasn't expecting it to, but it did. That stuff from Ecclesiastes kept ringing in my head: "Everything is mean-ingless."

What's the point of anything we're doing?
Which of these kids will it be in the coffin next?
Will God lead us to the most urgent cases first, or is it just potluck?

I feel like the Boiler Room has become some kind of spiritual ER with cases flooding in all the time. But it's not, is it? We can't do prayer triage and find out the urgent ones. We just have to take them one by one—and often they don't want our help anyway. Often we have nothing to offer but prayer.

Adam was one of the more hopeful ones. He had a strong conscience, he stood up for others, and he was intensely loyal. Yet his addiction was his downfall. Did we help at all? Did being at the Boiler Room these last nine months make a lasting difference? The vicar at the funeral thought so, but he confessed he never knew him. The family wanted people to make donations to us—so kind—but can we do any better next time? What about all the other Adams?

Today I feel more adrift, more hopeless, than I think I have since all this began ... and yet I feel more determined than ever not to give up. Maybe it's only one more prayer away. Maybe the person I talk to or care for today might be dead tomorrow. It's that real. There are no rehearsals here anymore.

We cried "C'mon!" We grabbed God's coattails and ended up here among "the hurting and dirty" and, yes, even among the dying. What will our response be? I've got nothing left to give except me. Maybe in our weakness and pain is where God's voice is at it's loudest. Maybe the place we've spent years trying to run away from is the very place God wants us to be.

*Andy Freeman, Reading Boiler Room, U.K.*

**For Further Study:**
2 Corinthians 12:7–10

# IN THE BEGINNING ...
[AUSTRALIA. CANADA. GERMANY.
INDONESIA. JAPAN. MEXICO. SPAIN.
SWEDEN. SWITZERLAND. U.K.
U.S.A.]

IN THE HELTER-SKELTER RUSH OF LIFE, I have sometimes withdrawn into myself and wondered if it was time to stop this glorious Moravian adventure and get on with the rest of our lives. We have vowed to stop when God does, so I often find myself with a finger to the wind or scanning the horizon for signs of a change in the season.

May 2002 was a watershed. Kerry, who had pushed us to persist in prayer at the end of our first month, was moving on to a new task helping to resource Christian students. She had been a key voice and inspiration within 24-7, and it was painful to watch her walk out the door. Samie's poor health was also a persistent tug on my heart, strength, and emotions. She was still having regular seizures, which were making life very difficult and keeping me unusually involved in the care of our children. Meanwhile, for 24-7, massive growth in a short period of time was introducing its own pressures; for instance, Pete Worthington was struggling to maintain such a big website almost single-handedly—we either needed to shut it down or allow it to grow; there didn't seem to be a middle path. And as I held my finger to sense the winds of the Spirit, I sometimes thought I could detect a slowing down of the pace. Was it time to wind things down, to stop resourcing the prayer rooms, updating the website, mobilizing mission, and all the other tasks?

Heavy with such questions, I poured out my heart to Paul Weston, my old friend, the wild man who had first caught the 24-7 idea right back at the start and with whom I had been running shoulder to shoulder ever since. Was it time, we wondered, simply to stop?

## STILL OUT OF CONTROL

Within days of that conversation, God stepped up to my little ear with His very large megaphone and pointed out in no uncertain terms that 24-7 was not mine to stop or start at will. It had not been my idea—it had been His, and it was ultimately not my responsibility either. "I am in control of this thing," He said, "and I haven't even started yet!"

The megaphone was a gathering of 24-7 people in Reading at the Boiler Room. It was only meant to be a meeting for U.K. team members, but, as if sent by God, all sorts of other crazy people turned up from other countries as well!

First, Jonah Bailey was there from Spain with wild reports of the ways in which God was moving through our bases in Sweden, Australia, Canada, and Germany. We were reminded that the movement was growing in Indonesia and that a youth church network in Japan had taken 24-7 on and was seeking to develop it there.

Markus Lägel wasn't there, but in his own inimitable style, the kid from Leipzig had sent a gift as a token of his ongoing friendship: a battered 1970s German recording of an Elvis impersonator called Shakin' Stevens.

Next Lyndall Bywater from the Salvation Army brought an extraordinary report of the impact 24-7 was having on her denomination in the U.K. and increasingly in other countries too. Some of her stories left us just shaking our heads in amazement at the ways in which God was moving in prayer rooms all over the world.

We heard about a church in Tulsa, Oklahoma, that had recently completed several weeks of 24-7 prayer. The gifted and popular pastor had confessed to adultery the year before, and the prayer room walls were covered with prayers of pain as the community wrestled with their sense of disappointment and anger. The room had been a place of healing in which the community was able to lament, exorcizing their pain and discovering grace and fresh vision to move on.

And then it was the turn of a Mexican group that had showed up, having sold their possessions to travel to England and Germany to connect with 24-7. The leader of the gang was a good-looking twenty-two-year-old named Carlos Sanchez with shaggy hair and a big, cheeky grin, the sort of guy who can make falling over in the street look cool. And it was probably as Carlos shared his story of the way in which God was moving in Mexico that I finally got the message. I could almost hear God laughing at my earlier talk of termination. Without doubt, this crazy, holy move of God was still spinning out of our control, spreading like wildfire, and it wasn't going to make much difference if I tried to shut it down!

I glanced across at Paul Weston, who was smiling and shaking his head, sharing my sentiments. Meanwhile, in a lazy, Mexican-American drawl, Carlos was describing how he had become a Christian two years previously in Chicago. Returning to Mexico, he had simply gathered friends and started a little 24-7 prayer room. However, as often seems to happen, others had heard about their prayer room, and from that one cell group, 24-7 had started spreading around Mexico, particularly among young people. To cap it all, they had been offered the possibility of a magnificent old leper colony in the heart of Mexico City as a Boiler Room and wanted to know how to do it! Carlos was being described as "the national director of 24-7 in Mexico" and he asked if this was okay!

We were still reeling from Carlos' report and the fact that these young Christians had joyfully sacrificed so much just to come and sit with us in a semi-derelict bar in downtown Reading.

Then Susanna Rychiger, our old friend from Thun, Switzerland, stepped forward holding a videocassette. She had brought another mind-blowing report for us, this time from Switzerland, and she had it on film.

Her nation, she told us, was still reeling from a succession of disasters over preceding months: the Nazi Gold Bullion scandals, the bank-rupting of SwissAir in the wake of September 11, 2001, a shooting in Zug (a Swiss regional parliament), and a big fire in the Gotthard tunnel. Many in the room nodded, recalling coverage of these events on CNN and the BBC. But in response to these traumas, Susanna and her friend Matthias Kuhn (Kuno for short) had decided to call the young people of the nation together to take a stand in prayer and fasting.

Their idea, Susanna explained, had been to gather people at a par-ticular place in the Alps, known as the Reutli, on March 30 that year. "Switzerland was formed in 1291 when three guys gathered on the Reutli to commit themselves to each other and to God," Susanna explained. "After so many humbling scandals and tragedies, we figured it was time to give things back to God. We were also sick of the passive Swiss stereotype of mediocrity and pacifism. We were once a nation of warriors and wanted to rediscover this radical heart for Jesus."

They had no idea how many would come, especially since you can't drive to the Reutli—you can only get there by boat or on foot, hik-ing for miles through a forest. There were no big names or flashy publicity. But as Susanna's video flickered onto the Boiler Room wall, we saw an awesome sight. Some 3,000 Swiss young people had convened that day to recovenant their nation to God. For some it was the culmination of a forty-day food fast, so deep was their long-ing for change. "Prophetically, all 3,000 of us made a huge cross on the ground, visible from the sky," recalled Susanna. "We also shared bread and wine, laying down the flags of all twenty-six cantons (states) to make a statement that we are one!"

After these unexpected reports from Mexico, Switzerland, America, Indonesia, Japan, and all over the world, I needed no other persuading. I had lifted my finger to check for the wind and been knocked over by a tornado of encouragement! As we broke for refreshments, Paul just simply said to me, "Pete, we couldn't end this thing even if we wanted to."

"I don't want to," I laughed. "This is the most amazing time of my life!"

---

Back home that night, I replayed the Reutli video, sitting alone in the room where I had wrestled with God so many months before. On July 2, 1999, I had written, "Okay, Lord, this is it. Here in the middle of the night I have finally reached the end of a long road with nowhere left to turn but to prayer." The irony was thick.

I watched once more those thousands crossing the lake by boat, their songs drifting up through the pure mountain air while others filtered down through the forest on foot to converge in an Alpine meadow on a hazy day in March to pray and pledge themselves to the King of Kings. Watching these Swiss warriors rising up, I found myself replaying in my mind the vision granted to a longhaired, carefree student on the cliffs of Cape St. Vincent.

"Thank you," I whispered to the one who hears my every prayer.

Something is stirring from nation to nation. But the crowds in Guildford, Valladolid, Dresden, and at the Reutli express a greater meeting still—the meeting of solitary figures kneeling in prayer in the middle of the night from Tulsa to Tumbi Umbi, conspiring alone with their Commander in Chief, their Father in heaven, their friend. Upstairs, Samie and the kids were sleeping peacefully, and around the world I knew that people were praying. I switched out the lights to go to bed and saw an eerie glow outside: Silently and slowly in the darkness of night there was a red moon rising.

## JOURNEY

## WRITING ON THE WALL

what have we begun,
when we pray like this?
What have we done?
Can we ever know—
what seeds we sow
what lights we show
what dreams we throw?
here playing like kids
in danger places
atomic seeds
hidden graces
radiation
kingdom come.
what have we begun?
here we see angels,
burning like the sun.
here we juggle destinies
what is this thing we've done?
what army gets commissioned
kneeling in this way?
What passion finds expression
when wounded soldiers pray?
are nameless heroes rising?
tomorrow's chosen ones
carriers of Jesus
what plague have we begun?
What dreamer writes upon the wall?
What wonders hem me in?

When we lit that three-way candle
What fires did we begin?

*Anonymous, found on prayer room wall, Chichester, U.K.*

# CONCLUSION

MOST THINGS BEGIN WITH A PLAN, A proposal, and a strategy. 24-7 began by accident. No plan. No budget. No expert in sight. For the first couple of years, we just kept hoping a grown-up would walk into the room and tell us what to do.

And yet, within a matter of months, we found ourselves with bases in several countries, a massive website, mission teams, monasteries, and prayer rooms from Utah to Ukraine. It's been quite a ride!

The most amazing thing of all has been the hunger, so many people from such different backgrounds just desperate to pray. We've never tried to persuade anyone to open a prayer room. People just do! This is remarkable because you can't make people want to pray. You can make people feel like they ought to pray. You can tell them they should pray. But when thousands of people all over the world spontaneously develop such a longing for God's presence that they will rise in the night and sacrifice food, such a hunger comes from God alone.

Perhaps there really is an army of young people being mobilized, Ezekiel's bones rattling in our time. The vision I received that night on the rocky cliffs of Southwestern Europe is coming true in the strangest, most amazing way. God has done "immeasurably more" than all we could possibly have asked or imagined. But where to next?

---

I was sitting in a large leather sofa sipping my usual double-shot latte talking to a young entrepreneur named Andy about 24-7. I wanted help from his business brain on how to get organized without turning into an organization. That was the question. But the businessman first wanted some kind of a road map for our future …

"Where do you want be in five years' time?" he asked.

"Five years from now," I stammered, "I guess we want to be friends. Still friends. And we want to be dreaming together. Still dreaming."

He was young and trendy in a dishevelled sort of way, already on his fifth business venture, with a razor sharp mind hiding under a nondescript baseball cap. "Yeah, but where do you want to be?" he repeated. "What do you want to have achieved? What are your goals? What's your strategy for success?"

I repeated my answer. "That's got to be the ultimate achievement, right? Still friends? Still dreaming? I guess some of the stuff we dream up will work. Some won't. But failure's more useful to God than success anyway! Maybe in five years' time we'll be a bigger bunch of friends doing even more stuff. That would be nice. But along the way every person who joins the movement will also change the movement. They will bring their own dreams and skills to the mix, which could in time change our entire direction. So it's hard to say what the future holds."

I sipped my double-shot latte and wondered if I was making any sense at all. A man at the next table lit a cigarette.

"The thing is," I continued, "if we were a business, we could cook you up a five-year plan no trouble. Might even have a PowerPoint to show you. But 24-7's an accident; it's like an adventure into the unknown. Success might mean that we don't even exist as a movement in five years' time, and if 24-7 stops, we've all got other things to do with our lives …"

Under the baseball cap, I thought I could detect a glimmer of amusement in Andy's eyes. Maybe he was "getting it," or maybe he just thought I was hopelessly naïve. Another sip of coffee; try another approach:

"Most organizations define themselves around a fixed goal; a set of pre-defined corporate ambitions. That goal can be turned into a five-year plan, broken down into monthly steps, and then you celebrate once you've ticked all the boxes and hit your targets," Andy was nodding as if he recognized the scenario. "Along the way," I continued, "I guess you hire and fire, wheel and deal, to get to that all-important goal. But what happens if you're not sure where you're going, only who you're going with and how? What happens if you're in it for the ride rather than the results? What happens if friendship is more important than function?

"I guess it's impossible to say where we'll be in five years' time. 24-7 might not exist. But we do want to remain friends, still loving each other, loving God, and loving His ideas into being. That would be success."

Andy was shaking his head with a bemused grin of recognition, his brain doing some kind of gymnastics routine worthy of the Olympics. "Okay," he said, "Count me in!" Andy Stehrenberger, a brilliant young entrepreneur, has worked for us ever since. And, of course, when he joined, we changed just a little bit more.

This book is a story of friendships and dreams. The next chapter is anyone's guess. Maybe God is challenging you to get involved, to find us wherever we are, make friends, and conspire together for Jesus.

We know it's about prayer, mission, and justice. We know it's about marrying intimacy with God and involvement in his world. But, in the words from *The Matrix*, "Where we go from there, is a choice I leave to you!"

C'Mon!

*Pete Greig*
*www.24-7prayer.com*

## DEEPER

## VISION AND VALUES

> *"24-7 prayer exists to transform the world*
> *through a movement of Christ-centered*
> *and mission-minded prayer."*
> —*Malaga Round Table, October 2002*

**1. Obedient to the Holy Spirit**—Like Jesus, we only seek to do what we see the Father doing. We acknowledge His right to break our rules and offend our sensibilities. *John 5:19, Psalm 127:1, John 3:8*

**2. Relational**—We are a community of friends with shared vision and values, driven by friendship rather than function. *John 15:14-15, Luke 10:1-22, 1 Peter 4:7-11, 1 John 4:7-12*

**3. Indigenous**—We respect, value, and honor cultural diversity. *Revelation 7:9-10, Daniel 1, 1 Corinthians 9:20-21*

**4. Inclusive**—We work with anyone provided they share our vision and values, regardless of race, age, gender, or church background. We build unity and enjoy diversity. *Colossians 3:11, Ephesians 4:3-6*

**5. Like Jesus**—We seek to be like Jesus in the way we do what we do. For us, the means do not necessarily justify the ends.

**6. Deeply rooted**—We are committed to growth in maturity rather than size. *Psalm 1:1-3*

**7. Creative and innovative**—We embrace God-inspired creativity as integral to authentic expressions of prayer. *Exodus 35:30-35, Genesis 1:1-2, Psalm 45:1, Proverbs 8:22-31*

**8. Just**—We will pursue justice and freedom from oppression for humanity and the created world. *Isaiah 61, Luke 4:18-19, Romans 8:19-21, Isaiah 58*

**9. Good Stewards**—We take responsibility for ourselves, for those around us, and for the resources that God has entrusted to our care. *Matthew 25:14-30, 2 Corinthians 9:6-15*

**10. Sacrificial**—We believe that a lifestyle of prayer is costly at every level. *2 Corinthians 8:1-5, 1 John 3:16-18, Romans 12:1-2*

**11. Celebratory**—We believe that Jesus came to bring life to the full and that we have a Christian duty to celebrate all that is good. Fun and laughter are central to 24-7, and we do not need to justify these. *Genesis 1:31, Psalm 24:1, Matthew 11:19, John 10:10*

**12. Simple**—We are a network of like-minded people, not some new slick organization. In character we are wild and unpolished, passionate about developing people rather than our own profile. *Psalm 116:6, Luke 10:3-5, John 3:8*

# The
# 24-7
# PRAYER
## Manual

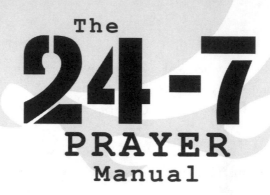

In up to 46 countries around the world, people are praying 24 hours a day, 7 days a week, with as many as 20 prayer rooms running concurrently.

This concise but detailed guide with CD-ROM will help churches, youth groups and Christian Unions set up prayer rooms for one day, one week or one month. It's full of creative, low-cost ideas that will help make the life-changing prayer room experience accessible to everyone.

"24-7 is making history as an unstoppable global prayer movement, and has caught the imagination of a rising generation, involving many tens of thousands in urgent, persistent, continuous, world-changing intercession, encouraging radical discipleship and effective mission. This brilliant book will inspire you with practical help on how to establish 24-7 in your own community."

**DR PATRICK DIXON**
**DIRECTOR, GLOBAL CHANGE LTD AND AUTHOR OF FUTUREWISE**

"24-7 Prayer is not a youth movement; it's not a great idea; it's one of God's ways of reminding us that prayer changes lives and even whole communities."

**STEVE CHALKE**
**DIRECTOR, FAITHWORKS AND TV PRESENTER**

PUBLISHED IN THE UK BY SURVIVOR (SURVIVOR. CO.UK)
LOTTBRIDGE DROVE, EASTBOURNE, ENGLAND, BN23 6NT.

# 24-7 PRAYER

**The 24-7 website connects
thousands of people in
hundreds of countries with:**

- Find out who's praying 24-7 right now

- Post a prayer on the Wailing Wall

- Share your thoughts

- Pray for the world with "Operation World" the ultimate prayer guide to
  every nation on earth

- Download prayer resources

- Visit the 24-7 store

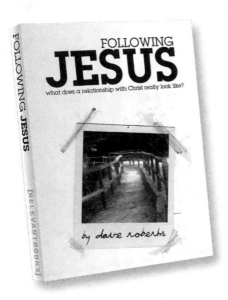